The Sociology of Culture

Boris Erasov
Yogendra Singh

RAWAT PUBLICATIONS
Jaipur • New Delhi • Bangalore • Guwahati • Kolkata

ISBN 978-81-316-0025-2

Indian Reprint, 2017

Published by
Prem Rawat for **Rawat Publications**
Satyam Apts., Sector 3, Jawahar Nagar, Jaipur - 302 004 (India)
Phone: 0141 265 1748 / 7006 Fax: 0141 265 1748
E-mail : info@rawatbooks.com
Website: rawatbooks.com

New Delhi Office
4858/24, Ansari Road, Daryaganj, New Delhi 110 002
Phone: 011-23263290

Also at *Bangalore, Guwahati* and *Kolkata*

Printed at Nice Printing Press, New Delhi

Contents

III
The Cultural Sociology of Developing Countries

Introduction

Human society is a complex phenomenon. And the range of sciences which sought to explain the various components of its structure took shape very gradually. This book will introduce you to a relatively new scientific discipline—the sociology of culture.

The general knowledge of arts, which everyone acquires in the course of their general education, is not enough to utilise culture for the solution of acute social problems. One needs specialised knowledge of the principles behind the functioning of culture and cultural structures, as well as an understanding of the way culture relates to the system of social regulation.

What does culture mean? Why must society understand culture? What kinds of cultures are there and how do they relate to one another? Is it possible and is it necessary to create a single world-wide culture? These are the most general questions answered in this textbook.

However, since the sociology of culture is directly related to the philosophical evaluation of society's existence, the authors could not limit themselves to a narrow examination of the social aspects of cultural functions. They wanted to present a broader picture.

First of all, they sought to define culture, i.e. its norms, values and its basic inherent principles. They also examined cultural functions and analysed the distinctive features of the social institutions related to culture.

The second goal was to demarcate the relationship between culture and economics and culture and politics. Culture is undoubtedly affected by both, however, it in turn influences them, too. Culture determines the degree to which economic activity is efficient and provides stability and legitimacy to political structures or, on the contrary, proves them ephemeral.

Cultural factors supplement the formative effect of economic and political factors on society and thus aid in the self-determination of various societies in the contemporary world. Therefore, the authors perceived their third goal as unfolding the significance of the cultural uniqueness of individual nations and civilisations, as well as showing how they can enter into constructive dialogues today.

These considerations helped shape this textbook. The contents unveil the distinctive features of the sociology of culture as a separate discipline, thus revealing the nature of its subject-matter. However, one should always bear in mind that the general laws and functions of culture develop differently in concrete social situations and depend on the nature and condition of the given society. At this time the industrialised nations have come to realise the inadequacy of a technological and scientific approach to the problems of social development. While the experience of the Third World has proved the limited usefulness of political or ideological approaches to solving many of the more complex problems inherent in self-determination and overall development.

Difficulties and contradictions affect, not only concrete regions, but also relations within the entire world. The prospects for economic and social progress in various countries, as well as the solution of global economic, energy and political problems, all require the realisation that culture is an integral component of both national and global regulatory systems. Thus, one constantly hears appeals to pay more attention to cultural factors in solving contemporary problems both in the United Nations and in many international research centres.

The changes occurring today affect culture as well. New forms of the production and dissemination of cultural values, knowledge and lifestyles have exercised an important influence on the contents and functions of global culture. An enormous ramified cultural industry has arisen, which demands huge capital investments. The newest forms of mass communication (mass media) spread its influence throughout the world, reaching into the most remote corners.

At the same time, the 20th century has been a time of increased cultural problems, and the rise of contradictions in the orientations and essence of various types of cultures. For instance, culture in the Soviet Union and a number of East European countries differs in social character and values from that in Western Europe. The national liberation movements have led to enormous changes throughout the world. Political liberation in Asia and Africa has been accompanied by the resurgence and reaffirmation of original national cultural values.

The concept of the universality of Western culture is unacceptable for other peoples, as they have their own unique cultures. Asian and African cultural systems have become the subject, not only of historical and philosophical, but also of sociological analyses. This required the significant broadening of the field of study, a restructuring of old approaches to the sociology of culture and the rejection of earlier scientific models, as well as special attention to the analysis of national and regional cultural variety and the unique features of their historical development.

All of these ideas provide the basis for this textbook. Dr. Boris Erasov, a Soviet scholar and specialist on Eastern cultures, uses global, as well as Soviet cultural expertise to unveil both the general and the specifically Eastern and Third World theoretical issues of the sociology of culture. One of the more typical examples of the East is India, which, thanks to its long history, socio-cultural variety and overall size, contains all of the more typical processes of socio-cultural development. The Indian sociologist, Yogendra Singh, a professor at the Jawaharlal Nehru University in New Delhi, wrote the chapter "Social and Cultural Change in India". In this chapter he provides a broad analysis of the historical aspects of the sociology of culture of India, as well as the on-going results of modernisation.

The authors hope that their example of co-operation will become only one display of the fruitful interaction possible between cultures and appeal to everybody to do the same.

PART I The General Principles and Subject-Matter of the Sociology of Culture

1

The Sociology of Culture as a Special Discipline

In this chapter, consideration should be given to the following:

1. What is the difference between a thorough scientific analysis of culture and the way an ordinary educated person views culture?
2. Why are there so many different definitions of culture?
3. How do an ethnographic and a sociological analysis of culture differ?
4. Is the sociology of culture relevant in your field?

Man is a thinking, creative being capable of creating cultural values. The cave drawings of primeval man, ancient manuscripts and temples, paintings and books, machinery capable of exploring outer space and the depths of our planet, buildings, parks and museums are all realities without which we cannot imagine human civilisation.

All highly-developed cultures are studied by various disciplines. Social consciousness is studied by philosophers, lawyers, and experts on aesthetics, religion and ethics. Communication is examined by linguistics and semiotics. Art and literature are the prerogative of the sociologists of art history. What does the sociology of culture study? And what are the practical applications of this discipline? One must define the parameters of this field to answer these questions. Thus we need to: 1) define culture as a subject and 2) define a sociological approach to the study of culture.

Analytical and Theoretical Culturology

One of the unique aspects of studying culture is that it requires first of all the ability to comprehend its products and monuments. A true understanding of its messages and imagery systems is impossible for a person who is uneducated or underdeveloped intellectually. This is why you must have art historians, literary experts and linguists working together to interpret and decipher cultural creations. A complete understanding of the essence of cultural phenomena is only possible after one has understood the imagery and significance of classical texts, works of art, architectural monuments, rituals and behavioural patterns. This is impossible to achieve if one does not thoroughly study all aspects of the cultural life of the society which gave birth to the given work. This approach allows for the comprehension of the inner meaning contained in a given work or intellectual phenomenon. This is why this approach is called analytical culturology or more properly hermeneutics.

Analytical culturology calls for an in-depth analysis of the inner meanings of cultural creations. This not only helps the researcher, be he philologist, ethnographer, historian, philosopher, etc., understand a certain cultural era, but also entails a certain input into the interpenetration of cultures, a translation of the ideas, images and style of the given work into the lexicon of another culture. Any theory remains a mere abstraction until one describes the given phenomenon and attempts to interpret the primary sources. The desire to study a given cultural phenomenon in-depth is natural due to unsatisfactory abstract theories, which do not allow for explanation of concrete cultural phenomena.

Nevertheless, no matter how valid such an inner perception of culture is, it is not the same as an analytical approach which must be correlated with a theoretical analysis. The logical result of a truly in-depth analysis is that the researcher turns into an adherent of the given philosophy or religion and thus loses, at least partially, his ability for critical and sober-minded analysis. Thus, the deification of the essence of the Koran reflects, not so much the divine enlightenment of the prophet Mohammed, as the deep need of the given society's consciousness for the absolutisation of the principle, which, to a great extent, determined the consciousness, will and intentions of the people, through words, norms and institutions.

Religious texts and relics serve merely as intermediaries for the contents of the given culture. Thus, one needs a theoretical basis, which goes beyond a hermeneutic analysis. It is well known that not everyone accepted the divine nature of the Koran, and this proves that the ones who doubted were not judging subjectively, but simply had a concrete need for a stronger creative and subjective elements in their spiritual lives.

Thus, we see that, in order to maintain a harmonic world-view, a person must, not only appreciate cultural values, but also learn to critically analyse them. This ensures a scientific approach to culture.

Culture as a Subject

The profound changes in the intellectual development of humanity were one of the causes for the growing awareness of culture as an important component of society both during the 19th century and especially during the 20th. Previously man and society, both in the East and in the West, were perceived as a combination of two opposing factors: natural versus divine (or cosmic). Man was half animal, half angel. He was an instrument in the hands of the gods. Mankind was both a race and a karma. Man and everything else on earth is presented either as the offspring or the component of the cosmological system in the cosmogonical mythology. This system represents the opposite of disorganised chaos. In many languages, the word "world", among other things, defines a general unity, which includes man.

Only as enlightenment proceeded, man and society began to be viewed as the result of joint activity by mankind, which was determined both by circumstances and by material achievements and intellectual values. Man's plane of development was separated both from the natural world and from sacred values or the supreme law, superseding all social structures. Many scholars used the term culture to define this plane, unique to mankind. Culture included everything inside and outside of man which did not exist independently in nature, but appeared due to human labour or his activities in the broadest sense.

This general definition of culture, which appropriates everything created by humanity (as opposed to everything in his natural surroundings or his own biological characteristics) exists to this day. Basically, it incorporates all aspects of society's life, including production and technology, economic and family ties, governmental systems and so on. Although this approach does stress the social nature of culture as opposed to natural or biological aspects, this overly broad interpretation can lead to a dangerous negation of the boundaries between the different spheres of human activity.

When using the term culture in the broader sense, one must be careful to differentiate between material and intellectual culture. The former includes objects which satisfy the material needs of mankind, such as instruments, utensils used for daily life, houses, clothing, transport, means of communication, and so forth. Intellectual culture comprises everything created in attempts to achieve the ideals of beauty, good, truth, and justice, the world of ideas born out of these attempts, as well as the sum of the social institutions and the artistic, communicative and other methods (such as symbolism or language) which express and affirm these ideas and ideals.

This division is relative. It is argued that the material and intellectual foundations for human activity are closely intertwined and cannot stand alone. It is true that any concrete material object must first be imagined, i.e., become an idea in someone's consciousness, before it is actually created (or embodied in a material form). At the same time, any idea or image can only be perceived by other people when it is vested in material form (a manuscript, picture, temple), that is, culture must be embodied. This is all true. However, there is a concrete difference between these two basic aspects of mankind's total activities, each of which is ruled by its own laws. This difference has engendered various sciences dealing with these aspects, in accordance with their unique characteristics. For instance, economics studies the material aspects of human existence, while the arts deal mostly with its intellectual factors.

Material needs and prerequisites call for both the production and consumption of food, clothing, housing, transport of cargo, and so on. Maintaining moral standards, a code of values, knowledge, and faith is tied to the organisation of intellectual activity, upbringing, education, and so forth. However, it is not always possible to separate the material from the intellectual components of human activity. Very often the two are closely intertwined. Take, for example, the variety of ethnic foods, clothing, trading practices, and so on.

Today, there are many definitions of culture. Many believe that it is impossible to find an adequate general definition of culture. This belief was strengthened after *Culture. A Critical Review of Concepts and Definitions* (currently a classical work for the sociology of culture) came out in 1952. Its American authors, Alfred Kroeber and Clyde Kluckhohn, listed over 150 definitions of culture. However, they then proceeded to demonstrate that most of these definitions could be combined and fitted into patterns, leaving only 3-5 variations depending on what a given researcher chose to emphasise. This means that the differences between the extant definitions of culture are not at all unsurmountable.

The term "culture" has two basic meanings. On the one hand, it denotes the quality or level of a phenomenon, according to how acceptable it is in the given society. Being uncultured is perceived as a negative evaluation. In this sense, the word "culture" goes back to the Latin word *cultura*, which meant the cultivation of soil or the raising of domestic animals. Cicero, the ancient Roman orator and philosopher, was already using it to refer to the improvement of human intellect. The word "culture" in the meaning of improving or perfecting various human abilities or behavioural patterns gradually entered the lexicon of languages throughout the world.

On the other hand it can be used to describe the uniqueness of the given society. Here you have differences between one culture, style or behavioural pattern and another. During the period of Enlightenment, the German philosopher Johann Gottfried von Herder (1744-1803) used the term "culture" to define the unique spirit of a given people, whereby the former determined the lifestyle and the overall image of the latter. Herder was also the first to use "culture" in the plural, which became an important step towards the recognition of the uniqueness of different cultures existing simultaneously and interacting with one another.

Only simpler societies, existing as independent, relatively undivided systems of relations can be defined as cultures. Ethnology (cultural anthropology) is devoted to the study of such societies. One term is not enough to adequately describe the more complex forms of societies where the development of systems of division of labour and social regulation is established. In such societies there is an independent sphere of production relations, which is linked to economic activities. There is also the political sphere, i.e., the relationship between parties or between society and the government. A complex society is laced with social interaction between classes or strata and categories of people (age groups, the urban and rural populations, professions, ethnic communities, and so on).

Economics, political science, sociology and jurisprudence, all deal with relevant spheres of society's activity and consciousness. These took shape as separate disciplines during the 19th and beginning of the 20th centuries. Sociology was at first defined as a general science dealing with social relationships and behaviour. However, it soon became necessary to separately study the contents and principles of intellectual activity. This led to the development of the discipline of sociology of culture, or culturology.

Sociology of culture is the discipline which studies the contents of intellectual activity within society as a whole and the specific role of intellectual components in the general system of social regulation, as well as the relationship of various types and levels of culture and cultural entities.

The Sociology of Culture in Relation to General Sociology

While the sociology of culture pursues its own direction of research, it does, in a certain sense, form a part of sociology in general. It is impossible to provide a complete analysis of the development of a given society without the sociology of culture. General sociological principles help determine the nature of the given social structure and its relationship to various components of the life of society. A sociological approach to economic problems teaches us about class relations, the difference between urban and rural inhabitants and various other social groups (such as youth, women, or immigrants). Industrial sociology is a factor regulating relationships in industrially developed structures. Political sociology examines the relationship between the government and society, the positions of various social strata, and analyses political processes, the behaviour of various social groups during elections, and so forth. Scientific sociology allows for an evaluation of the social factors related to the development and utilisation of scientific knowledge.

The sociology of culture, which deals with intellectual life as a social phenomenon, also examines the connection between intellectual matters and other aspects of society's life. It explains the effect of cultural factors on economic and political activity, on various types of social organisation, and investigates the role of various classes and strata in the intellectual life of the society on the whole, as well as their cultural characteristics specifically. This discipline also aids in the understanding of the nature of the relationship between different communities.

The existence of a specific theoretical basis for further research determines the place of the sociology of culture within the general scientific structure.

The Practical Applications of the Sociology of Culture

Scientific knowledge provides not only orientation for a world-view, but also aids in the practical analysis of life's realities. Let us apply this to one aspect of cultural life. There is a festival of folk music going on with performances by choirs, musicians, dancers, and so on. How does the audience view all of this? Usually the people take direct part in the festival, feeling themselves part of the stories, imagery and rhythms presented on stage. What does this event mean to an art historian? It is a rich opportunity for studying instruments, costumes, manners and styles of performance, symbols, and so forth. A historian who attends such a festival might use some of the performances to illustrate how historic events are ingrained in the people's memory, even if specifically interpreted. An economist, if he chooses to evaluate the performance from his own specialised point of view, may try to calculate the costs of such a festival. And all of these would be disparate, one-sided evaluations. On the other hand, a culturologist must provide a total sociological analysis of the given cultural phenomenon.

Here are some of the basic practical problems facing the culturologist:

1) unveiling the essence of the system of cultural values and norms within a given society, both as a whole and taken in its separate groups and strata;

2) demonstrating the interrelationship of various cultural groupings, both large and small;

3) determining the nature of the cultural changes occurring in various social strata both within urban and rural communities, as well as the effect of these changes on society as a whole;

4) determining the influence of cultural values and orientations on the economic and social spheres, and also on the nature of expectations in material production or in politics;

5) determining the degree of acceptance by the people of religious ideas and values, as well as the concrete significance placed on fulfilling religious rituals;

6) establishing the unique characteristics of the intellectual elite, which is the bearer of the highest level of cultural activity;

7) ascertaining the effects of the arts on the consciousness of the audience, which is classified according to social, ethnic or religious criteria.

Thus, we have examined the basic essence and aims of the sociology of culture as a separate discipline. We have only to emphasise the natural difficulties which arise before anyone who attempts to go beyond a purely academic analysis of the subject and strives to utilise it in his professional activities or in the social sphere.

All people evolve within a system of relationships and the cultural environment of their society and group. Even those acquainted with the theoretical principles and concepts have trouble understanding the uniqueness of the values and orientations of other groups and other environments. Only long-term practice results in the ability to master the details of the complex logic and the rules of applying sociological expertise. Also, sociology itself bears imprints of its source to a certain degree. Thus, in spite of the efforts of researchers, not everything in this field is always presented adequately in relation to reality. Constant corrections are necessary, which must be based on comparisons with reality.

Nevertheless, sociology of culture plays a vital role among the other humanities. It teaches one the principles of understanding one's society, with its intertwined norms, values and concepts. At the same time it also aids in understanding other societies with their unique approach to life and the purpose of man's existence. It is this mutual learning process which will guarantee the necessary degree of understanding and tolerance for the establishment of harmonious relations and the successful development of different societies.

If you wish to study the subject in depth:

1. Bromlei, Yu. V., *Ocherki teorii etnosa* (Essays on the Theory of Ethnos), Nauka, Moscow, 1983.
2. Markarian, E. S., *Teoriya kultury i sovremennaya nauka* (The Theory of Culture and Modern Science), Mysl, Moscow, 1983.
3. The entries on culture and sociology in *Filosofsky entsiklopedichesky slovar* (The Encyclopedic Dictionary of Philosophy), Soviet Encyclopedia Publishers, Moscow, 1988.
4. Zlobin, N. S., *Kultura i obshchestvenny progress* (Culture and Social Progress), Nauka, Moscow, 1980.
5. Kroeber, A. L., Kluckhohn, C., *Culture. A Critical Review of Concepts and Definitions*, Harvard University Press, 1952, Vintage Books, Cambridge (Mass.), 1963.

6. Kroeber, A. L., *The Nature of Culture*, University of Chicago Press, Chicago, 1952.

7. Kroeber, A. L., *Style and Civilisation*, Cornell University Press, Ithaca (New York), 1957.

8. Malinowski, B., *A Scientific Theory of Culture and Other Essays*, Oxford University Press, New York, 1960.

9. Malinowski, B., "Culture" in the *Encyclopedia of the Social Sciences*, Macmillan Press, New York, 1931.

10. White, L., "Culture" in *The New Encyclopaedia Britannica*, Vol. 16, Encyclopaedia Britannica Inc., Chicago etc., 1988.

11. Singer, M., "The Concept of Culture" in the *International Encyclopedia of the Social Sciences*, Vol. 3, The Macmillan and the Free Press, New York, etc., 1968.

12. White, L., "Culturology", in the *International Encyclopedia of the Social Sciences*, Vol. 3, The Macmillan and the Free Press, New York etc., 1968.

13. White, L., *The Science of Culture. A Study of Man and Civilization*, Farrar Straus, New York, 1949.

2

The History of the Sociology of Culture

In this chapter, consideration should be given to the following:

1. Why did the Enlighteners' attitude to culture prove to be ineffective?
2. What was the significance of the ethnological findings of the late 19th and early 20th centuries for the development of the basic principles of the sociology of culture?
3. Culture is permanent and yet constantly evolving. Is this not a contradiction in terms?
4. What is the difference between a properly sociological and a quasi-sociological approach to interpreting culture?

The sociological study of culture appeared fairly recently, only after most of the limits and possibilities of other approaches to culture as the main topic of humanities had been ascertained. Culture is unique in that one has to master it as well as understand it. Anyone who studies culture from a purely academic point of view as an object existing outside himself at the same time lives within his own cultural environment. This includes not only his immediate environment, but also the nation or civilisation to which he belongs. In this respect, he is, to a certain extent, the product, a bearer and a representative of his culture.

Let us examine the basic approaches to culture, which developed within social science world-wide and found an outlet in various countries, both in the East and the West.

The Approach Taken by the Enlighteners

The conceptualisation of culture first began in Europe during the Age of Enlightenment. European thinkers, such as Voltaire, Vico, Montesquieu, Goethe, Herder, Schiller, and Wilhelm von Humboldt perceived culture as man's inner intellectual wealth, based on his constant search for truth, good and beauty. Culture enabled man to get over the fact that he only lives once and that his life is quite short, and to see that he is part of nature, society, the past and the future. This view of culture was humanitarian in essence, which was primarily reflected in the enormous attention expended on ethical and aesthetic matters. Good and beauty became the main goals of human activity and were to transfigure the world.

The Enlightenment thinkers rejected religious scholasticism. They exposed the intolerance and fanaticism of the Church and the unwillingness of the feudal structures to change. They also affirmed the significance of man as a rational creature capable of independently determining his actions.

In Europe, and later in other countries, this approach to culture in many ways enriched intellectual life and furthered the development of education. However, it was limited in both ideological and theoretical terms. The Enlightenment thinkers wanted to radically improve society, but concentrated their efforts only on the intellectual sphere and ignored the economic and socio-political factors. They failed to see the social contradictions and the fact that the world is usually ruled by evil and vice instead of by good and beauty. The Enlightenment thinkers had concentrated on European civilisation. This approach was proved limited when Europe learned of the existence of totally new and unique cultures, possessing their own religions, systems of morality, and political and social structures.

The Enlightenment thinkers believed that the main creators and propagators of culture were members of the educated elite, who were isolated from the system of material production and thus were immune to any selfish personal interests, which warp the search for truth, good and beauty. Thus this elite was entitled to guide society in all matters concerning the values and meaning of life.

The masses were thought to be the bearers of superstitions, though these could be overcome through education, logical explanations and visual demonstrations of true beauty and virtue. This is why they believed that the broader masses would eventually learn to appreciate cultural values if they are better educated and provided with more leisure, books and works of art accessible to them.

The illusory belief and optimistic hopes that enlightenment would transfigure society slowly faded away during the 19th century. This led to the romantic withdrawal of the individual from society's faults, vices and problems into the world of an elevated nature and idealised relationships. Then realism replaced romanticism, whereby life was evaluated realistically.

The Evolutionary School

The French and English revolutions of the 17th and 18th centuries gave rise to various theories concerning the evolution of society from the old order to new capitalist structures. During the latter half of the 19th century, the concept of evolution predominated in evaluations of non-Western cultures. The classical interpretation of evolution appeared in the works of English thinkers, such as the philosopher and sociologist Herbert Spencer, the ethnologist Edward Burnett Tylor, and the religious historian James George Frazer, the American historian and ethnologist Lewis Henry Morgan, and other well-known researchers. From the very start, cultural anthropologists sought to use the multitude of available data as a basis for a theory of the birth and evolution of human culture. They wanted to find that common mechanism, the universal "grammar of culture", which would allow them to decipher the cultures of various peoples.

The evolutionary theory basically consists of the following points: 1) mankind is one species and thus developed culture in the same way, 2) development is a linear process, progressing from simple to complex, and 3) social phenomena gradually grew more complex and differentiated and yet united at a new level of organisation.

The 19th century was a period when information about various cultures was being gathered intensively.

The evolutionary theory was applied to these cultures and a scale was developed ranging from savages and barbarians to the most civilised, i.e. educated Europeans. According to the evolutionists, even the developed Eastern cultures, such as Chinese, Indian, and Islamic were only subject to partial approval. The features which did not answer to European standards of civilisation were perceived as superstitions, condemned and eradicated.

The Structuro-Functional Method

The qualitatively new empirical data gathered in mass quantities by anthropologists during numerous field expeditions beginning with the early 20th century made the evolutionary methods useless for a scientific analysis. Social scientists developed the term functionalism to describe the method of examining objects as integrated, mutually related entities, executing strictly defined functions, which were pre-programmed by unified systems.

The advocates of the structuro-functional method rejected historical and evolutionary principles when explaining social phenomena. They viewed culture as a subsystem of a single socio-cultural structure, where every element performed a separate function within the overall regulatory system. The British and American anthropologists (including Alfred Louis Kroeber, Ruth Fulton Benedict, and Edward Evan Evans-Pritchard) worked within this framework and gathered a lot of data on the customs, mores, idea and lifestyles of such so-called primitive peoples as the Indians of both South and North America, various African tribes, and the Australian aborigines. The lesser peoples of India, the countries of South-East Asia, and so on, were studied later. Two British researchers — the culturologist Bronislaw Malinowski and the ethnologist Alfred Reginald Radcliffe-Brown — summarised all of these data and developed the three basic postulates of functionalism:

1. There is a functional social unity which is expressed through the interconnection and interdependence of all of its elements.

2. All of the elements within the cultural and social

structure, such as customs, ideas or religions, all perform vital functions.

3. All of the elements are necessary to maintain the unity of the given culture.

The methodology of functionalism was first utilised in social anthropology. Malinowski and Radcliffe-Brown worked independently and almost never communicated with one another. Yet both formulated the basics of the functionalist approach to the cultures and the social organisation of archaic ethnic groups in the same year (1922). They deciphered culture as being an integrated entity wherein every element performs its given function in satisfying human needs and desires. At the same time, the constant repetition of these elements (production skills, ritual dances, religious rites, etc.) helps preserve and strengthen social structures, i.e., the established interrelations between the individuals.

The phenomena that social anthropologists dealt with seemed to be perfectly suitable for functionalism. The Australian aborigines, the tribes of the Pacific and Indian oceans, and the smaller ethnic groups of Indochina and tropical Africa all seemed to have frozen forever at one point on the ladder of socio-cultural evolution. They constantly reproduced, but did not change, their social organisation, cultural traditions, and the material and intellectual attributes of their daily life. Social anthropologists regarded these all as various remnants of a stable social organisation, having a simple but steady socio-cultural structure, which survived into the 20th century. These models of traditional social organisation, coexisting with modern society and existing within its framework, were defined as the analogues of earlier stages in human development.

The illusory socio-cultural stability of such entities, where all development had practically ceased, led to functionalism being treated as the absolute, the universal and the only suitable method for analysing the structures of archaic societies and the factors which helped them survive. Functionalism became more than just a method. It was perceived as an independent branch of social anthropology. Later functionalism was applied to sociology, political science, socio-linguistics, and other social sciences.

Functionalism did prove to be effective for an evaluation of simple social units, such as ethnoses, and communes as organic and relatively stable, unchanging communities. However, it turned out to be unsuitable for evaluating the relations between such communities, because contradictions strongly manifested themselves here. The relations between the communities did not fit into the functionalist structures. They evinced destructive tendencies, which only a force larger than either of the given communities could counteract.

The American sociologists Talcott Parsons and Robert K. Merton furthered the development of functionalism, when they utilised it for analysing the more complex modern industrial urban societies. They affirmed that the organising centre of any social system can be found in common values and meanings, created by the given society's cultural system. However, the elements within this system are not restricted to prescribed functions, but fulfil different tasks. Parsons and Merton separated functions from structural units, thereby striving to demonstrate that social development was a displacement of functions, which occurred under pressure from the goals formulated in the values sphere.

The methodology of functionalism and structuralism inevitably led to the evaluation of the given entity (the socio-ethnic unit) as existing outside historical time, as a closed system, unchanging and not evolving, but only constantly reproducing, regenerating its own structure. The functionalist and structuralist models developed within cultural anthropology and sociology proved useless for advancing from social microstructures to the macrostructures of national societies, or from a static description of social ties and functions to a theoretical analysis of dynamically evolving social processes. It also became apparent that kinship ties and systems, traditionally believed to be the base of social organisation, were themselves changing noticeably and becoming more integrated into a system of broader socio-economic, political and cultural relations.

Functionalism did succeed in affirming a unified approach to culture and abandoning the system of comparing individual elements in terms of their place in the evolutionary scale. Marriage within one's caste and extravagant festivals and rituals had their place within the given system of relations and could only be changed taking account of general principles. Thus, it is unjustified to claim that one culture is higher or lower than another.

The logical conclusion was relativism, in as much as the cultures of primitive African or Asian tribes were accepted as being equal to the cultures of the most developed nations. However, the retreat from evolutionism also led to a denial of the historical principle. For instance, it turned out that the English culture of 1069 (the year of the Norman conquest) was just as advanced as it is nowadays.

Everyone agreed that culture was a component within a general complex of social activity and regulation. The argument between ethnologists raged over what should be considered as the determining factor. Kroeber believed that it was social structures, while Radcliffe-Brown and Malinowski retorted that it was cultural factors. However, studies of more complex societies also revealed a need for a distinction between general sociology and the sociology of culture. Some well-known sociologists, for instance, the American Pitirim A. Sorokin, affirmed that one could not separate social and cultural components. According to this point of view, social relationships are closely tied to intellectual phenomena—appraisals, knowledge and religious beliefs. For instance, family ties or class relations cannot form without the appropriate values system and ideological beliefs. However, in essence, the issue at hand concerns the relations between these components. We are fully justified in separating the intellectual elements from social relationships on the theoretical level. In real life, social elements far from always correspond to cultural ones in developed societies. Thus, art and literature can get to the essence of the dominant type of social relations, thereby helping restructure them.

Talcott Parsons, one of the leading Western culturologists and sociologists, believes that it is necessary to differentiate between social and cultural systems. He defines the social system as the interaction and relationships between individuals which arise under the influence of biological and material factors. The cultural system includes meanings, values, and knowledge, which are expressed in language, rituals, and symbolism. It provides reference points and thus steers human activity into a certain framework.

The Comparative Historical Method

This method is utilised in culturology for comparing social phenomena from various stages of historical development or ones that exist simultaneously, but in different societies. The combination of comparative and historical methods allows for the determination of the changes the given phenomenon underwent and of developmental tendencies.

This method is used in the evaluation of many different intellectual phenomena, such as art and literature, religion and philosophy. It has been applied very successfully in the study of civilisation (see the works of the British historian and sociologist Arnold Toynbee, the modern Western sociologist Schmuel Noah Eisenstadt, and many others).

The Symbolist Theory of Culture

Back in the 18th century, the German philosopher Immanuel Kant believed that man exists in a world of phenomena, separate from objective reality, be it natural or human. The phenomena are symbols of this reality, but not directly bound to it. Man creates culture, which is expressed in symbols, to guide him in this sphere of phenomena.

The German neo-Kantian philosopher, Ernst Cassirer, is one of the best known advocates of the symbolist conceptualisation of culture in the West. His three-volume work, *Philosophie der symbolischen Formen* (The Philosophy of Symbolic Forms), was published between 1923 and 1929. He believed that what was important in all cultural creations was not the material used (that was for art historians to study), but the form, which alone was the bearer of meaning. Man, unlike animals, has a system of symbols and is characterised by his unique behaviour. He has an extra ability to evaluate reality, in addition to natural and biological abilities. This is evident, for instance, in the noticeable difference between organic reactions (found both in animals and in humans) and strictly cultural behaviour, which is mediated by a complicated process of consciousness.

Language, mythology, religion and art are all components of that unique Universe which is home to humankind. As this cultural sphere develops, physical reality recedes further and further into the background. Man exists mostly in a set of cultural symbols—imaginary structures which are indirect expressions of his aspirations, hopes, fears and illusions. This is true not only for his inner world, but also applies to his relationships with others and even his practical activities. Culture cannot be reduced to merely rational forms, ignoring the co-existing emotional aspect, expressed by mythological and poetical means.

The symbolist conceptualisation of culture eventually gave rise to semiotics, the discipline which studies the characteristics of systems of symbols (natural and artificial scientific languages, programmes and algorithms in cybernetics, myths and art in the communication field, and so on).

It is perfectly justifiable to examine symbolism as an independent sphere within intellectual life. At the same time, culture is irrevocably linked to material and intellectual creation as part of the on-going process of man's mastery of his environment, both natural and social. Maintenance of this link gives living meaning to myths, religion and art, while its weakening or total interruption leads to the elimination of intellectual symbols from the everyday life of society. And though these symbols may be preserved in museums and libraries, they cease to be a part of reality.

Sociological and Quasi-Sociological Methods

A general and unified approach to society's life requires taking account of the independent significance of such different components as the economy, social structures, politics and culture. Sociology avoids overestimating the influence of culture, but demonstrates how value systems, norms and ideals affect the functioning of other spheres of life.

However, there is also a fairly influential group among culturologists which stresses, above all, the social roots and ties of cultural phenomena. If one then accepts social factors as determining, all intellectual processes are perceived as the results and mirror images of social factors. This means that the works of each artist or adherence to each artistic movement are evaluated on the basis of the social class or stratum to which the given artist or movement belongs.

This one-sided and rigid interpretation of the relationship between intellectual activity and social factors leads to crude quasi-sociological conclusions, usually tied to economic materialism. Cultural values, ideas, intellectual tendencies, art, and so forth, are perceived as direct expressions of class interests and the psychology and ideology of the given social stratum. Such crude quasi-sociological methods neglect the ties and interrelations between the various social groups and classes which make up society, as well as the latter's unity and contradictions. Thus, these methods make it difficult to achieve a proper understanding of the general social significance of culture, its unity and its continuity.

This interpretation often shows up in distorted Marxist criticism. The latter is simplified and ideologised, and the dialectical and critical approach to analysing reality, which is inherent in Marxism, is ignored. Use of such a vulgar interpretation of the dependence of intellectual life on social factors can lead to intellectual life being perceived as a reflection of the petty-bourgeois way of life or the interests of the wealthy classes, i.e., as being tied to large fortunes. Those who take such a view sometimes indulge in apologia of proletarian art and merciless criticism of capitalist art, all the while ignoring the proper place of each in the general scale of values. Works of art or religious ideas may be perceived as outright lies or as disguised attempts to vindicate the selfish, mercenary interests of the ruling class. The ruling class is presented as dominating the cultural life of every antagonistic society and suppressing the intellectual life of all the other social groups. For instance, ancient storytellers, minstrels and preachers are always presented either as expressing the sentiments of the ruling class or those of the oppressed classes, whether urban or rural.

This approach is justified only to a certain degree, after which it ignores the significance of art and culture as a whole with their overall social values. For instance, the ancient India epics *Mahabharata* and *Ramayana* glorify the rulers and generals, as well as norms of class society. However, this in no way diminishes the enormous significance of these epics as the expression of mythological worldviews, which reflect the essence of Indian culture during its earlier stages of development.

The limited size of this textbook has made our description of the ways of the development of social science which led to the formation of the sociology of culture as an independent discipline very generalised and schematic. It is important to remember the general principles which lie at the base of the sociology of culture, in order to understand how they unfold in the course of studying culture. However, it is first necessary to define the role of culture in the general system of social creativity.

If you wish to study the subject in depth:

1. Tokarev, S. A., *Istoriya zarubezhnoi etnografii* (A History of Foreign Ethnology), Vysshaya Shkola, Moscow, 1978.
2. Engels, Frederick, "Socialism: Utopian and Scientific", Karl Marx, Frederick Engels, *Collected Works*, Vol. 24, Progress Publishers, Moscow, 1989.
3. *Culture and Social Anthropology. Selected Readings*, Ed. by P. B. Hammond, Macmillan Press, New York, Collier-Macmillan Press, London, 1964.
4. Herder, J. G., *Reflections on the Philosophy of the History of Mankind*, Chicago University Press, Chicago, 1968.
5. Parsons, T., *The Social Structure and Personality*, Free Press, Glencoe; Collier-Macmillan Press, London, 1964.
6. *Social Change. Sources, Patterns and Consequences.* Ed. by A. Etzioni and E. Etzioni. Basic Books, New York-London,1964.
7. Sorokin, P., *Sociological Theories of Today*, Harper and Row, New York-London, 1966.

3

Culture and Systematic Intellectual Production

In this chapter consideration should be given to the following:

1. What is the nature of intellectual activity as a form of production and consumption of intellectual values, norms, and knowledge?
2. What is the difference between material and intellectual production?
3. List and describe the basic forms of intellectual life.

The approaches to culture examined in the previous chapter reflect varying interpretations of culture, which developed depending on which aspects of culture the given philosophers and sociologists chose to emphasise, be it social structures or social development, the communicative relations inherent in society or aesthetic factors. We will now turn to the general principles of evaluating cultures. The principles developed within the philosophical theory of activity, particularly the concept of intellectual production, are of the greatest importance here.

Culture and Activity

Culture is a form of human activity. At the same time, it has an independent existence, so to speak, from each individual and from each society at any given moment in time. Culture gathers and concentrates within itself the following factors:

1) the sum total of forms of activity, existing at the present;

2) the past experience of the given society's evolution;

3) the innovations and discoveries which propel society into a new stage in its development.

The power of the overall results of human activity over individuals is evident in all spheres of life. In the economy, living labour depends on accumulated labour (i.e. means of production or capital). In politics, the individual, group or class is subordinated to the state. In the cultural sphere, they are subordinated to moral and legal standards and restrictions, as well as to intellectual values and symbols. All his life, man has to conform to the demands, standards, and principles expressed through culture, and at that much more than to the realities of the tangible world he immediately perceives around him.

Thus, not all human behaviour belongs to the cultural sphere. When behaviour violates the frameworks of culture, it becomes anti-cultural and anti-social. For instance, violence damages or ruins various social structures. Culture includes only the activity which is truly significant for society. That is why there is a difference between culture and non-culture.

The difference between culture and non-culture is often conventional. Eating and wearing clothes simultaneously satisfy biological needs and express some sort of new aspirations or involve the observance of certain social norms.

Karl Marx provides a comprehensive and consistent analysis of aggregate production. He unveils the general essence of labour activity and its social significance. According to Marx, "Labour becomes the source of wealth and culture only as social labour,"[1] i. e. within society and through society.

Marx's theories concerning aggregate production, which is divided into material and intellectual, is highly significant for sociology in general. Emphasis on the connection between culture and social production led Marxists to approach culture as the sum total of all the achievements of social development, both material and otherwise, to see it as a specifically human form of activity, namely the self-improvement of man in all spheres of endeavour. Such definitions proved to be too general. They excluded the possibility of isolating the unique features of the intellectual aspects of production. And yet

[1] Karl Marx, "Critique of the Gotha Programme", in: Karl Marx and Frederick Engels, *Selected Works* in three volumes, Vol. 3, Progress Publishers, Moscow, 1973, p. 14.

intellectual production does possess unique features and a logic of its own, which distinguish it from material production. Culture is the essence of intellectual production. The latter is the fount of the uniqueness of culture and the basis for its realisation.

One line of thought pursued by many culturologists is based on the reduction of intellectual creativity to the social consciousness, which is treated as the antipode of social existence. In this case, consciousness is merely a reflection of existence. And even though reflection is undoubtedly one of the functions of consciousness, the latter cannot be defined solely as the antipode of existence in general, but is an integral component of existence. One can only ascertain the unique qualities and meanings of the material and intellectual components of social endeavour after one analyses their complicated interrelations. We should be examining the material and intellectual aspects of society's aggregate activity not as contradictory elements or as one being subordinate to the other, but within the framework of their interrelations.

The Essence of Intellectual Production

One cannot reduce intellectual production to the formation of social consciousness either in intellectual or aesthetic forms. The real significance of these forms is related to their place within the total framework of social production. No matter how great the aesthetic or philosophical value of a given temple, painting or text, they participate in intellectual life only as "de-materialised" objects, i.e., they are subject to interpretation and realised in the nature of the interrelations and activities of individuals and groups. Cultural heritage is an important prerequisite for intellectual production. However, the latter's nature is delineated by the sum total of everyday factors, above all its relationship with economic activities and social relations and not achievements or discoveries of the past.

Intellectual production also includes material elements (such as schools, publishing houses, church buildings, museums, and means of mass communication), people who carry it on (the clergy, and the lay intelligentsia), and social institutions (such as the Church, educational institutions, and research centres). All the above elements are mutually interdependent, for one cannot build a church or write a book without the necessary material basis. However, in this case it is culture which serves as the determining factor.

When culture is incarnated in material forms, it undergoes a type of "otherness", which is only a conditional facsimile of the intellectual aspect. At the same time, intellectual production is an important prerequisite both for production in general and for social relations as a whole — relations subject to the influence of the values, knowledge and principles developed by culture. Thus, we can place in the cultural sphere all forms of creativity which serve to develop the available intellectual heritage, introduce new ideas and concepts, and give expression to values answering the new requirements of social existence.

Culture is a system of intellectual production encompassing the creation, preservation, spread and consumption of intellectual values, standards, knowledge, concepts and principles. It shapes the intellectual worlds of both individuals and society, provides society on the whole with a multi-faceted system of knowledge and principles necessary for all forms of endeavour practised in the society at that given point in history. The ideas, standards, and aims utilised by society in regulating its activities are formulated within this system. At the same time, culture aids in the intellectual integration of society and the various social groups it contains. The products of this production exist outside the mind as well, as they are incarnated, i.e., given material garb. The latter appropriates the characteristics of a symbol or an entire system of symbols (languages, ideology, religion, artistic or literary style, etc.). Each generation must work to preserve, reproduce, and select the necessary values, knowledge and principles, and then renew them and modify them according to the changing realities of life. Thus, you need appropriate institutions and professions, i.e. everything comprised by the educational system, religious institutions, and secular culture.

The Specific Character of Intellectual Production

The means utilised in intellectual production are also unique. The actual implements are often the same in essence as the implements utilised for material production. They are objects or sets of objects which man interposes between himself and nature (such as in the natural sciences). However, the main instruments used by a writer or a painter are not their pens or brushes (these are mere auxiliaries), but the vocabulary and phraseology of the language or the skilful combination of paints, which allow for the creation of an artistic image. The scientist and the philosopher use hypotheses, analysis and synthesis, induction and deduction, and other forms of logical thinking. These are the unique features of labour in the field of intellectual production that Karl Marx meant when he spoke of "intellectual productive forces."[1]

The division of labour which exists in intellectual production is not as distinct as that in material production. The product of the former is not necessarily the result of direct co-operation or the joint efforts of individuals. At the same time, it is the product of intellectual production which is more obviously the result of a general effort by all of society, for it synthesises not only contemporary experience, but also the experience of generations past.

Most products of intellectual production are unique. In order for them to be accessible to many people these products must be preserved and reproduced. Institutions such as archives, museums, libraries, and art galleries, serve to preserve outstanding cultural creations. Modern technological advances are utilised in the preservation of intellectual values, whereby unique works of art and literature are protected from the destructive forces of time. Modern technology also aids in the reproduction of rare works. We see rare books and rare paintings reproduced by the millions. Thus, the masses have the opportunity of appreciating unique works.

The preservation of intellectual values is not limited by

[1] Karl Marx, "Economic Manuscripts of 1857-58", in: Karl Marx, Frederick Engels, *Collected Works*, Vol. 28, Progress Publishers, Moscow, 1986, pp. 156, 426, and Vol. 29, Progress Publishers, Moscow, 1987, p. 93.

their protection from oblivion or physical destruction. It also entails guaranteeing continuity in the development of intellectual culture, that is, the selection of intellectual values. In the broader sense, the preservation of cultural values means guaranteeing their role in the cultural life of the new era. This is the true purpose of preserving intellectual values as functioning elements within the intellectual culture of society.

The dissemination of cultural values occurs primarily through the educational system (general, specialised, political, economic, and so on). The quality of intellectual life within a given society depends on the number of educational facilities, the education standards, the qualifications of the educators and the availability of all forms of education to the worker. The mass media, primarily television and radio, as well theatres, museums, philharmonic societies, clubs, libraries, lecture halls, exhibitions, and so forth, also play a major role in determining the quality of intellectual life.

However, the state of the means of disseminating culture and their potential (statistics about the number of books read by the population, the attendance of concerts, theatres and cinemas, the number of newspaper and magazine subscriptions, etc.) do not provide an adequate picture of the given society's intellectual life, for they do not describe the quality of the disseminated values. The intellectual development of people depends first and foremost on the essence of the culture accessible to them. Thus, the quantity of schools, libraries, and cinemas, and the size of radio and television networks do not in themselves show whether the culture these institutions disseminate among the masses is progressive or conservative.

The distribution of the vast range of creative activities of the members of the given society among the various types and forms of intellectual production necessitates an exchange of values, which, in essence, entails intellectual communication between people and the exchange of production expertise, scientific achievements and the products of artistic creativity. Individuals engaged in science need the products of artists while the latter need the information the scientists have amassed, and so on. Culture cannot develop without such mutual exchanges.

The products of intellectual production, just as those of material production, are meant to be consumed. However, the consumption of intellectual values differs greatly from the consumption of material goods, whereby the product is either destroyed (food) or used up (clothing, footwear, furniture etc.). Intellectual values can be re-used many times by many people. By their very nature, they are not subject to individual monopoly, even though, under certain social conditions, unfortunately this is precisely what occurs.

The consumption of intellectual products may be passive, though it is essentially an active process. In a certain sense, reading a book, listening to music, or watching a play or a film, is a form of co-creation. Preference for one or another cultural value depends on the intellectual needs of the given individual or social group. And, in turn, these needs depend on the developmental level of production, the socio-political system and the ideology of the class to which the given individual belongs, as well as on his social (including his cultural) environment and his individual qualities, taste, and habits. Intellectual needs are an active force which leads people to mastering the available cultural values and creating new ones, and meeting other people. In other words, to actively participating in the society's cultural life. The greater the cultural development of an individual, the richer is his inner world, and the more varied and unique are his intellectual needs.

The production of intellectual values lies at the foundation of intellectual culture. For, in order to preserve, distribute, and consume cultural values, one must produce them. At the same time, the consumption of cultural values and the evolution of the cultural needs of the masses have a reverse effect on the development of intellectual production, as it determines the nature of the demand and guides the producers' activities. As for the preservation, distribution, and exchange of cultural values, they serve as the intermediaries between the production and consumption of the latter and ensure the permanent functioning of culture.

The Different Forms of Intellectual Life

Usually, the study of intellectual life in developed societies, including the classical Eastern civilisations, is divided into such categories or spheres as religion, politics, law, ethics, literature, art, music, philosophy and science, or, to be precise, the sciences as concrete spheres of empirical data. This division is justified, even though, as many researchers have emphasised, the delineation of such spheres in reference to past epochs, when intellectual life as a whole was subordinate to religious principles to a great degree, is conventional and thus it is necessary to keep in mind the syncretic nature of both the arts and sciences in those epochs.

The above forms of intellectual life constitute the sphere which many researchers (Pitirim Sorokin being the originator) loosely label "mentality". However, the term intellectual life is more appropriate if one is discussing both psychological and intellectual, rational and religious, ideological and behavioural, personal and social, contemporary and archaic, and mass and elitist factors.

Intellectual life also encompasses the broad sphere of the unconscious, i. e., that which the individual is unaware of, and which is not apparent in public opinion but which always influences the life of society through the forms, means and symbols utilised by culture. Each form of intellectual life is studied by the appropriate discipline: political science, studies of religion, jurisprudence, and ethics, literary criticism, art history, and so on.

Thus, we have defined the essence of intellectual production as that socially significant sphere of endeavour which encompasses the creation, preservation, dissemination, and consumption of intellectual values, standards, knowledge, and concepts. As we will see further on, it is the laws of intellectual production which, for the most part, determine the social significance and functions of culture, its position in relation to the other elements of social endeavour, its quality and its developmental dynamics.

If you wish to study the subject in depth:

1. *Dukhovnoye proizvodstvo. Sotsialno-filosofskiye problemy dukhovnoi deyatelnosti* (Intellectual Production. Socio-philosophic Problems of Intellectual Activity), Nauka, Moscow, 1981.
2. *Culture, Ideology and Politics*, Essays for E. Hobsbawm, Routledge and Paul, London, 1982.
3. Sorokin, P. A., *Society, Culture and Personality. Their Structure and Dynamics: A System of General Sociology*, Cooper, New York, 1962.

4

The Components of Intellectual Culture

In this chapter, consideration should be given to the following:

1. How do customs and norms influence individual's needs and his motives of behaviour?
2. What is the relationship between the emotional and rational factors of human behaviour?
3. Do values represent permanent ideals or are they situational principles?
4. What are the general types of values?

There are certain components within intellectual life which possess unique qualities and thus have differing influences on society. At the beginning, every individual, group, or society retains a certain amount of freedom for the expression of emotional moods. When love or hate, inspiration or anger, horror or repulsion overwhelm an individual, they become the source of his actions. However, society as a whole can also experience surges of enthusiasm or apathy, outrage or satisfaction. This depends on the given situation, and the various factors it involves, which, to a greater or lesser degree, affect the society's basic interests or are interpreted as a threat to further survival. One important feature of such sentiments is the need for immediate (or almost immediate) gratification of the passion which overwhelms either the individual or the society, i. e., a need to "ease the tension".

When such emotions become the object of artistic endeavour, one first of all tries to get down to their inner meaning. Politics is supposed to take such emotions into account and direct them towards the satisfaction of the long-term interests of society. Social psychology is to provide a detailed analysis of the above. The sociology of culture also analyses these elements of individual and social behaviour.

Culturologists usually follow the lead of the outstanding German sociologist, Max Weber, and relegate emotional actions to the irrational category, in contrast to the various types of rational behaviour, where cultural components are the determining factor.

Customs

In the simplest of human communities, culture is primarily based on patterns of behaviour as unified wholes. The patterns stress the part of activity which should be imitated. For example, bringing up a child within a given culture or introducing an adult to a new cultural environment. In such cases, inclusion into culture means acquaintance with certain models: "Behave like that specific adult or like the people surrounding you." The essence of the behavioural patterns is not explained. Instead, the individual is acquainted with the custom which functions as a model of necessary behaviour. The model may be either positive (you should behave like this) or negative (this is how not to behave).

This most primitive form of culture exists not only at the earlier stages of social development. It is inherent within any cultural system. Socially accepted models turn into customs, that is, into the basis for the transmission of social experience from generation to generation, and individual to individual. Customs include traditional forms of labour, behavioural patterns, lifestyles and systems of upbringing. Customs are generally accepted and consolidated by the power of mass habit. They usually remain unexplained, and the members of the group are not always consciously aware of them. If you ask them, "Why do you behave like this?", they will usually answer, "That is how our ancestors behaved."

Norms

Any society has to strain to maintain an equilibrium in the social system in order to diminish the tendencies leading to chaos and arbitrariness. It also has to co-ordinate the actions of individuals and groups and prevent those which contradict the interests of the society as a whole. In this respect, there is an essential difference between societies founded on violence and exploitation and those where there is voluntary and conscious cooperation between people. Whereas the former cannot avoid economic and legal coercion and psychological manipulation, the latter depend on motives and needs compatible with socially accepted aims and encourage all sorts of creative activities.

All regulatory activity, since it pursues concrete aims, has to be founded on some sort of norms. The norms do not prescribe the details for any such activity, but lay down the basic principles or parameters for it, which allow for a certain degree of variation in behaviour, as long as it does not violate the established boundaries. It is incorrect to assume that people always really strive to get what they need, while society seeks to limit these strivings within some sort of boundaries or a set of norms. The desires, interests, needs, and abilities of individuals are determined socially, even though this determination is quite general, i. e., it allows for more variations than is always permissible in given social environment.

The function of norms consists in excluding the influence of purely subjective, chance motives and circumstances, and ensuring generally understood, reliable, predictable, and, to a certain extent standardised behaviour. Norms delineate the more rational and time-proven methods of action and resolution of conflicts, as well as further the formation of personality. They promote the establishment of ideals, values, and methods proven effective by science into real life. Norms either recommend or forbid the usage of certain knowledge, co-ordinate various types of cultural activity, and serve as symbols of social classes and cultural standards.

The actual contents of a given norm depend on the aims of the sphere of activity it pertains to. It is important to remember that various types of activity are standardised to different degrees, while the contents of norms and methods of devising them vary from culture to culture. The technological norms used in production are based on practical interests, the design of the machines and the properties of the materials. Agriculture has its own technical norms. Legal norms regulate the interrelations between individuals and social institutions. Moral norms and rules of etiquette control relationships in daily life and personal aspirations. Feeding children, changing their nappies, and training them to observe their hygiene all occur according to strict rules even in the most primitive societies. There are set norms for the time and quantity of both sleeping and eating. The choice of food does not depend on the biological needs alone. For instance, in Russia, it is not customary to eat snakes, dogs, frogs, or cats. And only a few peoples of the USSR eat horseflesh. While the Hindus never eat beef, and the Muslims never eat pork. In each case, the choice is determined by tradition, religion, or climate to some degree, and not the nutritiousness of the given kind of food. Most cultures have strict norms concerning the ingestion of alcohol and drugs, which are, however, somewhat relaxed within urban mass culture. There is no society which does not have a set of norms regulating sexual relations. In fact, there is no data available which shows that such a society ever existed. The choice of clothing is not entirely arbitrary either. The acceptable degree of nudity is strictly regulated. Society is also concerned about hairstyles, length of hair, beards, as well as how one walks, talks and shakes hands.

People are not usually conscious of all norms and not all norms can be expressed in rational formulas. The precision or definition of norms depends on the development and efficiency of the activity and on the specific features of the object of the norms. Norms are strict and definite in technology and economics. They are less precise in agriculture and stock breeding. And they are even more indefinite and intuitive when applied to upbringing.

Norms are applied not only to material activity and behaviour, but also to intellectual activity. Written and oral speech is regulated by grammar, while thought processes are ruled by the laws of logic. Memory, imagination, perceptions, fantasy, and other psychological processes are always standardised to a greater or lesser degree, since they take place within a given social environment. Their contents, direction, and intensity are dependent not only on the physiological activity of the psyche and individual tendencies, but also on moral, religious, and political norms.

Norms differ in degree of compulsion. There are motivational norms (improve yourself!) and proscriptive norms (do not lie!). Some norms, for instance, in the medical or scientific and technical spheres, are established consciously and based on rational thinking. While others, for instance, as regards social relations and daily life, are based on age-old traditions.

It is necessary to differentiate between norms common to all of humanity, class norms, norms established by various groups, and norms emerging in the personal relationship between two individuals. The demands of some of these sets of norms contradict those of others. The group may demand that its members perform certain activities which are condemned by society as a whole. Two individuals may follow rules in their relationship which they do not necessarily perceive as applicable to all. In fact, they may even object to their rules being turned into general laws. Then there are groups which tolerate infringements of norms which the society demands remain inviolate.

In the cases where interaction is impossible without observing some type of social distinction, such as in the relations between soldiers and officers, or students and teachers, there are special rituals, greetings, and tributes aimed at maintaining and strengthening this distinction. The norms applied to stronger emotions, such as erotic passions and ambition, tend to be more imperative. They help avoid the emergence of enmity between people who have to live and work together, as well as intimate relations which could breach set social distances.

The emergence and establishment of cultural norms is a very complicated process and a single mechanism is not enough to account for it. Most norms arise spontaneously, through trial and error. A new sphere of activity is first regulated by norms taken from other spheres. A set of norms unique to the new sphere is established in time. The norms may also be borrowed from other cultures or imposed by them. Habits can also be elevated into norms.

The stable nature of norms is related to the fact that they are part of the moral consciousness of individuals, and are often sanctified by the authority of religion or enforced by legal means. Changes are slow within sets of norms. Many norms are retained long after they cease to be effective.

Moral norms differ from all other types of norms. They are not unique in their contents, for there is no specific moral sphere outside of labour, social relations, education, and upbringing. They are unique in that adherence to them affects the most vital concerns of other people and society on the whole. Moral norms are also aimed at becoming a part of the individual's moral consciousness, and thus adherence to them is voluntary. Moral norms founded on ideological values, such as freedom, equality, fraternity, justice, etc., contain class elements for these norms are interpreted and revealed in the interests of social classes and groups. Norms which are based on the specific status of a given class and do not apply to other social units also pertain to class values.

Norms are not created in a day, with rare exceptions. Even when norms are established utilising threats and force, they are not accepted immediately. The difficulty in changing over from old norms to new ones lies in the fact that the basic norms operating in a given society are related to each other and form a system of sorts. New norms in any sphere tend to contradict the established system, and thus are not accepted easily. The possibility of new norms being accepted depends on the types of social relations, historic circumstances, technology, and other factors. It is impossible to change all of the norms at once. Most of the time, old and new norms tend to coexist, the former as rituals and the latter as practical rules.

One cannot speak of true or false norms, for they are regulatory principles and do not reflect concrete phenomena. However, it is possible to evaluate norms. The value of a norm depends on its effectivenes, correlation with other norms, flexibility, and its correspondence to social and personal concerns.

There are unnecessary bans and excessive restrictions in some cultures and certain spheres of social existence. An excess of norms is common in relatively poor cultures, where maintaining equilibrium is of primary importance. However, such excesses are often retained even in more developed societies. Excessively strict regulation or norms of behaviour result in an artificially limited variety of individual activity and thinking. Cultural creativity is thwarted and the society adjusts poorly to change. An excess of restrictions is just as damaging for culture as a complete lack of norms.

Values

Values play the deciding role at more advanced stages of cultural regulation. They reflect the orientation of individuals, social groups and societies, towards achieving certain significant, essential goals. However, the concrete goals may vary greatly, depending on many cultural, social, and individual factors.

Max Weber identified types of activity focused on value (value-rational action) and emphasised that they are aimed at carrying out the demands and commandments which the individual sees as most vital, and not at achieving a certain goal. Man ignores concrete circumstances and overcomes daily emotional motivation in order to focus his activities on such ideals as duty, human dignity, beauty, wealth, piety, and so forth. Value orientation can lead to conflicts with his immediate concerns or force him into ignoring negative consequences for the sake of duty or in the name of a higher ideal. Value orientation means choosing higher or ultimate goals, or those which are common to all of mankind. These are above ordinary, everyday events and are perceived as incarnations of good, truth, beauty, justice, order, or wealth. They are the antithesis of evil, lies, ugliness, injustice, disorder, or poverty. Values exist within the intellectual structures of society and are expressed in appropriate texts, images, rituals, and institutions. However, in the long run, their significance depends on the degree to which they are integrated into the inner world of individuals. When individuals behave, set their goals and guide their actions according to given values the latter help form a man of convictions, who firmly and consistently adheres to a chosen type of behaviour. When an individual fails to adhere to his chosen values, he usually experiences deep guilt or shame. It is a typical scenario for psychiatrists that an individual suffers from inner conflicts which are the result of his violating his personal values system.

Civil and religious values which apply to large groups of people tend to acquire significant imperative force. However, the variety of value orientations also results in the other spheres of individual, group, or social activity adhering to an applicable values system.

Every level and variation of value orientation operates in specific aspects of daily life or in given situations. Thus, it is useless to attempt to describe a society, group, or individual using definite, precise values. Nevertheless, one can discuss a system of values intrinsic to either society on the whole or single individuals. This system can encompass primary and secondary, central and peripheral, dominant and situational values. For instance, in Buddhist countries, not all individuals by far obey the commandment to respect all live creatures. However, the majority does treat live things with respect.

The higher values listed above (truth, beauty, justice, order, and wealth) are present as ideals in all developed societies. Some researchers mistakenly attribute to culture only specifically humanitarian forms of human activity, which reaffirm the principle of man being master of his fate. The choice of values in culture is actually much broader.

Culture affects all aspects of society's activity, both positive and negative. These very evaluations can only be made at a distance, i. e., from a point of view distinct from the bearers of the given orientation or the participants of the given ritual. For instance, the cruel and inhuman custom of *sati* (the self-immolation of widows) sometimes practised in traditional Hindu families is vehemently condemned by others. It turns out that the widow is often forced into adherence. This custom tends to serve as a cover-up for the selfish barbarism of the husband's relatives, who covet the estate and are glad to get rid of the widow and her rightful claims. Nevertheless, *sati* is still common among fanatical Hindus.

One can single out the following *types of values* forming the basis of cultural criteria:

1) *Family, relatives, the older generation.* These social elements are objects of respect, to some degree, in all cultures. This is expressed both in the behaviour of individuals (respect by younger individuals for older ones) and by verbal conventions. In many African and Asian cultures, senior age is respected as a sign of experience and wisdom, and is sometimes one of the cultural bulwarks. Individuals are identified in accordance with their ancestry, which does not exclude a broad spectrum of applications of this principle in different cultures. In some nomadic tribes it is a matter of honour to remember 9—12 generations back, while in modern industrial societies people seldom remember further back than two generations.

2) *Communocratic relationships.* Equal or hierarchal relations between individuals constitute one of the criteria for differentiating cultures. What a European perceives as submission, obedience, and the repudiation of individual freedom is perceived in other cultures as the acknowledgment of the right of a respected and influential person to leadership. The emphasis on individualism or solidarity is one factor which divides the East and West (we will examine this in detail later).

3) *Wealth.* One would think that material wealth is valued in all cultures. However, in reality, attitudes to wealth differ greatly and the material objects representing wealth depend on the nature of the given economic structure. For nomads, wealth equals herds, while for farmers land is wealth. In capitalist societies the basic sign of wealth is capital, which is actually concealed wealth. Under socialism priority is given to the harmoniously developed personality.

4) *Labour.* Labour is valued more in the cultures where social relations and the material level of the development of production guarantee a high return on labour to the individual or group. However, class factors play a larger role in this category than in any other. When the society is divided into distinct classes, whereby the ruling and wealthy classes appropriate the products of labour, the value of labour itself diminishes in the eyes of the workers. This is why the natural interest of work-

ers in their work is replaced by coercion. The coercion can either be direct (work from under a whip, or under threat of punishment) or take the form of purely economic necessity, i.e., physical survival or support of one's family.

5) *Time*. Attitudes to time differ greatly in various cultures, and the very interpretation of time depends on intellectual structures. Time began to be measured in Europe fairly recently. We will provide a detailed analysis of this type of value later on.

Values can also be classified according to social criteria. Each given social group works out its own set of values, which follow a strict hierarchal order. The values which prevail in times of conflict are called dominant. Sharp struggle can arise between dominant and secondary values within the inner world of individuals. Take, for instance, the argument between the god Krishna and Arjuna, the hero of the classical ancient Indian epic. Past family tries prevent Arjuna from joining the battle. However, Krishna convincingly proves that the duty of a warrior *(kshatriya)* is higher and must be obeyed regardless of other emotions, and Arjuna rushes into the fray.

The higher the level of values is, the stronger conscious faith in their meaning they arouse in people. This is why long-term and thorough efforts are necessary in instilling and nurturing higher values. The role played by religious institutions and the educational system endorsed by the given society in this process is enormous.

The unity and completeness of the intellectual life within a given society depends on the stability and mutual compatibility of its value orientations. Much can be said in favour of the effect such stability has on the inner world of individuals. However, there is always the danger of stagnation, which can result in obvious discrepancies between the previous values of the individual or society and the requirements of a new era. When the introduction of new values and norms leads to tension and contradictions within the intellectual and social spheres, there is ample basis for social conflicts. Sometimes, these conflicts then have to be resolved utilising political or economic pressure.

Goal Orientation

Weber's typology includes goal orientation (goal-rational action), which is characterised by the clear and unambiguous goals an individual sets for himself, in conjunction with precisely demarcated means for reaching said goals. Thus, both the goal and the means of attaining it are rational and expedient. All actions which could result in unwarranted and excessive losses are rejected. The expression "Pyrrhic victory",* which denoted an accomplishment attained at more cost than it was worth, has existed in Europe since ancient Roman times.

It is generally accepted that this type of intellectual orientation suits the political economy of capitalist societies, with its characteristic tendency to view profit and vested interest as the natural and main motivation of human behaviour. In essence, the main goal of capitalist society is profit gained through the accumulation of capital. Human personality and basic values are either subordinated or sacrificed, to a greater or lesser degree, to this goal.

Each society develops its own system of cultural orientation. This occurs because civilisation requires maintaining social norms and intellectual values as vital components of social regulation.

Even though a general system of regulation, whereby norms, values, and goals complement each other, exists in every society, contradictions do often arise between the three. This is clear, for example, from such expressions as "the end justifies the means" or "this is worse than a crime, it is an error", which are used to justify goals that obviously contradict the accepted norms and values. Such contradictions often arise in political acts which did not receive moral approbation and thus signify a gap between politics and ethics. However, the heated debates over the correlation between economic rationality and social justice, and scientific objectivity and scientific responsibility proves that the value aspect of human activity is not always a component of economic, political, or scientific success.

---

* Pyrrhus, the king of Epirus, defeated the Romans at Ausculum, but suffered irreplaceable losses in the process.

Knowledge as a Component of Culture

Knowledge is the result of the attempts to comprehend the outer world, which has been tested by sociohistorical experience and validated by logic. It is recorded in the form of concepts, judgements, theories, and notions. Knowledge varies in degrees of authenticity, and is relative at any of its levels. It depends both on the degree of development of the given society and on the individual development of each person. Animals also possess elementary knowledge, depending on biological laws, which they utilise in their behavioural patterns (searching for food, escaping their enemies, building shelters, raising their young, and so on). People can possess prescientific, practical, aesthetic, or scientific knowledge.

Practical knowledge is based on common sense and everyday perceptions. It is an important basis for the everyday behaviour of individuals. Scientific knowledge entails comprehension of facts within a conceptual system of a concrete discipline and is included into the structure of a general theory which forms the higher level of scientific knowledge. Scientific knowledge is a generalisation of verified information and discovers necessity and logic behind any chance event. This provides the basis for forecast.

Knowledge is the most flexible component of culture, as new information is being permanently gained and accumulated in the collective memory of the nation.

Thus, we have examined the basic components of the intellectual life of society—norms, values, and knowledge, which affect human behaviour. The role they play in social regulation depends on the degree of complexity and differentiation of the given society. The change-over to higher levels of values does not nullify the conventional norms developed within the given society, even though they may be allowed to play a lesser role.

Culture is a complex, "multi-storeyed" and multidimensional system, which manifests itself in different ways in accordance with social, class, ethnic, and political factors. The cultures of individual societies differ from each other. The norms and values described above are universal and inherent in all cultures inasmuch they reflect the unique features of any society.

If you wish to study the subject in depth:

1. The entries *Norma* (Norm), *Tsennost* (Value), and *Obychai* (Custom) in *Filosofskaya Entsiklopediya* (the Philosophical Encyclopaedia), vols. 4 and 5, Soviet Encyclopaedia Publishers, Moscow, 1967, 1970.

2. Ember, C. R. Ember, M., *Cultural Anthropology*, 3rd ed., Prentice-Hall, Englewood Cliffs (N. Y.), 1981.

3. Herskovits, M., *Cultural Anthropology*, Knopf, New York, 1955.

4. Parsons, T., *Social Systems and the Evolution of Action Theory*, Free Press, New York, 1977.

5. Weber, M., *Economy and Society: An Outline of Interpretative Sociology*, University of California Press, Berkeley, 1978.

5

The Functions of Culture

In this chapter, consideration should be given to the following:

1. What are the main functions of culture?
2. What are the main differences between the functions of culture in traditional and modern societies?
3. What are the characteristics of the scientific rational functioning of culture?
4. How is the significative function of culture carried out?

In the previous chapter, we determined the contents of culture as a system and ascertained the elements which make up culture. Now let us examine the functions of culture in all societies, regardless of the variation in content. Certain norms, values, and knowledge take shape during intellectual production. What is their role in society?

Sociologists actively debate over the basic functions of culture. For instance, Max Weber emphasised the ties, be they positive or negative, between intellectual values and economic activity. Emile Durkheim, the outstanding French sociologist disagreed. He perceived culture's main function as integrating society. Later, Talcott Parsons identified four basic imperatives of culture in any society, be it simple or complex: 1) determination of goals, 2) adaptation to the surroundings, 3) the correlation and integration of all components in a system, and 4) the continuity and stability of a society.

* In this chapter, I utilised the work of the Soviet culturologist Elmar Sokolov, an expert on the relationship between culture and society..

Parsons believed that the cycle of activity in a given society (or any social unit) begins with the definition of a goal and the mobilisation of energy to achieve this goal. The activity will succeed only if the participants cooperate. At the same time, adaptations must be made to the existing conditions and circumstances. Each cycle of activity entails constant repetition and the retention of the initial paradigm, even if somewhat modified.

This scheme was criticised primarily for its inflexibility, as it did not encompass the possibility of progress or the sequential development of society. Yet renewing society through the transfiguration of its intellectual orientation is one of the more important functions of culture.

It is a customary view in the sociology of culture that culture has the following basic functions to perform:

1) the function of gathering, preserving, and transmitting of values, knowledge, and experience (i. e., informative).

2) the significative, or symbolic function (i. e., the expression and entrenchment of meanings, knowledge, and values within a system of symbols).

3) the communicative function (ensuring communication between people during the process of various activities and the promotion of unity and interrelations between the members of a given society).

The Function of Gathering, Preserving and Transmitting of Values, Knowledge, and Experience

Since culture, just like technology, is the vehicle and expression of man's control over the spontaneous forces of nature, as well as the social conditions of human existence, it encompasses the sum of knowledge which reflects these accomplishments.

Culture allows for the transmission of social experience both from generation to generation and between nations and peoples during the lifetime of a single generation. Only culture can fulfil this vital function, as it is a complex system of symbols, which preserves the social experience of a generation in concepts, words, mathematical symbols, scientific formulas, and various devices used in art, which have a lot to say about man and his creative abilities. In this sense, culture is the collective memory of society or the storehouse for the experience society has accumulated.

Information is transmitted not only through intellectual, but also through material culture. Every instrument of production or consumer article bears a functional meaning (it satisfies some human need) and at the same time it includes information about the person who made it or the social relations of the era he lived in. One can judge about the social relations which existed in past eras on the basis of various artifacts and utensils.

The instruments for the accumulation and storage of information can either be natural memory or physical means of recording information, such as manuscripts, books, records, paintings, and films. In both cases, in order for information to be recorded, systems of symbols and certain methods of organising and categorising the information according to value and content must exist. In most cases, the spoken language serves as such a system, while the methods of organisation include oral tradition, emanating from an authoritative figure, dogmatic systems of belief or logically and semantically devised systems of knowledge, i.e., a scientific worldview.

Natural memory, direct imitation, and oral tradition serve as the basic mechanisms for cultural continuity in primitive societies. However, natural memory is not a reliable mechanism. Information of general significance is diluted in a live collective consciousness and is garnished with a layer of fantastic notions. In the course of the struggle to prevent the dispersion of information, custom and tradition guarded the integrity and immutability of collective knowledge and beliefs, and prevented innovations. This hindered the recombination of knowledge and the restructuring of concepts about reality. And the inconvenience and inefficiency of such methods of transmitting information resulted in some of them being irretrievably lost, in spite of the tremendous wealth of folklore.

At the very dawn of history, written language revolutionised the transmission of information. Once literacy appeared, information was rapidly accumulated, systemised, filtered, and changed its structure. It began turning impersonal, that part of it which was relevant to all of society, i.e., neutral information, was separated from the part significant for some individuals only, and objective truths from opinion. Written language allowed for a stable synthesis of independent images and meanings into a more or less systematic picture of the world, unfolded within space and time. Understanding the world was now interpreted as vision.

The better organised the presentation of information was, the more valuable it became in practical terms, and the more variety became possible both in individual behaviour and in the creative enrichment of culture on the whole. Gradually, the transmission of cultural information was separated from its practical utilisation.

As human activity grew more complex, individual elements and components of it became relatively independent. People were becoming aware of their motivational stimuli, goals, means, plans, and models of action. At this point, the cognitive structure of their activity was separated from its value structure, that is, knowledge was freed from assessments, norms, and beliefs. Society's collective memory now retained and transmitted along historic channels, not individual instances of activities, but their abstract characteristics, such as knowledge, norms, and general principles of behaviour.

Before written language was created, the constant threat of the dissipation of information related both to vital means of social regulation and to knowledge of the world gave birth to extensive oral mythology and folklore preserved in the memory of bards and elders. The immobility of this cultural structure was perceived as a guarantee of the stability and survival of the commune or tribe in the culture based on written language, there was a greater variety of information, as a result of recording its various (general and specific) types. Information recorded in a text could be accumulated and preserved regardless of the fate of its creators and users.

In those days when most societies had no written language, those cultures which did have it and were based on it were forced to defend themselves from the eroding influence of the former by utilising dogmatic and canonical definitions of the basic perceptions about the world. Religious dogma furthered the maintenance of basic philosophical categories and the consolidation of information related to the functioning of the social systems.

The highest authorities blessed dogmatic principles, which they claimed to be universal. Individual consciousness was relegated to a very insignificant role in the realisation of a given programme. Dogma ruled over practical experience, the essential results of which were not recorded in the collective memory of society. Dogmas changed slowly, and the changes were further hindered by the resistance from those whose livelihood depended on religion.

The more complex and varied society's activity became, and the more information was accumulated, the more often the dogmatic method of its classification clashed with the need to acquire further knowledge.

As the various aspects of social relations developed and types of activities became increasingly specialised, a new, rational and scientific method arose of identifying elements of reality, and synthesising knowledge about them, as well as methods for recording them in intelligent and logically organised systems. Specific categories of knowledge were isolated according to the properties of the cognisable object and its relevance to humanity. The unique value of each category was ascertained and specific rules for the synthesis of information were developed for each.

The rational partition of information led to the development of historical, ethical, scientific, political, and other classes of knowledge. A new type of person evolved, the scientist, whose consciousness became the incarnation of the scientific method of transmitting knowledge. The highest form of social control of information and its transmission consists of providing not a ready-made model for imitation or commands to carry out certain specific tasks, but a dismembered programme, and one is expected to take creative approach to it. The individual consciousness reproduces the demands of the system and chooses a method of their implementation. The successful functioning of the system on the whole not only allows, but even requires individual innovations and creativity. The rational scientific method of transmitting information is meant not for a passive executor, but at an active, energetic individual, conscious of his social responsibilities.

Each sphere of society developed and matured at its own pace. Thus, all three types of cultural transmission, traditional, dogmatic and scientific, tended to exist within the framework of a single culture in a single society.

The invention of the printing press intensified the conversion of practical experience into significant, generalised information. The appearance of mass periodic publications accelerated the formation of opinions and increased the influence of written culture and theoretical concepts on everyday life. Many new categories of learning appeared. The general store of information grew rapidly, which led to the "information boom" of the mid-20th century. There was also a parallel development of technological means of storing and transmitting information, such as radio, television, films, records, tapes, photography, polygraphy, video recorders, and so on. Then came machines with electronic memories, which could be utilised for the creation of social centres of unlimited quantities of information.

This information is always available for scientific or educational purposes. The mechanical machine-oriented method of preserving and transmitting information has made knowledge totally impersonal. It requires a strict and well-grounded division of information into functional classes and a single system of coding.

Culture will serve society the more effectively, the more information is accumulated, and the freer the access to it. This information must correctly reflect the characteristics of the given culture, as well as the features of the surrounding world. In class-based societies, certain irrational beliefs or taboos form a sort of screen, which interferes with a clear vision of certain aspects of reality and hinders the development of scientific knowledge and rational behavioural norms in the given sphere. One specific feature of totalitarian ideology is the desire to obliterate historical memory and interrupt cultural continuity.

Modern art is concerned with the theme of lost heritage and the loss of collective and individual memories. George Orwell, in his novel *Nineteen Eighty Four*, depicted a society which practised conscious distortion of history and turned it into a policy regressing into the past. The authentic historical documents have long been destroyed. The people working in the enormous so-called "Ministry of Truth" are busy re-writing, re-drawing, and re-photographing all printed materials from the past in order to make it conform to the prevalent opinions and reigning authorities.

In his well-known novel *The Day Lasts More Than a Hundred Years*, the Soviet writer Chingiz Aitmatov presents the terrifying image of a *mankurt*, a man deprived of his memory. He was kidnapped by nomads as a child. In order to turn him into an obedient slave, they pulled a piece of fresh camelskin over his head. As it dried, it shrunk and pressed against his skull, leading to loss of memory, so that he even forgot his own name and did not recognise his own mother. Severed from his past, he was in essence dead, while still alive.

The intellectual well-being of a society depends on its ability to remember events from its own history. Lapses and distortions in an individual's memory or the one-sided recording of some events at the expense of others are signs either of a partial psychological disorder or the absence of self-control. Just as the self-awareness of a healthy individual organically encompasses all of his experiences, so must a healthy society be aware of its past. An individual must remember who he is, where he came from and where he is going. While drawing support from one's past success and finest hours, one should not forget one's incorrect decisions, nor can one help deploring one's past errors. A society which fears to face its own past and strives to forget about it is behaving contrary to its own interests.

Nowadays, social development is directly related to science, which is turning, as it were, into a distinctive branch of industry. New types of labour, such as chemistry, automation, and electronics are primarily based on knowledge, instead of past production experience, which used to play the leading role in older types of labour. In the developed industrial countries, the "knowledge industry", which produces and consumes information, instead of goods and services, dominates a huge part of the economy. Thus, in the USA in 1986 the information sphere in some form occupied 63 per cent of all workers. In the 1970's the volume of scientific information doubled every five to seven years, while in the 1980's this process took only twenty months, and in the early 1990's it should turn into an annual cycle. The information boom is having an enormous effect on the functioning of society on the whole (see Chapter 9 for more details).

The information boom necessitates radical changes in the methodology of storing, organising, and accumulating information. These changes will entail the transformation of the entire system of education, library science, the methods of mass communication, and the organisation of scientific research.

The Significative Function

All knowledge and values are expressed in a system of signs which may contain no information in themselves, but without which it is impossible to convey any information to anyone. The reception of information and the development of meaning are processes which do not coincide. Meanings are developed, perfected, and classified in the course of many centuries. They are expressed in visual images, sounds and conventional signs. They can also be found in gestures, words, greetings, adornments, rituals, details of clothing, and so on.

What determines man's need to develop meanings and designate objects, as well as his own actions and emotions?

In the first place, man cannot be satisfied by instinctive motivations, which form the natural system of orientation in the environment for animals. Man possesses reason and can abstract from his own experiences and the phenomena he observes, and then actively, freely, and consciously react to them.

In the second place, man is a social creature, who participates in a complex network of social interrelations. He must co-ordinate his inner aspirations with social and group interest, as well as cultural requirements. When the various sides of his personality enter upon reciprocal relations with his environment and when he runs into contradictory situations he learns to construct a behavioural strategy and forgets about his immediate desires and the sensations assailing him at the given moment. The same incentives and motives acquire different meanings for him and he evaluates them according to his role in the situation or his social status.

In the third place, man exists not so much in the natural world as within an artificial cultural environment, which he created himself. Each cultural phenomenon contains a much greater number of elements than are apparent from direct observation. The outer appearance of a cultural item very often tells one nothing about what it is used for or how one should approach it. An intermediate complex system of meanings is necessary before man can incorporate trains, planes, telephones, and calculators, as well as a divine image, into his everyday life. The prerequisite of the correct usage of a product of culture is a complex chain of intellectual activity making use of the appropriate meanings. Inasmuch as social existence and culture are growing more complicated, the intellectual modelling of the phenomena one has to handle and behaviour itself is becoming more and more the universal method used by man in relation to reality.

In the fourth place, man runs into many standard and repetitive situations, and is forced to record his experiences in generally accepted symbols, which can be correlated, systematised, and transmitted to future generations.

Culture provides the means to create bright, easy to remember names, which allow for the reproduction of the image of the object within the imagination when the object is not present physically. Names also allow for listing and combining objects in any order. Culture gives rise to multi-faceted systems of meanings, which help distinguish the fine nuances of one's experiences and the phenomena of the visible world. The ensuing complex hierarchy of evaluation gathers the experience of untold generations. When man names and evaluates phenomena, he classifies, comprehends, and interprets the outer world and his existence within it. He is then able to find his bearings in reality.

Naming an object is the first step to comprehending it. The name affixes the object in one's experience and allows one to recognise it upon a further meeting. Thus, outside of systems of cultural meanings, there is no difference between a king and a courtier, a saint and a sinner, or beauty and ugliness. Meaning makes culture a unified ensemble of phenomena, for it erases or relegates to the background the empirical spatial and temporal differences between the inanimate and the animate.

Objects, human actions, or psychological processes in and of themselves do not form culture. These are just cultural building blocks. Once given meaning, they are "drawn into" culture, systematised, and included into the functioning of social institutions and the lives of individuals. Culture provides meaning for the crucial, determining moments of life, such as birth, love, death, struggle, victory, and defeat. Meanings can also pertain both to natural phenomena (the arrangement of the stars, sunrise and sunset, rainbows and hurricanes) and to man's inner state.

Meanings incorporate motivational and cognitive elements, as well as the process of evaluation. The first ones help man approach life practically, the second—theoretically, and the last one shows him the place of things and his own actions within the general hierarchy of values. The motivational elements of meaning are very apparent in ethical terminology: good, evil, duty, baseness, and generosity. The theoretical interpretation of the world occurs in the concepts and images, which make up scientific and philosophical systems. The evaluation of phenomena is based on criteria such as truth and falsehood, beauty and ugliness, tragedy and comedy, sacred and secular or honest and criminal. In everyday life we do not draw clear distinctions between motivation, cognition, and evaluation. An in-depth analysis is necessary in order to isolate these cultural elements.

Meaning reflects the objective qualities of the given phenomenon. On the other hand, many qualities of things which man considers important are established utilising meaning. Meaning can turn stones into religious artifacts, toys or adornments. And sound can signal danger, or express either triumph or love. Unusual acts are interpreted either as heroic feats or the actions of a madman.

The experience of each individual is unique, therefore "the worlds of meanings" of any two people are always somewhat different. The formation of meanings shared by large groups of people depends partly on the identical and proper functioning of sense organs and partly on the standard reaction of people to given behaviour. The basis of communication is the existence of shared meanings, which are interpreted the same way. When people hear words pronounced, they react to their meaning. Mutual comprehension depends on the degree of agreement on what exactly is being indicated.

Meaning is developed during the process of active socialisation and during the thinking process. Meanings may be retained in memory or books and can be accessed and unveiled when needed utilising maps, charts, and dictionaries, as well as clocks, sextants, compasses, barometers, and other instruments. Meanings concentrate human experience in relation to natural and social phenomena. The broader the cultural experience, the richer the world of meanings, and the finer the distinctions within it.

In any organised group, the interaction of individuals and their reaction to external stimuli are guided by the cultural meanings recorded in language, moral standards, and convictions. These meanings can be compared to the rules of a game. It is impossible to understand anything in a culture or the events occurring in a given society if one does not know these rules and cannot relate people's activities and needs one observes to a system of meanings which they accept and conform to.

Meanings consolidated in concepts and beliefs not only reflect the past experience of a given group, but also determine the direction of social practices and human endeavour. A developed system of valuations and concepts reflecting natural processes did not exist during the Middle Ages. This is partly why nature attracted so little investigative interest, which instead was concentrated on the divine and otherworldly. Observation and experimentation were barely developed. Christian morality perceived natural human urges as being base.

The artists of this period ignored landscapes, portraits and genre scenes. There were relatively few scientific discoveries and inventions during the Middle Ages. The natural sciences and medicine were persecuted. The moral and aesthetic cult of nature which reigned during the Renaissance encouraged active scientific research and changes within practical morality. These cultural changes were the result of the development of economic relations. However, one must remember that economic relations affect human behaviour indirectly, refracted through principles, norms and reasons for actions, i. e., through a system of meanings.

The Communicative Function

People enter into relations with one another during any type of work activity, just like they do in the procreation of the human race. Co-operation and the division of labour is the foundation of any sort of production. However, every individual and each social group enters into some kind of relationship with others long before they join the process of production. Both the upbringing of the individual and the co-ordination of actions or the maintenance of unity on the whole are impossible without the existence of various forms of cultural communication.

Verbal language, which accompanies all forms of activity in society is the most important means of communication between people. Language is the key to mastering any given national culture.

Non-verbal forms of communication such as symbols, facial expression, and gestures are also important. However, all cultures develop unique artistic languages in music, theatre, and painting, which help achieve mutual understanding and self-expression.

Along with natural language, we also have artificial scientific languages, as well as specialised languages—mathematical, physical, chemical, and other symbols and formulas.

During the scientific and technological revolution human relationships have become significantly more extensive and complicated. During previous historical eras, direct contacts prevailed over indirect communication. Today indirect communication, utilising technological aids, predominates. The appearance of mass media (the press, radio, television, cinematography, records, and video) has become a crucial factor in the dissemination of culture and contacts between various social groups and nations.

Thus, culture, which is an embodiment of intellectual production provides the framework for the accumulation, preservation and transmission of the values, information, and experience necessary for the functioning of all social structures. As it records important experiences, culture identifies phenomena, objects, and processes. This promotes the preservation of accumulated intellectual accomplishments within society. Culture provides an important form of contact between people and coordinates human activity within the framework of society on the whole.

If you wish to study the subject in depth:

1. Sokolov, E.V., *Kultura i lichnost* (Culture and Personality), Nauka, Moscow, 1972.

2. Cassirer, E., *An Essay on Man. An Introduction to a Philosophy of Human Culture*, Yale University Press, New Haven, 1956.

3. Harris, Ph. R., and Robert, T. M., *Cultural Anthropology*, Harper and Row, New York, 1983.

4. Smith, A. G., *Communication and Culture*, Holt, Rinehart and Winston, New York, 1966.

6

Culture in the System of Social Regulation

In this chapter consideration should be given to the following:

1. What is political culture?
2. What are the functions of ideology within the system of intellectual orientation?
3. What is the relationship between ideology and mass consciousness?
4. What is the role or religion within the intellectual sphere?
5. What are the basic social institutions which promote intellectual production?
6. How can the arts be organised?
7. What is the role of the intelligentsia in intellectual production?
8. What is the social significance of dividing culture into elite and mass culture?

Social regulation is carried out, not only through culture, but also through other components of social existence, including social structures and politics. There is a considerable difference between social regulation in pre-class and class societies.

Cultural anthropology which primarily investigated primordial ethnic (or quasi-ethnic) groups was based on examining a single body of common meanings and preferences inherent in all of the members of a given ethnic group. For instance, Emile Durkheim based his conclusion that it is collective perceptions which were the basis for integration in the primordial human groups on this postulate. Of course, even then there was differentiation according to age, sex, or kinship. However, in all cases, this differentiation was less significant than the general values and orientations.

Culture and Class Structure

A completely different situation unfolds in the complex social systems studied by sociologists. In spite of the existence of several integrating principles, there are serious differences between elements within each system, the most important ones often being class distinctions. This necessitates an examination of the concept of class culture. Class distinctions in culture have been studied in-depth by the Russian Marxist philosophers Georgi Plekhanov and Vladimir Lenin. This concept was then further unfurled by such people as the outstanding Soviet cultural figure Anatoly Lunacharsky, the Italian philosopher Antonio Gramsci, and the Hungarian philosopher Georg Lukács, and the members of the Frankfurt School.

The division of society into classes and social groups also manifests itself in the differentiation of its culture into sub-cultures. Sub-culture is defined as the culture unique to the given social environment which serves the specific, particular interests of the given class or group. Some examples of class subcultures include the cultures of the old landed gentry or large-scale financiers, the middle class or the blue-collar workers, and so on.

Lenin's views on the social significance of culture are exceedingly well-known. He perceived the culture of any antagonistic society as divided into progressive and conservative. Lenin believed that "the *elements* of democratic and socialist culture are present, if only in rudimentary form, in *every* national culture, since in *every* nation there are toiling and exploited masses, whose conditions of life inevitably give rise to the ideology of democracy and socialism. But *every* nation also possesses a bourgeois culture ... in the form, not merely of 'elements', but of the *dominant* culture." * The Marxist-Leninist concept of culture is not limited by a sociological evaluation. It also includes a broad programme, which entails "the *develop-*

* V. I. Lenin, "Critical Remarks on the National Question", in *Collected Works*, Vol. 20, Progress Publishers, Moscow, 1972, p. 24.

ment of the best models, traditions and results of the *existing* culture" * (this will be discussed in reference to developing nations in Chapter 16).

The existence of distinctive social types of culture can be traced both in everyday life, in manners, norms, interests, and language, and in intellectual values and ideology. The products of culture, from items of everyday use to art all bear the imprint of social factors.

Class culture can be viewed from many angles. Many sociologists devote themselves to the "culture of poverty". This applies to the poor both in urban and rural communities, who are identified in the social sphere by a lack of steady employment and thus means of livelihood. In the cultural sphere, this situation leads to degradation of everyday lifestyles. Such analyses should be rounded out by examining the "culture of wealth", which is characterised for the main part by showy and prestige-oriented spending, hedonism, and the abhorrence of physical labour.

Now that we have determined the specific functions of culture, as well as its relationship with social structures, we can examine the relationship of culture with other components of social regulation, such as politics, ideology, and religion.

Culture and Politics

Political relations are determined not only by the correlation of forces or the nature of the social structure, but also by the intellectual principles, perceptions, and values generated within the given society. Political activity is also affected by cultural heritage, which provides (or does not provide) society with the substantiation of contemporary models of political organisation, which must be justified (legitimate).

Power, the central component of the political world, can also be examined as a component of the cultural world. Culture provides a prism through which politics can be understood better. For instance, it allows one to understand who values power and how much and what kind of it he needs, as well as the relations between vari-

* V.I. Lenin, "Rough Draft of a Resolution on Proletarian Culture", *Collected Works*, Vol. 42, 1977, p. 217.

ous values, such as power and property, power and prestige, power and religious sainthood, or power and morality.

The variety of cultures throughout time and space clarifies the reasons why some political systems, appropriate for certain conditions, were defeated when the conditions changed, or why the same actions directed at one nation produce the expected effect, but fail when applied to another nation. The variety of cultures equals the variety of ways of perceiving reality, evaluating it, and thus the variety of methods of action.

Politics primarily depends on political action and means of mobilisation. Politics utilises parties, the government apparatus, courts, police, jails and security forces. Culture, on the other hand, is maintained by knowledge, norms, and values. It primarily functions through education, publishing, museums, the mass media, works of art, theatre, holidays, language, and so forth.

The effectiveness of politics is greatly dependent on political culture. The legal views within the population, the relationship of mass consciousness and ideology, and so on, are all important components of political culture. An analysis of political culture can provide a lot of information concerning the mechanism of correlation between authoritarianism and democracy or hierarchal and egalitarian structures, as well as the tendencies towards bureaucracy and corruption. Culture influences the formation of democratic or authoritarian tendencies. It can further corruption or foster the awareness of the significance of duty to society. Policies answering the needs of the society can be formulated only with the aid of political culture.

In traditional societies, the main components of the political system are the ruler and the bureaucracy. Both are supposed to act within the boundaries of a given political culture, which provides the necessary legitimacy to them. History has shown that both these components are capable of going beyond the legitimate boundaries. They usurp and monopolise power as the source of wealth and blame each other for the inevitable failures. Sometimes they use force against the discontented, as well as against each other, either by replacing and exterminating the bureaucracy or by overthrowing and replacing the ruler.

However, these methods are only partially effective. Sooner or later, public opinion will demand a strict accounting, and then both the ruler and the bureaucracy are in trouble, even though the demand for either a "just" ruler or "honest officials" may arise anew in some situations.

Political independence is exceedingly important for the self-determination of the countries of Africa, Asia, and Latin America. This forced social scientists to concentrate on studying the roles of politics and government, which were perceived as vital formative and constructive factors and the motive force of development.

As politics developed and society discovered the limits of political activity and experienced upheavals, coups, collapses and total re-structuring of political systems, as well as dramatic failures of attempts to modernise on authoritarian lines. Thus politics, in spite of its seeming omnipotence, requires a firm grasp on reality, interaction with the other components of social regulation, and continual legitimacy. In order to evaluate the degree of legitimacy, and thus the stability of a given government, as well as the efficacy of its action, one must determine the nature of the political culture.

Culture and Ideology

Ideology has a tremendous impact both on politics and on culture. Ideology guides social consciousness, affects the establishment of a values system and the behaviour of the masses, and regulates their activities. Ideology is a developed form of theoretical consciousness. It not only affects mass stereotypes, but is subject to their influence itself. The system of political and ideological propaganda is an important means of restructuring the consciousness and behaviour, both of society as a whole and of individual classes.

In countries with a mature structure of social production and developed legal institutions, social interaction and regulation are ensured by various economic, legal, cultural, and political methods. Thus, to a great degree, bourgeois ideology is based on the comprehension of the production and movement of commodities, and is also used as a justification of certain legal standards. The situation is different in societies which are still in the making. There firm economic ties and mature class structures have not yet evolved. The majority of these nations are also only beginning to take shape, and national and political unity is still precarious. Therefore, ideology serves as one of the most important factors in the formation of social movements and the unification of both individual strata of society and the society as a whole.

Karl Marx analysed both pre-bourgeois and bourgeois ideologies and proved that all of them were conventional and had a distinct bias. Ideology is more a guide for practical activity under conditions of social contradictions, than an explanation or reflection of reality. Ideology ignores important aspects of social reality. It seeks to restrict public opinion to certain specific areas, neglecting ambiguities and complexities, and giving distinct meanings to phenomena. It rejects ideas unacceptable to it utilising criticism and repudiation, thus directing the consciousness and will of the people into prescribed channels. Whereby, the price of such choices is the decreasing significance of other aspects of reality.

Let us look at a concrete example. Emotional and psychological factors are closely related to various ideological currents in contemporary developing nations. The leaders and ideologists of these countries, which were once colonies of the major imperialistic powers, are extremely sensitive to attempts to force a choice of social orientation for their countries. They view this as interference in their internal affairs or as infringement on their sovereignty.

Their ideological fervour often causes perplexity abroad, where it is viewed as exaggeration or even distortion. However, what is important here is not the emotional aspect, but the fact that the leaders of the newly independent nations are ruled by ideologies pervaded with morality. This shows the enormous role of subjective factors in such societies. Verbal ideological formulas, even the extreme ones, reflect the awareness of real and serious contradictions and express the subjective rejection of some aspects of reality, while also evincing readiness to act.

Ideology, in conjunction with political action, is an irreplaceable means of influencing the subjective factors amongst the masses and their behaviour and social psychology, for ideology is a way of ascertaining the direction of social activity and forms of social structure. Ideology is an important tool for the awakening and activation of the masses. It can be used to instil pride and optimism in them, under circumstances when it seems as if a "sober-minded" evaluation could lead to disappointment and lack of confidence in one's abilities. Ideology allows the mass consciousness to determine the unerring route amidst a complicated mesh of various external and internal impulses. Ideology can guide the masses through serious conflicts and unite them around clear and appealing goals. At the same time, ideology should be based on a sober analysis of reality and reflect the character of the activity of the masses.

Ideology and Mass Consciousness

The acute problem of correlating ideology and mass consciousness arises when ideology functions in a socially and culturally backward environment. The ideas visibly outstrip the practices of broad social strata and expand the gap between two levels of consciousness: the everyday (mass) and the ideological. A complex relationship arises between evolved theories and the limits of mass consciousness, as well as the culture of the society as a whole and its psychology.

Ideology bridges the gap between the traditional stereotype-oriented consciousness and modern forms of thinking. It strengthens the rational elements within the consciousness and allows for the restructuring of traditional behaviour through the conscious overcoming of the established way of life.

Ideology adjusts to the specifics of mass consciousness, but it can be deformed or change its character. Sometimes, it becomes prisoner of the same slogans which it produces on the practical and utilitarian level. Ideology opposes mass consciousness only after it reaches theoretical maturity and becomes firmly institutionalised.

Such lack of co-ordination between levels is also evident in the difficult relationships between "highbrow" and mass culture, and in various spheres of social consciousness, such as art and literature, morality, law and jurisprudence, education, and so forth. The extreme importance of culture and mass consciousness as some of the factors which mould social life is confirmed by such phenomena as ebbs and setbacks in the political and ideological sphere, the unexpected transformations of ideological doctrines, excesses and ruinous results of attempted cultural modernisation which does not correspond to the established forms of behaviour and consciousness, or ineffective political reforms, reduced to merely economic and social aspects.

The utopian character of ideological programmes is often caused by the special role of subjective, emotional and psychological factors within mass consciousness. Ideology, as a source of belief in the expediency of a given policy or system of actions, reflects the innermost aspirations of social groups and whole nations. These aspirations require long-term and persistent efforts before they are realised. Therefore, it is not surprising that ideology sometimes becomes a vehicle for all sorts of expectations, a formula for miraculous programmes, where assurances of solidarity with one's confederates goes hand in hand with rejections of the position of the given ideology's opponents.

Culture and Religion

The problem of the relationship between culture and religion is complicated to a great degree by the comprehensive intellectual essence of the major world religions and their structural intermeshing with other social institutions. To a greater or lesser degree, religion is related to the intellectual life of society on the whole, not only to the crucial problems of existence—those of life and death, but also to the regulation of ordinary behaviour. Thus, a definition of the ideological contents of religion is not enough to understand the roles of Christianity, Islam, Buddhism, Hinduism, or paganism in the life of society. They encompass a system of beliefs, morality, law, philosophy, and lifestyles. At the same time, they are both vital components of the social structure and social institutions themselves.

The basic difference between the specifically religious and secular elements of culture is evinced through the paired concepts of "sacred-secular". First Max Weber and Emile Durkheim and then other sociologists and culturologists, utilised these antipodal concepts to examine antithetical methods of regulating intellectual life and social behaviour. The idea of the sacred stands out from culture as a whole because of its unique status and the role given to principles, some of which are elevated to the rank of highest. Howard Becker, the American sociologist, developed a gradation for both of the above principles. He asserted that the sacred occupies the higher level. It is identified by the intensity of emotions experienced and the unconditional acceptance of its value. The sacred is unchanging, in spite of all the vicissitudes the members of the society can go through, and any emotional states they may have. The following concepts come after the sacred: 1) loyalty, which entails a greater formalisation of these qualities, 2) the inner saintliness, identified by a strong inner attachment to the sacred (this is, however, restricted to one's subjective state), 3) moralising saintliness, which amounts to moral exhortation, and finally, 4) the outwardly sacred, which is merely an outward adherence to the commandments.

According to Becker, the secular is characterised by greater conventionality and vagueness. Social principles are the most important. They are often related to laws, which can be changed only after elaborate procedures. Secular norm and value criteria are subject to transfiguration and interpretation according to social class interests or the dynamics of society as a whole.

The accepted belief is that religious consciousness reflects the unity of nature, society, and man. In every religion, divine will (or the supreme law) rules the universe, and an individual's perception of this supreme principle can never be totally exhaustive. The individual lacks the awareness of his own significance and doomed to a slow comprehension of divine will. This signifies that when a religious worldview predominates in a society, culture has not yet become a specifically human sphere of endeavour. Hence, it is not man who determines the state of his environment through culture, but the environment which shapes man utilising its own essential principles, transcendentally distinct from the individual.

Christianity played an enormous role in the development of European culture. It predominated in the consciousness and intellectual lives of both the upper and lower classes for many centuries. However, it was not all-powerful. The image of the knight as the embodiment of courage and honour was glorified along with priests and monks. There was also a well-developed folk culture. And yet, it was Christianity which shaped the basic values and concepts in Europe throughout many centuries.

Biblical imagery and subjects, abetting the cult of Christ, the Virgin and so forth, dominated painting and sculpture for a very long time. The best examples of medieval European architecture, the churches, were meant to glorify God and the Church. Church music and singing instilled Christian principles in people. Biblical aphorisms, images, and stories (the "heavy cross", "the way to Calvary", the Tower of Babel, Sodom and Gomorrah, the Last Judgement, king Herod, the traitor Judas, the fratricide Cain, etc.) shaped the system of views, assessments, and moral principles. The moral system of society was moulded for centuries by the most important dogmas and postulates of the Church, such as the salvation of the soul, the redemption of sin, and the One God.

During the 16th and 17th centuries a mass protest erupted in Europe against Church domination which had bound the entire life of Society. This led to a radical restructuring of intellectual life. The Reformation was primarily expressed in the freeing of the individual from obedience to the Church hierarchy, the affirmation of the personal responsibility of the believer before God, and the dependence of man on God's will both in his successes and his failures. Personal responsibility and personal guilt, and not the authority of the Church became the criteria for evaluating the behaviour of believers. The elimination of the essential difference between the clergy and the lay freed society from Church rule and allowed for democratisation. This led to the gradual secularisation of European culture and the abatement of the influence of religion, which became, for the most part, the personal business of the individual.

The Eastern secular cultures encompassed doctrines which called for an evolutionary rise of man above nature (not his break with it) and the distinction of subject and object. However, this potential never did unfold enough and culture remained bound to the sacred sphere.

Religion remains an important factor in the majority of Asian and African countries. Its influence is growing due to the fact that the Eastern religions, unlike Christianity, never experienced a true reformation. They do not see the established differences between the secular and the sacred spheres, and the earthly and the otherworldly, or religious and legal commandments. Islam, Buddhism, and Hinduism possess comprehensive systems for controlling the behaviour of believers. These systems encompass cult, legal, and educational functions, and regulate family and marital relations. These systems affect all aspects of life in the society.

Today, just as in the past, religion is a stable factor, barely penetrable for economic or political pressures, alien intellectual influences, or rapid modernisation. This observation came as a bit of a shock for theoreticians used to dealing only with the economic, social, and political spheres. Religion disrupts and blocks the free interaction of economic and political forces, and thus has proved to be an important independent component of society's life. Religion not only provides accessible forms for expressing class and political interests, but is also a concentrated expression of the interests of a given socio-cultural unit.

The history of Christianity in the West witnessed a long, complicated, and sometimes painful process, whereby religion was separated from other spheres of society's life and now plays a unique, yet rather limited role. This has not been the case in the East and Africa. In spite of a growing differentiation of social spheres, the relationship between the sacred and the secular or the transcendental and the earthly remains stable. Reform movements have definitely become widespread and influential, but have not yet succeeded in unconditionally delineating these spheres. The definitiveness of religion, as well as its stable historical continuity, its comprehensive (and systematic) character owing to its inclusion not only of specifically spiritual aspects, but also moral, social, political and economic factors, make religion an exceedingly significant component of society's life.

Culture as a Social Institution

Each component of social activity has appropriate forms of organisation, i. e., institutions maintaining it and allowing it to influence society on the whole. The economy cannot function without certain forms of ownership of the means of production, productive groups, associations of businessmen and workers, etc. Politics is primarily expressed in the activities of governments and political parties.

It may seem that culture is more difficult to institutionalise than other spheres. The special role of creativity in it correlates culture with the individual activities of scientists, artists, writers, and actors, all of whom do not take well to attempts at regulation. The fame and popularity achieved by many great scientists, painters, novelists, and musicians turned their work into significant concentration and expression of social life, both in the past and in modern times. Thus it is important to study not only the actual works of art and literature, but also the lives of their creators.

In essence, the above is an example of the high degree of specialisation, which must exist in order to achieve perfection in any type of production, including the intellectual sphere. Nevertheless, all creativity is dependent on social conditions, and each artist is bound to a given social environment.

Religion provides the main sphere for intellectual activity in pre-industrial societies. This entails the existence of a special group of people, who are not engaged in purely material production (or pure politics). The production and preservation of intellectual values is concentrated in their hands. They are the clergy, the "traditional" intelligentsia. This class always possessed, at least formally, a higher status even than the rulers or the wealthy. At first, this elite consisted of clerical "intelligentsia" separated from their native tribal environment and the previous ruling groups. Confucian scholars, Hindu Brahmins, Buddhist monks, and the Islamic ulema—all embodied this apolitical and unpropertied, but intellectually powerful elite: "Kings rule people, but learned men rule kings". Priests and monks, organised in accordance with internal hierarchy, enjoyed the highest status in all religions. The ruling class always came second, forming the uppermost rank in the lay hierarchy.

Spiritual institutions are obliged not only to maintain and preserve the original teachings, but also have the much more important task of developing them, in order that they answer the requirements of civilisation and thus the needs of other elites, and broad strata of the population.

However, the arts began to take shape already during the earlier stages of human society. These required special groups of people for its maintenance. The rulers usually kept a certain number of them at court, as did wealthy patrons. Panegyrics, the main poetic genre gratified the patron, and elevated his prestige, while satires served to disgrace people. Court receptions entailed poetry readings, musical performances, and flowery speeches.

However, this only existed for the elite, there were also the fairs and markets. Those were places where every day, and especially on holidays, one could listen to and watch theatrical performances based on classic subjects. In China, there was the "Three Kingdoms", while in Russia there was the Petrushka puppet theatre.

This kind of art also found its way to the homes and palaces of the rich. Very often the same people performed there. The poetry of the tavern appeared at palace feasts, while folk plays were polished for educated audiences. Tales or roguish adventurers were translated into refined verse, accessible only to real connoisseurs.

The usual classification of these arts is this: 1) the patronage type, whereby the nobles and the rich supported or paid poets, writers, musicians and architects, 2) crafts, whereby an artifact was made on order or to be sold locally, 3) commercial art, part of modern industrial societies, and 4) state-controlled art.

It was only natural that the arts to a great extent depended on the level reached by material production and the degree of variety attained by public life. Even in the earlier periods of history, the arts mainly existed in the towns, where most of the trade and handicrafts were practised.

Culture and the Market

Artifacts and works of art were commodities to a greater or lesser degree in all societies which had trade. For long periods, patronage and the market complemented each other in the support of artists.

Market-orientated production meant that the work of art was a commodity, irrespective of whether it was unique or existed in many copies. Thus, the success of an artist was measured by the demand for his works at the market. Under capitalism, the market became the main form of material support for cultural activity, even though it did exist earlier and is preserved to some degree under socialism. The artist and the writer, the scientist and the philosopher must create certain products, such as paintings, books, music, and so on. These satisfy the needs of other people, who purchase them. Naturally, the wealthier part of the population is able to order and purchase works of art, thereby providing commercial pressure on the artists, who are forced to work for a living. These conditions gave rise to the difficult dilemma between creative freedom and the dependence of artists on commercial success.

The relationship between the market price of any physical incarnation of intellectual culture (paintings, novels, or scientific discoveries) and its intellectual value is very mutable indeed. We know how precarious was the financial situation of such outstanding 19th-century writers as Honoré de Balzac, Alexander Pushkin and Fyodor Dostoyevsky. Artists and those who buy their works continue to argue to this day. Only a few artists are able to achieve material success or at least relative well-being, if they only depend on the market. It is well known that it is not necessarily the best works which are most marketable, but the ones which best suit public tastes. Thus, the great Dutch painter, Vincent Van Gogh, died in poverty, rejected by all, and yet his works proceeded to beat all records on the market and go for millions of dollars.

The market did free the artist from state or Church control. At the same time, it makes him highly dependent on the fluctuations of commercial demand.

Cultural Institutions and Organisations

The various cultural institutions and organisations which have arisen in modern society can be classified according to function. There are social institutions which are meant to actually engage in intellectual production (publishing houses, film studios, theatres, amateur unions, clubs, folk art groups, etc.). Others are meant for the dissemination and consumption of culture (cinemas, lecture halls, concert and tour organisations, and so on). These are also the main functions of universities, schools, libraries, and museums.

The cultural system also includes specialised institutions, which organise and plan cultural activities and guide the cultural process (state cultural organisations, artists' associations, institutes for scientific research, and so forth). These are joined by such a unique social institution as scientific and artistic criticism, which influences the work of the creators of intellectual products, as well as the consumption of cultural values by the masses, for to a certain degree it shapes their aesthetic tastes and fosters elevated intellectual needs.

Naturally, this classification of cultural institutions is conventional. Cultural institutions tend to be multifunctional, as they often both produce and disseminate cultural values.

Culture and Education

The state of education among different social groups plays a special role in the history of culture, as do any changes in this state, occurring within a given period. Aside from the independent significance of education as a purely intellectual sphere of social existence, which encompasses, whether directly or indirectly, all classes and social groups, it plays a vital role in all aspects of intellectual life. Education considerably affects the degree to which the masses assimilate the accomplishments of professional intellectual creativity and the nature of the relationship between such creativity and the everyday intellectual activity of the masses. Scientific theories and artistic values penetrate the mass consciousness primarily through education. On the other hand, the more educated the masses and the more elements of the scientific worldview in their everyday consciousness, the more effective is the influence of mass consciousness on culture. In other words, school (from kindergarten to college) is the main link between the different levels of society's intellectual life.

The state of the educational system is more directly dependent on the socio-economic and political systems within the given country, the policies pursued by the ruling class and the alignment of class forces than other cultural spheres. Constant battles raged between representatives of various classes and political parties over the problems of organising education, for instance, the role of the government in the creation and financing of educational institutions, the age limit for compulsory education, relations between church and school, teacher training, and so forth. These battles clearly showed the differences between various ideological positions, be it those of the extremely conservative, liberal or radical capitalist or the working-class strata. The battle was even more fierce over the ideological principles of education, and the subjects to be studied, and even the actual teaching methods. In essence, this was a battle between democratic and conservative tendencies over questions which affect a broad range of people, for there are children in most families, whose future depends to some degree on the standards and nature of their educations.

Education, like other spheres of intellectual life, or even very likely to a greater degree, combines elements from various subcultures and the ruling culture with non-class-related elements shared by all of humanity. Quick wits, fast reactions, and the ability to find the right solutions and apply them are not "tied" to a given social system and a given subculture. Economic stimuli force the capitalists to go against their political interests and further the development of some of the intellectual potential of the workers. The habits and knowledge acquired through education allow for the assimilation of higher democratic intellectual values.

This is especially true in the case of literacy. A person who has learned to read has performed a crucial qualitative leap in his intellectual development. He masters the system of sounds which records and identifies the knowledge about nature and society accumulated by humanity. In other words, he has access to newspapers and books, even though this ability is not always realised. And the printed word allows for the assimilation not only of true intellectual values, but also of destructive ideas, vulgar pseudo-ideas and pseudo-art. However, literacy is potentially the primary foundation of culture. It is the starting line from which one has to go on to acquire knowledge. And as a rule, this line is crossed while still in school.

School education is one of the most important methods of transmitting the accumulated human experience to new generations. It is a form of socialisation of the individual during his formative years and his adaption to the social relations which he will encounter in life and at work. These are the objective possibilities inherent in the idea of systemised education. They may be limited, curtailed or even distorted, however, to a greater or lesser degree, they still manage to overcome all obstacles.

In societies bound by class distinctions the same functions of culture are perceived differently by people, depending on their social status. Each class and social group perceives cultural norms and values incompletely, based on the limits of their own interests.

The regulatory functions of culture in many ways interact with politics, as a totally independent sphere of social regulation. Political culture is a result of such interaction, despite the possible contradictions and conflicts between these two spheres. While politics can utilise various forms of physical coercion of culture, culture can retaliate with persuasion, criticism, condemnation, and so forth.

Ideology and religion are closely related to politics and yet pertain to the cultural sphere as well. They utilise the same elements as culture (values, knowledge, conceptions) and cannot function independently of the cultural environment within the given society, with all of its social variations.

Thus, we see that the complex nature of social regulation requires a thorough analysis of all societies and each concrete situation. Only such an analysis will unveil the role and essence of the components of social regulation.

If you wish to study the subject in depth:

1. Burlatsky, F. M., and Galkin, A. A., *Sotsiologiya, politika, mezhdunarodniye otnosheniya* (Sociology, Politics and International Relations), Mezhdunarodniye Otnosheniya, Moscow, 1974.

2. Wiatr, J. J., *Socjologia stosunków politycznych*, Państwowe Wydawnictwo Naukowe, Warszawa, 1977.

3. *Kultura i politika v stranakh Azii i Afriki (Culture and Politics in the Countries of Asia and Africa), Nauka, Moscow, 1986.*

4. *Zarubezhny Vostok i sovremennost* (Modern Times and the Countries of the East), Vol. 3, Part 5, Chapter V, Nauka, Moscow, 1981.

5. Levada, Yu. A., *Sotsialnaya priroda religii* (The Social Character of Religion), Nauka, Moscow, 1965.

6. Marx, K., Engels, F., *Ob iskusstve* (On Art). Collected Articles, vols. 1 and 2, Politizdat Publishers, Moscow, 1976.

7. *Massovaya kultura — illyuzii i deistvitelnost* (Mass Culture: Illusion and Reality), Iskusstvo, Moscow, 1975.

8. *Intelligentsiya i sotsialny progress v razvivayushchikhsya stranakh Azii i Afriki* (The Intelligentsia and Social Progress in the Developing Countries of Asia and Africa), Nauka, Moscow, 1981.

9. *Khudozhestvennaya kultura v dokapitalisticheskikh formatsiyakh. Strukturno-tipologicheskoye issledovaniye* (The Arts in Pre-capitalist Formations: a Structural and Typological Analysis), Leningrad University Press, Leningrad, 1984.

10. *Khudozhestvennaya literatura v kapitalisticheskom obshchestve. Strukturno-tipologicheskoye issledovaniye* (Literature in Capitalist Society: a Structural and Typological Analysis), Leningrad University Press, Leningrad, 1986.

11. *Ideology and Cultural Production,* Croom Helm, London, 1979.
12. Mannheim. K., *Essays on the Sociology of Culture,* Routledge, London, 1956.
13. *Political Culture and Political Development,* Princeton University Press, Princeton (N. J.), 1965.
14. Weiner, R., *Cultural Marxism and Political Sociology,* Sage, Beverly Hills-London, 1981.
15. Williams, R., *The Sociology of Culture,* Schoken Books, New York, 1984.

7

Society and Intellectual Production

In this chapter, consideration should be given to the following:

1. What is the basic difference between pre-industrial social relations and the ones currently existing in capitalist societies?
2. What is the relationship between religion and mythoiogy?
3. What does solidarity mean in traditional societies?
4. What is the traditional interpretation of the relationship between egalitarianism and hierarchy?
5. How do the masses traditionally interpret power?
6. What are the ways in which commodity-money relations determine the character of culture in capitalist society?
7. What are the basic values of capitalist societies and why do some of them contradict others?
8. What makes socialism a radically new form of intellectual production?

Intellectual production is closely related to production in general. Therefore, we will begin by examining the basic intellectual characteristics of three types of social structures which existed in the course of human development: the traditional pre-industrial, the industrial capitalist, and the post-industrial socialist. If one sees the differences between these three types on the level of basic factors, one can then ascertain the principal variations of intellectual production and thus the cultural values and ideas which arose within each of them.

Industrial Production and Communocratic Relations

In pre-industrial social structures, production was based on the predominance of living labour over accumulated labour, of natural factors over transformed labour, and of social labour co-operation over material prerequisites. At this point, man was still heavily dependent on nature. To a great degree, both labour and his very 'lifestyle were determined by geographic and climatic conditions. Thus, the type of social relations found within traditional society was essentially different from the market relations developed under capitalism. Pre-industrial social relations were basically communocratic.

Karl Marx showed that the social ties found in structures, which were not transformed by commodity exchange, were perceived "at all events as their own mutual personal relations, and are not disguised under the shape of social relations between the products of labour". * Communocratic relations serve as the framework for the interaction between individuals and groups of producers, the division of labour and co-operation, as well as the merging of the individual with the objective prerequisites for production. Membership in an existing group, be it a community, an ethnos, a caste, or a clan was usually all one needed to ensure access to means of subsistence. Everyone received what they needed for survival. This mechanism ensured the existence of many population groups which did not own land or were not engaged in productive labour.

While analysing the economic systems of the medieval East, sociologists have proved that forms of distribution tied to communocratic relations were significant both on the primary (i.e., within the actual unit of production) and on the overall national level. On one hand, distribution guaranteed the preservation of various groupings, that is, their ability to survive and their unity. On the other hand, it coincided with the accepted system of labour duties, the division of the spoils of war, and so on. These factors minimised the freedom of the producer to do what he liked with his products.

The principles of distribution ensuring the continua-

---

* Karl Marx, *Capital*, Vol. I, Progress Publishers, Moscow, 1984, p. 82.

tion of communocratic relations differed from the principle of private property which generally remained undeveloped and never achieved absolute status. In the precolonial era the right to private land ownership never did take final shape even in the most developed countries such as India, China, Persia, and Turkey. This led to the enormous viability of communal or caste ties, which opposed the development of class structures.

What are the basic sociological features, intrinsic to non-Western societies and which, as we shall see, are closely related to the nature of intellectual production?

1. Solidarity and antagonism in communocratic relations. In pre-capitalist structures the individual was not independent. He belonged to a group of a certain type or level, such as a family, clan, tribe, caste, estate, or religious sect. In capitalist societies, the individual is free from all forms of personal dependence. He is only dependent on others insofar as he takes part in the production of exchange value and is involved in commodity-money relations. Family, ethnic, communal, tribal, and caste ties ensure the survival and socialisation of people, however, only on the condition of conformity in behaviour, lifestyle and thinking. Excessive wealth and zeal, or unexpected success are condemned. Attempts to escape the established frameworks are thwarted or punished.

The isolation of the members of the given group, clan, family, or community from the surrounding groups, which are perceived as outsiders, is the reverse side of localised solidarity. Very often, distinctions here are made on the basis of secondary cultural criteria, such as dialect, the minutiae of daily life, names, and so forth. Under circumstances of economic disunity, these differences are difficult to overcome.

Pre-capitalist social structures could not be united by the conditions of production. The economic factors (the fragmentation and the small-scale character of production) are in themselves not enough to ensure integration, but instead increase isolation.

Even today, the sphere of influence of the communocratic relations described above is rather significant. They survive not only within the framework of non-commodity production (in some countries almost three quarters of the population are involved in it), primarily in the countryside, but also within small-scale commodity production, even though the market does affect them. These relations also have a significant influence amongst the urban population and have their impact on the relationship between town and countryside.

Commodity-money factors also do not control a significant part of hired labour, which is often tied to pre-capitalist relations, and is not meant to produce surplus value, but satisfy immediate needs, which are different for every class. This type of hiring is practised in the enormous sphere of services, which requires more labour, than the production of goods.

Commodity circulation in traditional societies is greatly affected by the forms of distribution and the norms of communocratic relations which distort labour and use value. Thus, in terms of their labour value, commodities are perceived as "impenetrable" for social, "human" interest. They are primarily evaluated on the basis of how well it satisfies certain specific needs. For instance a particular kind of clothing can either protect one from bad weather or confirm one's status. Religious restrictions and caste prohibitions are utilised to curb certain needs and preserve the status-orientated hierarchical principle in the usage of certain items.

The exchange of goods in pre-industrial social structures is often presented as the exchange of various types of mutual services, even if they are essentially unequal in value. Goods are not only sold, but mainly redistributed, and are sometimes exchanged for a specific form of relationship. They can be given as gifts, awards, ransoms, dowries, privileges, and so on. The situation remains essentially the same even if money is given instead of goods, before it has been turned into capital.

In such circumstances, trade performs not only purely economic, but also socio-cultural functions. Thus, the Eastern bazaar is mainly a place for trade, but it also serves as a centre for direct personal contact and interaction, i.e., a general "convention", when purchases become services and the prices of the goods waver dramatically, in accordance with purely subjective factors. There is also a dynamic exchange of information and cultural values. It is no wonder then that the bazaar, which serves as the site for important events in people's lives, is a beloved setting for both medieval and modern literature.

In traditional societies, classes and various other social groups were identified on the basis of status, power, and wealth. Trading, urban, professional, bureaucratic, and aristocratic social elements are mature enough to formulate their interests and demands, and invest them with institutional trappings. However, as a rule, these remained group claims and did not evolve into common social ones.

The plurality of pre-industrial societies was based both on the mutual isolation of homogeneous nuclei and their heterogeneity, that is, their differentiation according to ethnic, linguistic, cultural, caste, and religious characteristics. For instance, in India, there are approximately 200 major and 2,000 minor caste groups. Apart from that, there are 179 languages and 544 dialects.

Thus, the basis for the formation of traditional structure lay not only in solidarity (which, as we have seen, was very often enforced) within a given group, but in the conflicts inherent in the relations between groups. An Arab proverb illustrates this perfectly: "I am against my brother, my brother and I are against our cousin, my brother and I, together with our cousin, are against outsiders." Solidarity usually includes only "our own" and excludes all outsiders, whether they belong to other clans, villages, communities, castes, or religions. However, even among "our own" there are numerous gradations of higher and lower: old inhabitants versus newcomers, man versus woman, those who own land versus those who do not, and so forth. Ethnic, caste, religious, and other barriers reflect the struggle for more favourable land ownership and usage or better access to goods. Less privileged groups struggle for the right to use wells, temples, credit, etc.

2. *Social hierarchies and systems of exploitation.* Communal, tribal, caste, and ethnic relations are both forms of internal solidarity and components of hierarchal systems of domination and subordination. In the context of a social hierarchy, the individual is either a member of the ruling group or the object of domination and exploi-

tation. As Karl Marx once wrote, in pre-capitalist societies "we find everyone dependent... Personal dependence here characterises the social relations of production just as much as it does the other spheres of life organised on the basis of that production".*

The fusion of the producer and the conditions of production leads to various forms of communocratic domination, from direct enslavement to the establishment of a strict hierarchy of social prestige, playing a significant, often predominant role in the system of exploitation. The attributes of such prestige can be degrees of power, military ranks, position in religious, ethnic, caste, or tribal hierarchies, and so forth. In traditional societies, exploitation is disguised. It is embodied in a system of "mutual responsibilities", wherein a leader, Brahmin, landowner, merchant, money-lender or boss show their "fatherly concern" for his subordinates, "weaker" people or provide them with vital or imaginary assistance (lends them grain or money, helps them out in times of trouble, prays for them, and so on). These services are paid for not only with labour and goods, but also with moral gratitude, which firmly binds the individual to his "benefactor". In essence, the labourer ends up in the situation where he can save himself from life's blows or cross beyond the narrow boundaries of everyday existence into a wider world only through the intervention of a "strong" person, one who has access to power, influence, and wealth.

At the same time, communocratic relations also placed limits on the privileged classes in that they discouraged the total alienation of the worker from the objective factors of production (for the main part, this concerns land), allowing only for the endless deterioration of the conditions of their unity. The greater the proportion of the surplus product was which was diverted for consumption by the ruling class, the more this class could grow. However, there was always a ceiling, after which the workers were denied the goods essential for their subsistence. Thus, to a great degree, distribution was regulated by customs, developed as one of the methods for

* Karl Marx, *Capital*, Vol. I, Progress Publishers, Moscow, 1984, p. 81.

maintaining communocratic relations. The threat of transgressions against them constantly nourished strong egalitarian tendencies in culture.

3. *The state within traditional systems of relations*. The main characteristic of the state in the East and pre-capitalist societies in general consisted in its far greater role there in comparison with the West. To a great degree, this role was based on the fact that state control was supposed to nullify the contradiction between the fragmented nature of production, splintered into small and tiny units, and the necessity of providing that same production with all the basic elements. Thus the state served as the co-ordinator of production and division of labour within the society as a whole. The isolation of primary groups directly threatened their very survival, as it gave rise to exhausting petty conflicts and weakened the ability of smaller social groups to resist encroachments from the outside. These groups badly needed socio-political unity, which would regulate their internal relations, as well as their contacts with the outside world.

In pre-industrial societies there was always, on various levels of social consciousness, the perception of the state as the patron and defender of society and the guarantor of its unity and well-being. This perception reflects the enormous need for the state as the embodiment of the unity of primary groups (tribes, communities, villages, clans, etc.), as an effective instrument for mastering nature, beating off external invasions, resolving conflicts and creating more large-scale forms of division of labour.

The rise and development of the state was a complicated and contradictory process. No matter how dire was the society's need for the unity provided by the state, no existing state could live up to the hopes associated with it. Engels put it well, in his description of the tendency, inherent in the state, to rise above and dominate the society which gave birth to it: "And this power, arisen out of society, but placing itself above it and alienating itself more and more from it is the state." *

* Frederick Engels, "The Origin of the Family, Private Property and the State", in: Karl Marx and Frederick Engels, *Selected Works* in three volumes, Vol. 3, Progress Publishers, Moscow, 1973, p. 327.

Mythological Consciousness and Society

How do the above-described characteristics of pre-industrial society affect the contents of its intellectual production? We have seen that in pre-capitalist societies, human activity and relationships are not embodied in either commodities or laws. However, this does not yet mean that man appears in traditional societies as his true self, i. e. as the independent creator of his being and his relations. In pre-capitalist structures, consciousness was based on other forms of social fetishism, in which the communocratic relations play the dominant role. In this case, neither commodities nor legal standards, which combined separate individuals into mutually interacting social units of different sizes, did not serve as vehicles for social relations there. The individual's religion and language, and his acceptance of certain customs, behavioural norms, and historical experiences became the main buttress of the unity of his group and the main condition for his membership in a given group, outside of which his chances for survival were slim. These factors became super-significant for consciousness.

In addition, the nature of consciousness in pre-capitalist societies was determined by the close connection between the material and intellectual aspects of everyday activity, the amalgamation of individual and group interests, and unity between man and nature. All of this gave rise to a mythological vision of the outside world. This vision identifies social and natural processes with that which takes place within either the individual or human society. The outside world, for instance, is perceived as being directly affected by customary social relations. Some people believe that rifts between relatives can cause natural disasters. Control over nature depends on the level of moral perfection and harmonious relations within the group as a whole. Mythological conceptions intertwine with magical perceptions of the outside world, based on the assumption that symbolic deeds or verbal spells can affect people and objects.

Research carried out in recent decades has demonstrated the continuity of mythology, which can be traced through the entire history of various societies. Primordial peoples or early archaic cultures were not the only possessors of mythology. Nor is it restricted to the type of consciousness and artistic creativity of various peoples which existed in the classical periods, where mythology was already built into a more developed system of intellectual life. In this system it coexists with other, de-mythologised forms of consciousness and pertains to its more rational versions.

The tenacity and stability of the mythological consciousness was reflected in more developed structures, as well, such as religion, ideology, philosophy, and artistic creativity. The conceptions this gave rise to unveil the deep foundations of human existence and the human psyche which are the site of the formation of the fundamental elements of culture. This theory is advocated by such scholars as the Austrian psychiatrist and psychologist Sigmund Freud, the Swiss philosopher Carl Gustav Jung, the German philosopher Ernst Cassirer, the Western theologian M. Eliade, and the French sociologist Claude Levi-Strauss, as well as the Soviet researchers Alexei Losev, E. M. Meletinsky and V. N. Toporov. Their work unveils the mechanisms which mould the symbols and images of mythology as an expression of the cultural phenomena inherent in various human societies.

In traditional societies social consciousness also reflected the complex and contradictory nature of reality, but vested it in mythological garb. Their view of reality manifested itself in pairs of concepts opposite to each other: up and down, left and right, near and far, inner and outer, large and small, hot and cold, wet and dry, light and dark, and so on. This applied to the physical world (earth and sky, earth and underworld, earth and sea, north and south, east and west, night and day, winter and summer, sun and moon), to the sphere of social relationships (one of ours and stranger, male and female, older and younger, higher and lower), to the correlation of social and natural elements (man and cosmos, house and forest, village and desert), to numerals (odd and even), as well as to man's existence (life and death, happiness and misery, gratification and suffering). There were also widespread systems of classification based on the correlation of man and the cosmos or combinations of the basic elements: earth and water, fire, sky, sun, etc.

There are many different opinions, some of which are

totally opposite, concerning the relationship between mythology and religion. Usually, mythology is viewed as the primary level of world perception, tied to the oneness of consciousness and action. Modern culturologists have studied the oneness of consciousness in-depth. It is reflected in vague distinctions between an object and sign, a thing and a word, a living being and its name, a thing and its attributes, single and plural, spatial and temporal, or a source and a principle, i.e., origin and essence. World religions overcome this unity by "expelling" primitive pagan myths, but then in turn create their own myths to corroborate the new faith. At the same time, mythology may be recognised as the more fruitful form of consciousness, which is linked to man's ability to overcome his dependence on external forces through fantasy.

Both the mythological and religious form of consciousness are fairly independent, despite their obvious interrelation. Today, just as in ancient times, mythology can exist without undergoing religious sacralisation and fulfilling, to a great degree, explanatory functions. Mythological consciousness is nourished not only by old, established images, but also by new infusions. It is often a form of the mass comprehension of new realities, the course of history, and fates of nations. Exaggerated descriptions of the accomplishments of ancient heroes and kings, who aided the glorification of the nation, exist to this day in national histories. Although such cults further the formation of national self-awareness, they can also herald the opposition of one nation to another. The same is true for the newest myths of the 20th century. They arise both within and outside religious boundaries and do not exclude naive or even ruinous attitudes, which hinder progress.

On the level of mass culture, the principles of worldview, linked to primeval forms of society and the life of the masses, arise time and time again, despite all attempts at de-mythologisation. Re-mythologisation, which swept through various aspects of European culture in the first half of the 20th century, demonstrated that even in this developed region mythology is neither archaic nor the exclusive domain of either mass consciousness or artistic endeavour. An analysis of the role of political myths in mass culture demonstrated the stability of mythological perceptions. Jung introduced the term "archetype", which became a broad denotation for the previous cultural experiences, accumulated in the collective sub-consciousness, out of whose depths mythological images and symbols rise again and again.

The enormous role of mythology in the life of traditional societies illuminates the importance of verbal activity as a vital form of influence on subjective factors and thus the regulation of individual behaviour. This activity encourages for example, oral poetry where verbal praise (of courage, generosity, loyalty, etc.) was a way to elevate individual prestige, while verbal accusations (of weakness, cowardliness, breaking one's word, dishonesty, lack of noble ancestors, immorality, adherence to unacceptable habits, such as eating pork or dog meat, lowly occupations, etc.) were means of damaging the moral and social status of one's opponent. In this case, words serve as effective weapons in social battles. The ruling class uses words to raise its prestige, while the lower classes utilise them to shame their masters and describe their woes. Verbal activity is used in an analogous fashion in contemporary cultural and political life.

The Values of Traditional Culture

The principles of solidarity, which serve as the basis for relations in traditional structures, demand the psychological subordination of individual interests to various kinds of social or group ones. This creates a system not only of identical behavioural patterns for individuals, but also imparts uniformity to their very consciousness, whereby their thoughts are purposefully subordinated to the interests of the given social whole. Many sociologists attribute the predominant moral orientation towards a sense of shame instead of guilt in these societies to the lack of a developed individual element within the mass consciousness there. A sense of guilt means the individual's inner admission of his misdeed. A sense of shame means the individual's concern over how others regard his qualities, which leads to his desire to prevent anyone else from learning about his errors, weaknesses, dependence, and so forth. Ruth Fulton Benedict introduced the sociological concepts of guilt culture and shame culture. Shame culture is more localised, as it focuses the individual consciousness only on his own community: shame exists only in relation to one's "own". Worth and dishonour are related to external forms of control, i. e., either condemnation, punishment, and derision or approval, praise, encouragement, and so on.

Eastern cultures are usually classed as shame cultures. However, just as in any "high" culture, guilt or the stress on the individual's responsibility for his actions and for his qualities does exist to a greater or lesser degree in these cultures. This pertains, for instance, to the Hindu principle of karma. Karma requires that the individual not only accept the burden of previous incarnations, but also answer for his actions in his current life. And yet, guilt is less significant than shame, which is the more apparent and mass system of influencing individual behaviour. Confucianism also assiduously cultivated a sense of shame.

The antithesis pride versus shame currently plays a major role in the functioning of social consciousness and practical ideological and political battles. Nevertheless some established stereotypes of shame and pride may be seen as undesirable from the point of view of various political interests and thus various means, including mass terror and total control over the individual, may be utilised to eradicate them.

The moral virtues advocated by traditional societies, which have been extolled by many thinkers (honour, courage, justice, honesty, generosity, pride, respect for others, etc.) turn out to be relative, for they are to be observed only within the boundaries of one's "own" community. In relationships with members of other communities they are sometimes turned inside out and if necessary metamorphose into mutual distrust, hatred, and treachery. Antagonism is the reverse side of such solidarity and its indispensable counterpart, creating the psychological mechanisms for the rejection of, and disdain for "strangers".

Of course, the crux of the matter lies not in the excessive amount of aggressiveness, as some writers claim when they compare this with the English philosopher Thomas Hobbes' "*bellum omnium contra omnes*". Antagonism is an integral component of the normative mechanism of furthering internal solidarity. Increased interaction between communities undoubtedly widens the boundaries of solidarity and eliminates the excesses engendered by antagonism, but this does not abolish it entirely.

Hierarchies and egalitarianism. Traditional societies are characterised by a slow increase of the means of production. This gives rise to the idea that the sources of means of subsistence are limited (the stereotype of the "constant pie"). Thus, the adherence to the habitual norms of distribution of the existing means of subsistence is an important concern within such societies. Their violations lead to fierce conflicts and a strong desire to "restore justice".

Egalitarianism is to a great extent nourished by the sentiments of the lower classes, who mainly depend on redistribution for survival. Egalitarian demands are a means of protecting the interests of the lower classes, limiting the desires of the ruling classes, and the degree of exploitation, and preventing excessively prestige-orientated and parasitical consumption by the wealthy strata.

However, egalitarianism in and of itself does not call for a transition from the old mode of production to a new and more advanced one. An egalitarian approach to the gross product hinders the utilisation of accumulated labour for increasing production. In the more primitive societies, accumulated wealth is simply destroyed in extravagant feasts, war, and raids. The need to set up a stable system of division of labour and differentiation of roles results in a shift towards the organisation of society based on hierarchal principles, which are applied both to production and the lifestyles of the different social strata. The ensuing system of division of labour inevitably leads to some people dominating others.

In traditional societies egalitarianism co-existed in a complex, intertwined fashion with hierarchal principles, which were firmly established in the consciousness. The degree and nature of the hierarchy varied greatly depending on the level of social differentiation. Rank, caste, and class distinctions, which were expressed in external signs and behavioural norms, became the incarnation of the inner value of the individual in the consciousness as well. This system encouraged not only obedience, but also servility and sycophancy in relation to superiors, and domination and scorn in relation to inferiors. Dominance and subordination were perceived as components of the system of solidarity, whereby the superiors (good monarchs, landowners, leaders, officials, etc.) adhered to the principle of *noblesse oblige*, while the common people repaid the former with obedience.

The correlation between these ambivalent value orientations (solidarity and antagonism, egalitarianism and hierarchies) entails complicated dynamics, which depend on the actual state of a given community and society in general. Solidarity within different social communities and between them could turn into grave disturbance and open clashes, which will die down once the potential of the given conflict is exhausted. Strict dominance systems tend to rouse egalitarian tendencies and engenders active movements, which brings about the reestablishment of hierarchal structures.

Each society attempts to avoid the actual confrontation of these opposing orientations by developing a mechanism of self-control, which prevents eruptions. Religion plays an enormous role in this respect. However, such eruptions are sometimes institutionalised as "ritual rebellions" in folk mystery-plays and carnivals, where all hierarchal structures are temporarily abolished, allowing complete freedom to reign.

In such structures, the attitudes towards wealth and labour are based on principles of solidarity and hierarchy. The traditional mass consciousness is primarily orientated not on the increase of the material prerequisites of labour, but on the satisfaction of immediate vital needs. However, these needs are strictly delineated by the position of the given group or individual within the general system of relations, i.e., consumption is limited in nature. Thus, the consumption values inherent in mass consciousness are subordinate to the values discussed above, which can be viewed as basic. The former are embodied by such ideals as wealth, health, longevity, many children, strength, wisdom, and so forth. All of these are supposed to strengthen the group or individual in relation to his enemies or adversaries.

Qualities related to procreation, i. e. the production of the true wealth of traditional societies, man himself, are also extremely significant. Erotic folk symbolism (both visual and verbal) developed on this level is closely linked to the general emphasis on the maximisation of natural abilities. This can be seen in the stubborn resistance of the traditional consciousness to the idea of birth control.

Folklore, in all of its forms, is a reasonably valid reflection of the values inherent in mass consciousness. Folklore usually extols certain characters, endowed with authority and all sorts of virtues, even if at the expense of others. Folklore reflects the inequality of people: friends versus strangers, nobles versus commoners, rich versus poor, strong versus weak, and so forth. In general, folklore tolerates cruelty and injustice if they are a source of someone's power and success. At the same time, social criticism plays an important role in folklore. It expresses the resentment of the lower class against the behaviour of the upper classes and their protest against the customs of patriarchal families, the cruelty of the caste system, the hypocrisy of the clergy, the bribery of officials...

The previously mentioned orientations also determine the attitudes of the masses to such crucial factors as labour and wealth. Traditional societies value labour and the skills it requires. It is perceived as the source (even if not the only one) of the acquisition and consumption of material goods. Labour for the sake of accumulation and savings, meant for the development of the material factors of production is condemned not only because it leads to increased exploitation, but also because it strengthens the tendency towards the withdrawal of the growing section of the common wealth and creates new sources of welfare for these propertied strata, unavailable to others. Excessive savings were to be redistributed, either directly of indirectly, between all members of the community in the form of feasts, presents, aid in times of trouble, religious donations, and so forth.

The limited nature of productive forces and relations in traditional societies results in a situation whereby the individual's position is but little affected by his industry. Instead, it is determined primarily by "fate", the amount of land he inherits, the size of his family, his caste and religious status, nature's "good will", and other factors which man has little control over and which make up his karma. However, a lot depends on the quality of the relations of the individual with his group or the person he is dependent on.

In traditional societies, the well-being of both the individual and the group as a whole was determined to a considerable degree by communocratic relations. The perpetuation of these relations (festivals, rituals, joint discussion, etc.) taken from the point of view of pure production, rather resembles leisure, which often provides grounds for sarcastic criticism (or envy) by bourgeois sociologists. A significant part of accumulated wealth is utilised for the perpetuation of these relations.

This system did not close the door for the growth of demand for and the consumption of material values, either in the past or in the present. Instead, consumption (individual and social) is viewed as the basis for the development of the qualities of both the individual and the group as a whole. Secular culture, as well as many religions, perceive wealth as a factor, which strengthens solidarity. This applies when wealth is utilised for religious purposes, festivals, charity, the upkeep and entertainment of relatives, fellow-tribesmen and neighbours, the upkeep of multitudes of servants and spongers, distributed according to "stirrings of the heart", and so on.

In traditional social structures, wealth is the prerequisite for going beyond the narrow boundaries of one's existence prescribed by low levels of production and rising to a higher level of consumption, a source of prestige both in this world and beyond. The main traditional channels for the utilisation of accumulated wealth are the subsidising of production costs by the wealthy and the support of rituals and religious cults, which are both sanctioned by the established norms and religion. The same consciousness which condemns excessive accumulations easily accepts making debts for the sake of prestigious activities (weddings, funerals, etc.) This often results in the enslavement of the individual or even his entire family for many years or even future generations.

On the one hand, there were fantastically rich individuals, which gave rise to the myths of Eastern extravagance. On the other hand, the broader masses suffered from extremely limited possibilities for consumption. This was sanctioned by customs and religious principles aimed at encouraging acceptance of the existing situation. The privileged classes confiscated all goods which were above the established minimum subsistence level. However, accumulation often turned out to be dangerous even for wealthy individuals, for the ruling class had claims to it. Thus, the source of the poverty of the masses lies not only in insufficiently developed production, or in the bounty of nature, which makes people lazy, but also simply in the stagnant social relations, which form part of the system of class domination and subordination.

The Attitudes Towards Power in the Traditional Mass Consciousness

Extremely strong urges to "socialise" the government and demands for legitimate power, which should reflect the interest of the entire society constantly pervade its existence. A thorough and impartial analysis of historic reality led to the renunciation of the concept of Oriental despotism, which once played a considerable role in identifying the laws governing the formation and functioning of socio-political and intellectual structures in the East. This concept portrayed the monarch as having a monopoly on power and the state bureaucracy as totally isolated from the other social groups. Contrary to this opinion, first Eastern and then African socio-political structures turned out to be much more complex entities, laced with contradictions and subject to intensive inner dynamics. Authority was necessary for the regulation of the general affairs within the entire society. Thus, it was often expressed in paternalistic, family-related symbols, based on the assumption that it protected the entire nation, not that it only served the privileged elite and the ruling minority. The latter was often perceived as an unnecessary impediment in the relations between the supreme ruler and the people. Protest movements directed at bad counsellors and officials, who were deceiving the ruler often arose as a result. And in extreme situations, there were mass uprisings against the bad reigning monarch in order to replace him with a good one.

However, despite the cultivated ideals such as "pious caliphs", the just king Asoka of Buddhism, the ideal king Vicrama of India, and so on, countless real monarchs were merciless, as they were guided by the pragmatic interests of the ruling class or even simply their own whims. This was the basis for the stable tradition of mistrust for the existing authority, as a hostile and oppressive force. The Buddhist monastic regulations contained in the Pali Canon, already put "danger from kings" before "danger from robbers, from fire, from water, ... from beasts of prey". *

Reality inevitably demonstrated the alienated essence of power. Increased oppression by the state resulted in the instability of the forms of social integration linked to it as the source of general moral standards and laws. When the class content of these precepts and the essence of the state itself became apparent, the masses became hostile to it, for they perceived that they had been victims of unjust laws and subject to manifest tyranny by the powers that be.

Internal problems were not the only grounds for upheaval. When social organisation was based on the identification of society with the government, clashes with external forces would lead to instability too. The desire to strengthen the given state was fraught with the possibility of exhausting wars. Even when they were successful, such wars drained the people's strength in the name of goals which were becoming increasingly foreign to them.

The government was perceived by the masses as a hostile and oppressive force, in contradiction to the cultivated stereotype of a "good government". The futility of protests against it nourished the tendency towards alienation from the government, escape into one's private life, i.e. a sphere where the authority could not reach one.

Mass movements arose during periods of instability. These movements stood for the creation of a "just" gov-

* Emanuel Sarkisyanz, *Buddhist Backgrounds of the Burmese Revolution*, Martinus Nijhoff, The Hague, 1965, p. 78.

ernment, which would reflect everyone's interests. These movements often engendered charismatic leaders, whose personal qualities allowed them to overcome the given state of the society and direct it towards new goals. Protests against class oppression and against a government isolated from the people brought enormous forces to the fore, which destroyed the established order. However, the positive changes proposed by these movements were inevitably utopian in essence. This led to their eventual defeat or metamorphosis, even in the case of initial success.

The contradictions and unreliability inherent in the forms of social regulation used by government authority led social consciousness to religion, which was immune to the corrosive influence of "earthly" politics, in search for a more convincing foundation for the expression of the interests and hopes of the people.

Commodity-Money Relations and Intellectual Production under Capitalism

Karl Marx and Frederick Engels stressed the importance of small-scale private property. In the *Manifesto of* the *Communist Party,* they wrote that property acquired individually through one's own labour is the basis of personal freedom and independent activity. In *Capital,* Marx stresses that when the worker determines the working conditions himself, he demonstrates all of his inventiveness and physical abilities and thus his individuality.

Individual labour based on the worker's small-scale private property became an important cultural phenomenon. It retains its importance even when large-scale industry engulfs the basic spheres of production. Independent handicraft provided the material basis for the arts, which produced fine works of art or architecture.

The development of capitalism deprived the individual of the property he earned with his own labour. This undermined the cultural foundation for his individual development as well. Independence, prudence, skill and will, all of which he needed when engaged in his individual labour, now became useless. The mechanical production process subordinates the individual, even though he is alienated from its results.

At the same time, individual labour does have serious disadvantages besides the advantages it has over large-scale production. One's development is considerably limited by one's constant physical strain and the significant subordination of one's labour to the insistent need to avoid poverty and one's uncertainty about one's future.

How does large-scale production, which takes final shape under mature capitalism, influence intellectual processes?

In capitalist societies, production is founded on the predominance of accumulated capital (tools, machinery, technology) over live labour. The labour is usually skilled, but the individual functions as the performer of this labour, either as worker or as employer, while the other components of his being do not affect production directly. Commodity-money relations link all production units, and thus, individuals as performers of labour. Therefore, the individual is bound to production by money, as a manifestation of functioning capital. This inevitably leads to the decay of previous social relations and their considerable individualisation.

The founders of Marxism believed that it was also very important to study ideological structures which sheltered these processes. Ideology significantly affected both economic and socio-political processes. For instance, the slogans of the Reformation (making the Church more democratic, less costly, etc.) and the Enlightenment (the restoration of violated natural human rights, the gaining of liberty, equality, fraternity, etc.) provided the necessary foundation for the unity of the classes making up the third estate, which Marx and Engels describe as the indispensable basis for the triumph of bourgeois socio-political revolution. The stable functioning of capitalism would be impossible without the preservation of the ideological formulas which arose during the period of bourgeois revolutions.

Mature commodity circulation (whereby labour is also a commodity) seems to embody individual freedom, however, it is a façade for capitalist exploitation. "...The process of exchange of exchange values developed in circulation not only respects freedom and equality, but is also their real basis, while they are its products. As pure ideas, they are idealised expressions of its various moments; being developed in juridical and social relations, they are merely reproduced in other degrees." *

Marx demonstrated that the relationship of domination and exploitation is hidden behind the façade of free relations between supposedly equal members of capitalist society. The discovery of surplus value, gained by the capitalists by means of consumption of the "independent" labour he has purchased, allowed for the unmasking of the vindicatory function of capitalist ideology.

In their work, *The German Ideology*, Marx and Engels write that the ruling class forces its ideology on the subordinate social strata. And this leads to the distortion of the real nature of things in the ideological life of society as a whole. The result is that formal or simply hypocritical proclamation of intellectual values can reflect the mercenary interest of the privileged classes. On the other hand, the subordinate class is denied the opportunity for asserting its alternative values which are underestimated and scorned.

The dominant system of values enforced by ideology creates a mechanism for the inculcation of principles which correspond to the general goals of the higher classes, and justify their activity and right to priority. Accordingly, this system ensures conformist behaviour from the subordinate strata, instilling in them tractability and acceptance of the enforced lifestyles.

On the institutional level, this correlation of class-orientated types of cultures is ensured by the education system and the mass media, which serve as a mechanism for the ruling of culture by capitalist governments.

The inculcation of commodity-money relations into all spheres of activity is characteristic of mature capitalist societies. This shapes the basic, dominating types of consciousness and culture. Nevertheless, internal contradictions, reflected in the intellectual life, are inherent in capitalist societies. The main contradiction lies in the opposition of values and goals linked to the functioning of

* Karl Marx, "Economic Manuscripts of 1857-1858", in Karl Marx, Frederick Engels, *Collected Works*, Vol. 29, Progress Publishers, Moscow, 1987, p. 475.

capitalist wealth, i. e. capital, and the values inherent in the independent development of each individual.

Property ownership lies at the heart of the bourgeois values system since property ensures an independent status in the world of property owners. The transformation of private property into the basis of social interaction makes social relations formal and impersonal. Relations between people are replaced with relations between capitals, incomes, and property statuses.

Thus, people seek to express themselves outside of pure production relations, in the sphere of leisure. Here they are free of the constraints of the law of constant growth of capital and the fierce battle of competition, where only the strongest survive, i. e., the most successful in the chase after profits.

If we keep in mind this structural division of intellectual life in capitalist society into purely business and non-business related spheres, we can understand the contents of the basic values which are usually considered as inherent in Western culture.

1. *Achievements and success* are values which often lead to the use of the word "achieving" in reference to Western culture. It is not by chance that the image of the self-made man is so popular in capitalist societies. These values are usually evaluated on the basis of financial and economic criteria. The methods used to acquire wealth are ignored.

2. *Individualism*. The underlying assumption here is the acknowledgement of the absolute rights of the individual and his freedom and independence from society and the state. Bourgeois individualism focuses the energy of independent individuals into the spheres of economic and political activity, thereby further increasing the rate of development of productive forces. The individualistic foundation of Western culture was not eradicated by the evolution of various forms of "corporatism", characteristic for state-monopoly capitalism. Individualism is closely linked in the bourgeois consciousness with such concepts as freedom, equal opportunity, competition and individual success.

However, the development of contradictions within capitalist society resulted in conflicts between the ideal of independent individuality and reality. As a principle of relationship between people individualism became antihumanitarian, as a norm for the relationship between the individual and society—antisocial, as applied to the state and legality, it turned antidemocratic, and within family relations it is metamorphosed into immorality.

3. *Activity and labour.*Commodity-money relations cannot function without the constant circulation of commodities and capital, which sets in motion the entire spectrum of elements of social and cultural structures. Social entities, technology and intellectual life in capitalist society are very flexible and dynamic. This often is reflected in the artificial introduction of new consumer goods and alteration of styles and fashions, which is mainly done for the safe of mobility.

Industry was originally the trait of capitalist enterprise which ensured economic success. However, the increase of social contradictions detracted from its importance in favour of the pursuit of quick profit.

4. *Consumerism.* The maturation of capitalist society and increased average incomes led to cultural changes, reflected in substitution of hedonistic values, such as material comfort and increased consumption, for the stress of humanitarian and intellectual factors, found in earlier periods. However, the lust for consumption is far from always matched by individual opportunities, which causes acute emotional stress.

5. *Universalism,* i.e., the extension of capitalist values to other cultures and civilisations. Universalism is fraught with destructive consequences for the latter or the social degradation of the inhabitants of the given lands.

It is important to understand that the above values of Western culture are primarily professed by those social strata which are most interested in the establishment of capitalist relations. They either already are or want to be entrepreneurs. The situation differs for those parts of the population, which do not have many hopes for achieving wealth and success. These people approach the values of capitalist entrepreneurship critically.

The inculcation of mass demand, with a growing system of its gratification, became an important method of re-orientating the intellectual demands of the workers in developed capitalist societies. According to some scholars, including the German-American sociologist Herbert Marcuse, it is this ability to satisfy the increased demands of a significant part of the working class which ensures the capitalist class control over the state of the society in accordance with its own interests. At the same time, the domination of mass culture does not allow for distinguishing spontaneous demands from those which were instilled by advertisement; they are usually artificial and the satisfaction of some of them is expected to increase one's prestige. In these conditions, individual requirements are closely linked to social ones, which in turn, are linked to those of capitalist society as a whole. The degree to which they are satisfied increases according to the gross quantity of goods, even though this masks intellectual poverty and a one-dimensional structure of desires. According to Marcuse, the rise in living standards and the standardisation and trivialisation of mass culture cement the system of class unity and hide the domination and subordination relationship.

Marcuse's conclusion can be reduced to an appeal directed at the leftist radical intelligentsia and various marginal and extremist groups to carry out a humanitarian revolution against the represssive culture of industrial society. This entails rejecting the repression of primordial (primarily erotic) urges and establishing avant-garde art, which combines real life with imagination.

Naturally, in modern society, the working class of developed nations differs dramatically from the 19th-century proletariat that Marx wrote about. However, this does not yet mean that it has been either socially or culturally integrated into the middle class. Impersonal labour devoid of content, the instability of the worker's role in social production, and their cultural isolation all lead to the formation of a stable sub-culture, which opposes the dominant norms and values, accepted by the middle class. Further technological advances should ensure that labour becomes more qualified and human in essence.

The moral standards and intellectual values which the workers would like to see realised in modern society are even more important factors, both for the development of production and for the transformation of labour, as well as for the enrichment of their personalities. The scientific and technological revolution requires not only ingeniousness and physical fitness from the actual producer, but also a store of knowledge and intellectual abilities which would allow him to work with modern technology and adapt quickly to further advances. This calls for a marked improvement in the training of workers and the increase in the proportion of engineers and technicians. The production of skilled labour requires further training and greater experience. The increased educational and cultural level of the modern worker, as well as his growing role in ensuring the functioning of complex production, have made him feel a need for taking independent decisions and participate in the management of both production and society as a whole.

The contradictions inherent within the social existence and intellectual life of capitalist societies have engendered mass movements which strive to overcome the negative aspects of capitalist civilisation, re-structure Western society itself into a society with other types of culture and limit the disastrous consequences of its expansion.

Intellectual Production under Socialism

The main goal of socialism is to further the surmounting of the restrictions which can be found in societies consisting of antagonistic classes linked to the economic subordination of the workers to the ruling class and their alienation from production. This entails an economy sufficiently developed to free man from excessive daily labour, and allow for his overall development. This also entails a radically different method of intellectual production.

Socialism should bring about the combination of culture with the creative activity of the masses. The workers metamorphose from passive consumers lacking initiative into an independent force. The domination of principles and authorities isolated from the individual is eliminated and he becomes master of his fate. The success of socialism depends on a level of productive forces which is higher than that under capitalism, a transfiguration of material activity which would allow the workers to abandon direct production not as expelled unemployed, but as individuals craving overall development. In such societies, labour is not only a means of ensuring individual survival, but the sphere for the realisation of the personality. Intellectual production is no longer isolated from and opposed to, material production, but instead is combined with it into one effective unity.

However, this is but one aspect of the overall evolution of society. The increase of the potential of intellectual production is another. Socialist culture utilises the achievements of world civilisations and gathers all of the best and progressive results of the creativity of thousands of nations and peoples, and includes the values of the past in the cultural life of the present.

The above type of society, which radically differs from the earlier traditional and industrial types, possesses the following intellectual characteristics:

1. *The drive towards the constant overall development of the individual* through the disclosure of his abilities and creative talents and the modification of the character of his needs. This is realised both in practical activities (production) and in social interaction.

2. *The approach to labour as a primary vital need*, as a sphere whose meaning consists of the realisation of the individual's potential and its use for the attainments of the goals of society as a whole.

3. *Focus on the constant accumulation and improvements of the material and intellectual components of production.*

4. *Stress on the gratification of the reasonable needs and desires of the individual*, that is, on moderation in relation to the contents, level, and methods of gratification.

5. *Solidarity in communocratic relations*, which leaves space for individual development and stimulates it. Such solidarity assumes mutual respect for individual freedom and human dignity. It requires that people are considerate towards and interested in each other, and that they are prepared to support each other in times of trouble and in a common cause.

6. *Humanitarianism*, which entails the acknowledgement of the value of the individual, his right to liberty, happiness and the development of his abilities. The good of mankind becomes the criterion for the evaluation of social institutions which plan human activity, while justice

becomes the desirable norm for relations between people.

7. *Internationalism* in relations between various peoples, based on friendship, equality, mutual respect and multifaceted co-operation.

8. *Universalism*, which shapes an orientation common to various peoples and social groups towards the transformation of reality and the building of a just society.

9. A revolutionary focus on the acceleration of social progress through increasing the political awareness of the masses and stimulating their participation in the transfiguration of society.

These features are far from always organically inherent in socialist culture during the earlier stages of socialist society's development, but serve as goals and ideals. Their introduction and dissemination occurs gradually, in the course of economic, political and cultural evolution of socialism.

Socialist culture encompasses traits formed by both religious and scientistic pragmatic cultures. Ideally, a member of socialist society should control his emotions and avoid excessive rationality, have lofty values and practical sagacity at the same time, in a word, he should be harmoniously developed and public-spirited.

It is worth noting that at present, socialist culture is not a unified whole. Only some of its components exist. During the building of socialism, the socialist countries ran into significant difficulties, which gave rise to serious problems. Social relations and intellectual life turned out to be bound by fetters artificially imposed by a bureaucratic political system, which controlled the main resources of society. The functioning of culture was also distorted. All of this required radical restructuring, which should unveil the true possibilities of socialism.

Such are the general characteristics of intellectual production in pre-industrial, capitalist, and socialist societies. To a great degree, these determine the contents and social functioning of culture. Each of these societies has its own type of social relations. Communocratic relations dominate in traditional society, commodity-money relations in capitalist society, and the free co-operation of producers in socialist society. Each type of social relations engenders a corresponding version of intellectual life. The focus on status or capital not only turns them into fetishes, but also creates contradictions in the cultural sphere. Socialism, on the other hand, has a type of relations, which annuls previous contradictions and leads to the focus on the comprehensive development of man, who becomes a part of a complicated network of relations with society and the world.

If you wish to study the subject in depth:

1. Alexeyev, V. M., *Kitaiskaya narodnaya kartina* (Chinese Folk Painting), Nauka, Moscow, 1966.
2. Bakhtin, M. M., *Tvorchestvo F. Rable i narodnaya kultura srednevekovya i renessansa* (The Legacy of François Rabelais and Folk Culture in the Middle Ages and During the Renaissance), Nauka, Moscow, 1965.
3. Gurevich, A.Ya., *Kategorii srednevekovoi kultury* (Categories of Medieval Culture), Iskusstvo, Moscow, 1984.
4. Erasov, B. S., *Sotsialno-kulturniye traditsii i obshchestvennoye soznaniye v razvivayushchikhsya stranakh Azii i Afriki* (Socio-cultural Traditions and Social Consciousness in the Developing Nations of Asia and Africa), Nauka, Moscow, 1982.
5. Losev, A. F., "Mifologiya" (Mythology) in *Filosofskaya entsiklopediya,* (The Philosophical Encyclopaedia), Vol. 3, Sovetskaya Entsiklopedia, Moscow, 1964.
6. Porshnev, V. F., *Sotsialnaya Psikhologiya i istoriya* (History and Social Psychology), Nauka, Moscow, 1978.
7. Tokarev, S. A. and Meletinsky, E. M., "Mifologiya" (Mythology), in *Mify narodov mira* (Myths from Around the World), Vol. 1, Sovetskaya Entsiklopediya, Moscow, 1980.
8. Benedict, R., *Patterns of Culture*, Houghton Mifflin, New York, 1961.
9. Eliade, M., *Myth and Reality*, Allen and Unwin, London, 1964.

8

The Ethnic, National and Civilisation Planes of Culture

In reading this chapter, consideration should be given to the following:

1. What are the existing types of classification of culture?
2. What are the basic characteristics of culture on the ethnic plane?
3. What shapes culture on the national plane?
4. What are the characteristics of civilisation as a type of cultural unity?
5. How does culture change on the various planes?

The connection between intellectual activity and social existence makes culture extremely multifaceted. The contents of culture, and its laws and dynamics are evinced in all of the spheres of society. They depend on the type of economic structure, social environment, or political system, and, last but not least, on the historical stage of development of the given society.

Sociologists usually divide cultural phenomena, either directly or by implication, into three basic types in accordance with the following criteria: 1) similarity (homogeneous units), 2) inorganic combination (heterogeneous congeries), and 3) organic unity (organic wholes). * Description according to similarity reveals either the functions of culture in various socio-economic units (urban, class, or age-related cultures), or the area where each given element operates (which is an important subject-

* Pitirim Sorokin provides this classification, even though in greater detail, in his *Society, Culture and Personality. Their Structure and Dynamics: A System of General Sociology* (see recommended reading for Chapter 3).

matter of ethnology). The similarity of various aspects of culture gives rise to meta-ethnic entities (i. e., uniting several ethnoses) such as ethno-lingual, cultural-cum-economic (according to similarity of material culture), historic-cum-ethnological (according to similarity in the arts and everyday life), and ethno-religious (according to religious unity) ones. These entities are based on similarities between the populations of different territories in some kind of shared characteristic (such as economic structure or language), but they do not encompass any other spheres of life of the same populations.

Heterogeneous congeries are based on characteristic features of different planes of cultural phenomena, which are either unrelated in terms of function or causality or related by external principles forced onto these phenomena (for instance by museum exhibits or libraries).

The organic whole presupposes the functioning of a cultural complex as a single entity, which may be a contradictory one, but is held together either by function or causality. Similarity criteria of cultures make it possible to distinguish three planes of culture: the ethnic, national, and civilisation, ones.

Culture and Ethnos

Cultural factors play an important role in the shaping of the ethnos. The ethnos is a historically evolved community of people with shared, relatively stable cultural and psychological features, a common language, aware of their own unity and their differences from other such communities, and having a name for themselves. The territorial limitations of ethnoses give rise to certain interdependent factors constantly operating in their consciousness. On one hand, these factors ensure their survival, due to their unity. On the other hand, they place one ethnos into opposition with another for some reason or other. The members of the group develop continual archetypes of belonging to a stable prototype, which is reflected in language, place-names, and so forth. As a result, ethnic features which in reality are relative are perceived as absolute. At the same time, many "secondary" characteristics are disregarded. Features turned into fetishes serve both as signs of belonging to the given ethnos and those of its distinction from others. The less developed the community, and the less differentiated its internal relations, the more natural (the less cultured) is its consciousness. As social differentiation increases, so does the significance of cultivated behavioural patterns. Thus, the influence of such natural features as kinship, and common ancestry, and customs is undoubtedly greater in the tribal environment than in an ethnos strictly divided into urban and rural populations. In ethnoses, the close connection between economic and religious relations leads to the syncretism of culture, which has not yet developed a fixed distinction between subjective and objective factors or between "I" and "we". The culture unites the past and present generations, while social relations are intertwined with man's relation to nature. The culture of an ethnos ensures not only its integrity and stability as a system. Various elements of such a culture lead a "dual life", for they also serve to show differences between ethnoses, becoming the basis for distinguishing "us" from "them".

The need for differentiation results in one of the components (language, religion, cultural and political structures or aesthetic features) becoming a system-forming factor, responsible for the identity of the given society as distinct from other societies. The significance of any cultural component is always relative. One ethnos may have a cultural feature another ethnos does not possess, and this constitutes one of the differences between the two. However, it is a neutral element in the contacts of the former ethnos with one which does possess this feature, too. The differentiating function of ethnic culture constantly manifests itself in the persistent maintenance of an "us" versus "them" relationship. This often leads to mutual alienation and conflicts between various nations. On one hand, consolidation of national culture eliminates internal disunity and on the other, it results in the increase of international conflicts. Antagonism is an integral characteristic of the mechanism whereby inner unity is strengthened. This is one of the main causes for the various forms of ethno-centric sentiments constantly surfacing in the mass consciousness. Developing relations between ethnoses undoubtedly broadens the boundaries of solidarity and eliminates excessive antagonism, but does not abolish antagonism entirely.

The attitudes of one ethnos towards others fluctuate, depending on various internal and external factors. It could be co-existence, which arouses interest, but does not lead to interaction. Mutual or unilateral penetration is also a possibility, whereby some elements are utilised, but the mutual alienation continues. Of course, some elements of inter-ethnic culture, which is the basis for interaction between ethnoses, emerge on this plane, too. The language of inter-ethnic contacts, which is not necessarily the native language of any of the given ethnoses, is one of the primary elements of such cultures.

Thus in Tropical Africa trade and economic contacts are effected utilising not only Swahili and Hausa, but also lesser ethnic languages, as well as various mixed jargons. However, such culture is too immature to ensure the intensive interaction of heterogeneous elements. Controversies and conflicts where cultural differences could serve as grounds for enmity or violence, make the establishment of stable unity on a higher level a vital necessity.

The interaction of ethnic cultures has some internal contradictions. On one hand, mutual absorption of cultural elements fosters integration, mutual enrichment, exchange, and so on, and on the other hand, it is accompanied by heightened ethnic self-awareness and the desire to preserve ethnic uniqueness.

Culture and the Nation

National culture encompasses a far greater variety of intellectual orientations and lifestyles than ethnic culture. It encompasses various subcultures, identified by ethnic, geographic, social, economic and class factors. It is often noted that nations are not formed through the achievement of uniformity. They are extraordinarily heterogeneous formations, incorporating various types of components, even though, in and of itself, each component contains the general cultural features which distinguish the given nation.

The inclusion of ethnoses into a nation does not mean that they assimilate the entire national culture. They only partially accept the nation's intellectual culture and form their own subcultures. Only a concrete analysis can show which features of the national culture were accepted by the subculture of the given ethnos or reveal how the integration of the given nations as a whole occurs.

Class distinctions manifest themselves in such spheres of national culture as law, morality, ideology and the arts. Class distinctions can also apply to different sorts of material symbols and attributes of social prestige, such as forms of greeting, adornments, manners, housing, clothing, etc.

Nevertheless, the differences between social groups within one nation do not extend to the cultural heritage of the nation as a whole. Cultural unity manifests itself in the language, and thus in the literature, the beliefs, symbols, everyday life, customs, and so forth. Intersocial cultural diffusion is also important, as regards class, occupation, way of life, etc.: for example, the mutual penetration of folk culture and aristocratic, urban and rural features, some characteristics of the settled and nomadic ways of life, and big city and provincial attitudes.

As a society develops, national culture serves as the framework for the formation of such means of social regulation of consciousness as law and morality (distinct from the accepted customs) and art and literature (as independent spheres of individual creativity).

History is an important parameter for evaluating national culture. On the purely ethnic level, time is basically reduced to constant repetition, linked to natural, economic, or human cycles or to a permanently remembered origins—a mythical forefather. The temporal boundaries of culture are widened on the national level, due to the accumulated experience and longer cycles of activity. National culture encompasses not only conceptions concerning the origins of the given people and state, but also records the history of the settlement of the people, their conflicts with their neighbours, and the flourishing or failures and disasters encountered along the way.

It is true, of course, that this memory is very selective. The social consciousness records only some, and not always the major, events, those which are perceived as examples of either failure or success. On the national level, political culture stresses the role of unification as a prerequisite for stability, power, and influence of the given nation as the basis for its prosperity. Strong government is seen as an important condition of unity, for this is necessary for withstanding internal strife and external enemies. This perception arises even when the given nation lacks sovereignty and is dependent or subordinate. The resurrection of symbols utilised by ancient states, even if their ethnic make-up and territory had nothing in common or barely coincided with those of the given contemporary state often provides the ideological grounds for its political independence achieved by a national liberation movement.

In such cultures, power is often vested in paternalistic symbolism, which implies protection not just of the ruling class, but the entire people. A "just" state ensures the continuity of the established (i. e. developed in the past) measure of solidarity and egalitarianism and prevents the total severance of paternalistic links. Under these circumstances the ruler is believed to be endowed with unique abilities and prerogatives. However, contacts with the really existing state gave rise to a different stereotype in the mass consciousness: the state as hostile and oppressive and power as the source of evil. This dual attitude towards the state often manifests itself in protest movements inspired by the dream of establishing a "good government". The latter is expected to regulate the interaction of the local cultures of various regions and the subcultures of various social strata. Even though high culture, embodied in law, political ideology, literature and art, and science, is to a considerable degree created in the interests of the ruling class, it still reflects the national spirit.

Civilisation as a Type of Cultural Entity

All nations have social, territorial and historic boundaries. Relative cultural homogeneity (despite all of the social differences) distinguishes nations from other nations. This leads to the complicated process of developing international relations, both on the political and the cultural levels. Even in ancient times, there were large international unions, far larger than nations in scope. Various terms have been used to denote these unions. The German culturologist Oswald Spengler used the phrase "high cultures". The Americans Alfred Kroeber and F. Northrop make use of "cultural formations with lofty values" and "world cultures" respectively. The Russian philosopher Nikolai Berdyaev spoke of "great cultures", the American sociologist Pitirim Sorokin of "extended cultural systems and supersystems". Arnold Toynbee's "civilisations" is commonly used, even though its meaning has been significantly modified.

Civilisation as a type of culture possesses the following characteristics:

1. Civilisation is based on the general socio-cultural connection between individuals and groups, which creates a large-scale unity in time and space. This connection is not just the result of commodity-money production relations. Communocratic relations, mediated by intellectual factors of social production, can also take on general validity, most obviously in the world religions. Social wealth which is typical of civilisations, is not merely material wealth. It also includes the wealth of human relations, which manifest themselves in both material and intellectual factors and methods.

2. Civilisation ensures a higher degree of variety in society's life. It furthers the progressive development of peoples, even though it may not prevent inequality and oppression. Civilisation is accompanied by the further division of labour (physical and intellectual, simple and complex). The interaction between material and intellectual production and urban and rural populations becomes simultaneously more complicated and more fruitful. This is primarily based on objective socio-economic mechanisms. The specific task of regulating various types of activity is accomplished by utilising subjective factors, i.e., intellectual mechanisms of interaction and of the motivation of activity.

Civilisation abolishes the contradictions between various ethnic and cultural groups, developed and undeveloped peoples, the central parts of the given country with its developed class division and the periphery, where class distinctions are still quite vague, the alienated nature of state power and the need for general regulation, and natural and historic parameters of social existence.

3. Civilisation embodies history. It provides continuity between past, present, and future.

It is impossible to understand the present or make forecasts for the future unless one turns to history. Knowledge of history is essential for existence of any society, for otherwise it may have to start from scratch, over and over again, repeating its past. Quite often, the glossing over of a given element from the past as being supposedly incompatible with present goals leads to the future restoration of a developmental stage which, it would seem, had long since faded into the past. The "vestige" is re-cultivated, and occasionally even "restored". In this case some of our accepted concepts turn out to be linked to a given cultural historical situation and are not always capable of reflecting the essence of intercultural comparisons.

History is primarily embodied in historical knowledge, which has its own sphere of existence. However, history is also recorded in cultural heritage, such as norms, knowledge, orientations, beliefs, meanings, and customs. The embodiment of this culture in signs, symbols, and texts is studied, interpreted, mastered and accepted or becomes the object of contention. In the latter case, the given cultural phenomenon is either absorbed into the lives of new generations or is changed, deformed, or destroyed.

The emergence of classical civilisations signified an important shift in the intellectual life of society, which was expressed in the formation of the individual's intellectual potential. In developed cultures, values and forms of consciousness were directed at the inner abilities of individuals and affirmed the possibility of intellectual and moral choice. The gnosiological, ontological and ethical components of philosophical and religious theories were centred at the individual.

The above functions have their inner laws, and interact with each other, although some of them contradict others. They had different manifestations in different civilisations and in the interaction between the latter. This has created an enormous field for comparative studies.

Of course, civilisation encompasses both material components (towns, handicrafts, etc.) and political structures (the state). However, the nature of intellectual production is what determines the character of various structures within civilisations. Civilisations reflect various types of cultural and historic community and dynamics. They co-exist and interact with each other. A given civilisation retains its structure and basic characteristics when it advances to the next stage of development. In fact, the characteristics and rhythms of civilisation exercise an important influence on social development, both past and present, as well as on the socio-cultural life of society.

We will not go back into history and examine ancient civilisations, such as Egypt, Sumer, Babylon, Greece, and so on. The contemporary situation worldwide makes it worthwhile to examine only the still existing world civilisations realising their potential to this day: European and North American (together they make up the West), Indian, Buddhist, Far Eastern, Islamic and Latin American. Some describe Tropical Africa as a proto-civilisation, which lacks a common religion, related to the beliefs prevalent in the area. This region lacks the "upper storeys" of culture. As a result of this "incompleteness", Christianity and Islam have spread through many countries of Tropical Africa and created the necessary spiritual and ethical levels of universality. Today, however, maturity is far from always perceived as being superior to "immaturity". The domination of religious orthodoxy in major centres turned out to be more of a burden in some ways than the "primitive" religions of African countries. On one hand, traditional orthodoxy of the classical Eastern religions is definitely weakening. On the other hand, the African intelligentsia is actively resurrecting the more universal and theoretical aspects of their own culture in philosophy and ideology, as well as in art and literature. The result is an undoubtable convergence of the levels of development of civilisations in different continents.

Cultural Dynamics

Intellectual production, which shapes the cultural life of society, is a complicated and multifarious process, wherein one can identify various tendencies. It requires maintaining both a complicated system of differentiation and social unity within the framework of ethnoses, nations, or civilisations. The nature of cultural development at various organisational levels was discussed above. It is also important to understand cultural dynamics, i.e., the mechanism of change within culture.

There are two basic types of such change:

a) the change of intellectual styles, artistic genres, interests, and fashions; territorial shifts of the centres of cultural activity, and social changes in culture, entailing the enrichment and greater variety of culture or of the relations between its various elements;

b) changes which lead to the weakening or total annulment of given cultural components, the simplification of cultural life, or even its stagnation.

Innovation (invention), inheritance (resurrection) and dissemination (diffusion) are usually perceived as the sources for positive cultural development. It is especially important to turn to the past, to accumulated knowledge and the established systems of values and symbols, when examining non-Western cultures. The cultural heritage of many centuries is an accumulation of those cultural elements which might re-enter culture under different circumstances.

1) Innovation entails the creation of something new by modifying old cultural elements. Thus, innovation is usually cumulative in essence, both in the spiritual and the technological spheres. Individuals and groups produce new ideas, norms and orientations utilising elements already present in society.

Innovation cannot come out of nowhere. Extensive studies of culture have shown that it has two reasons:

a) Creative abilities linked to the education standards achieved by the given society, to the social strata which most intellectuals come from and to the degree of activity of these strata.

b) Social demand, determined both by the state of the

society and the social stratum which is the most interested in expanding either intellectual or economic activity.

In Western society, it was the technological innovations which proved to be most attractive during the industrial boom, for success of the system of capitalist enterprise to a great degree depended on the level of the utilisation of the newest technology. Extra demands may be made on new political or intellectual currents during periods of social and intellectual change. This leads to the development of political, aesthetic, or intellectual views. For instance, 17th- and 18th-century England was famous for its jurisprudence and political philosophy, reflected in the systems of Thomas Hobbes and John Locke. Germany, on the other hand, was bound by vestiges of feudalism and produced outstanding philosophers, such as Kant, Hegel, Schelling and Marx only in the 18th and 19th centuries.

2) *Reference to cultural heritage*, i.e., the sum total of the cultural achievements of a given society and its historical experience, including that part of it which has been reappraised. All this has eternal value for society, in that it encompasses those achievements of different eras which can be transmuted to new generations in new epochs. The necessity of this transmutation is dictated by current social needs.

The dialectics of culture means a constant transition from the past to the present and the future. Everyday practice calls for constant analysis of previous experience, its adjustment, selection, interpretation, and enrichment. Within this sphere, linking the past with the present, excessive traditionalism can coexist with extreme pragmatism. At times, the professional study of the culture of the past engenders the view that only competent and thorough research and detailed descriptions of past cultural achievements can explain what has been accomplished. The importance attached to such research in the academic world and elsewhere, as well as the awards won by the authors of this research seem to be visible confirmation that the historic legacy has been preserved.

This is true to some degree. There is a certain sphere, both within the culture of each society and within worldwide culture in general, where heritage has an eternal life, and is safe from socio-political storms and turmoil.

This is culture in its physical manifestations, i.e., paintings, statues, and texts, that is, everything which can be stored in museums, libraries and published literary monuments. The maintenance of this sphere has evolved into a science with its own carefully developed methodology.

The preservation and mastery of cultural heritage is not only a vital component of the activities of social organisations and a mandatory task for the state. It also forms an important part of international projects. UNESCO plays an enormous role in this sphere.

Preservation is not the only concern. Traditional forms of creativity lost or half-forgotten must be resurrected. There is a fairly common tendency to present this heritage as the embodiment of some "living spirit" (culture), which has been preserved in the form of texts, symbols, paintings, and statues. This results in the belief that the comprehensive description and the preservation of a given monument actually constitutes the eternal existence of basic human values. Thus it may seem necessary to provide their consecutive, methodical descriptions, volume after volume, manuscript after manuscript, legend after legend, temple after temple. Symbols and images taken out of historical context could actually become part of the private world of individuals, but they do not necessarily become a part of their everyday life, nor do they have to be embodied in their new activities.

The values and meanings embodied in the monuments of the past are undoubtedly important factors in new culture. They not only have to be preserved, they must be reproduced, revealing their meaning for new generations over and over again.

The use of cultural heritage presents a constant dilemma for social consciousness. It reveals the deep contradictions inherent in the past itself, which invariably reflect the rivalry between various tendencies, inevitable in the classical model of the development of the given civilisation. This dilemma also reflects the variety of influences the West has had on the cultures of other regions.

Maintaining the stability and continuity of social regulation is one of the more important functions of cultural heritage. Those elements of cultural and social legacy which are passed on from generation to generation and preserved for long periods of time constitute tradition. The very existence of these elements for a given period of time provides their necessary justification and legitimacy. Tradition includes not only such imitative and routine activities as customs and rites, but also more differentiated and carefully appraised elements: values, norms, and social institutions. The mechanism of traditional regulation rejects innovations as harmful digressions. However, tradition can be a stable form of maintaining social regulation and cultural life only within relatively simple and isolated communities, where the intellectual sphere is almost inseparable from the practical one and the ancestor's behests provide adequate grounds for behaviour. More developed societies cannot be limited by traditions, thus their functions are reduced to the maintenance of the basic stabilising factors. Ideological battles, which reflect different social interests, engender various attitudes towards tradition. Different classes also have different attitudes towards previous norms and conceptions, interpreting some as positive and others as negative.

Attitudes towards tradition have special significance for people's movements, which comprehend activating principles through their customary forms of consciousness. Religious and revolutionary movements used ideas from the distant past, seeking to make them near and dear to the masses.

3. *The diffusive dissemination of culture.* If tradition is the transmission of culture through generations and time, diffusion is its dissemination in social or geographic space. Culture is disseminated among individuals, social groups, regions, and countries. This process can be either direct (through the influence of immigrants on the social milieu which absorbed them) or indirect (through the influence of mass media, consumer goods, cultural exchange, universities, research centres, etc.).

The factors which influence cultural diffusion include:

— The degree of intensity of the contacts. Constant or frequent interaction between societies leads to the rapid absorption of alien elements. Thus, the inhabitants of border regions or commercial centres usually absorb elements from other cultures faster than people in the inland areas.

— Conditions for contacts. Culture imposed by force

may be accepted by part of the population, but the wider masses will reject it.

— The degree of differentiation within a society. Peoples with social and cultural systems having greater variety accept alien cultural elements faster, and are confident that their uniqueness will not be destroyed thereby.

The character of cultural contacts in the modern world will be discussed in Chapter 18.

The above classification allows for the comprehension of the variety of existing cultural communities, and the changes they undergo. It does not contradict internal division into social subcultures examined in Chapter 6. Naturally, these two types of classifying culture intertwine in actual reality. Each one plays now a greater, now a lesser role, depending on economic or political factors.

The norms and values discussed in Chapter 4 are expressed differently in every cultural community. Cultural anthropology (ethnology) provides a detailed description of the specific cultural complexes which exist in various ethnic or national communities. In Part II, we will examine the cultural characteristics of Western and Eastern civilisations, as the largest complexes, which possess different historical heritages.

If you wish to study the subject in depth:

1. Bromlei, Yu. V., *Ocherki istorii etnosa* (Essays on the History of Ethnoses), Nauka, Moscow, 1983.

2. *Kulturnoye naslediye narodov Vostoka i sovremennaya ideologicheskaya borba* (The Cultural Heritage of the Eastern Peoples and the Contemporary Ideological Struggle), Nauka, Moscow, 1987.

3. Bagby, Ph., *Culture and History. Prolegomena to the Comparative Study of Civilizations,* Greenwood Press, Westport. (Conn.), 1976.

4. Braudele, F.; *Civilisations materielles et capitalisme (XV-XVIII siécles)*, t. 1—3, Colin, Paris, 1967, 1979.

5. Parsons, T., *The Evolution of Societies*, Prentice Hall, Englewood Cliffs, (N. Y.), 1977.

6. Steward, J., *Theory of Culture Change. The Methodology of Multilinear Evolution*, University of Illinois Press, Urbana, 1963.

PART II General Sociological Principles in the Study of Western and Eastern Civilisations

9

Modern Western Culture

In this chapter, consideration should be given to the following:

1. What was the role of Christianity in the formation of modern European culture?
2. What changes have occurred in the material basis of Western culture during the 20th century?
3. How do technological advances affect the intellectual life of Western society?
4. What are the reasons for the upsurge of irrational tendencies in 20th-century European culture?
5. What is the social character of Western mass culture?
6. What changes have occurred in Western mass culture within the past few decades?

We examined the basic characteristics of the type of intellectual production which exists in capitalist society in Chapter 7. The domination of commodity-money relations is reflected in the utilitarianism of practical activity, the rational attitude to material factors of existence, and the view of individualism and activity as the prerequisites for personal success in this world.

However, culture should not be reduced to merely functional components, needed to sustain a given aggregate mode of production. Therefore, capitalist society in the West is characterised not only by features which furthered its maturation, but also those which to this day keep going the more significant elements of its existence.

---

* In this chapter, I used works by the Soviet sociologists G. Ashin, Yu. Davydov and G. Sunyagin, all of whom are specialists on modern Western culture.

Christianity and Western Culture

Christianity has left a deep imprint on the entire social, political, intellectual and aesthetic development of the West. Its heritage is multi-faceted. It comprises not only independent established movements (Catholicism, Protestantism, Orthodoxy), but also various sectarian, heretical and secularised branches and elements. Nevertheless, these have the following common characteristics:

1. Monotheism, i.e., the belief in one God, transcendental in relation to man and the world. The deity is segregated from all creatures and objects, yet is perceived as the source of their being.

2. The view of the individual as a bearer of faith, who is directly responsible before God for his deeds.

3. The universality of sermons, regardless of all political and ethnic boundaries.

4. The precept that man must seek his own individual redemption before God, which is expressed in ritual, spiritual, or practical activities.

5. The separation of the spiritual sphere from the political one on the principle of "render to Caesar the things that are Caesar's, and to God the things that are God's".

Some sociologists believe that Christianity asserts the super-social essence of man, by removing him from the framework of purely social sanctions. However, this super-social essence is linked to general human principles of regulation, as they signify the triumph over the restrictions of the existing social structure.

Throughout the course of its history, Christianity developed various types of internal organisation:

1) the church as an institution controlling the entire society;

2) the sect as a closed group of the chosen opposing the rest of the world;

3) religious movements which are messianic and prophetic in nature.

During the 16th and 17th centuries, Christianity underwent a consistent and radical reformation, which resulted in the separation of Protestantism from Catholicism. Catholicism later underwent significant reform as well, adapting to the needs of the contemporary capitalist society.

The most important idea of the Reformation was the necessity of personal responsibility before God, without the mediation of the ecclesiastic hierarchy. Salvation could be achieved outside of Church rules. It could be achieved primarily through man's inner faith and his good deeds. The Reformation rejected the principle of ecclesiastic centralism and thus led to the strengthening of nation-states.

Protestantism played an important role in the development of capitalism. It encouraged worldly asceticism and personal faith, as forming the basis for the individual's set of values. However, this justification of the bourgeois way of life by religion was only typical at the early stages of development of capitalism. Later, capitalism breaks away from the Church and becomes purely secular.

Western Culture and Capitalism

Fundamental changes in the culture of the past accompanied the emergence of capitalist society. This led to a radical transformation in the existing system of intellectual orientation.

Man's individual freedom became the main principle of the new society, for, like Robinson Crusoe, man could now stand alone. This principle served as the foundation for the entire system of social relations. However, the average entrepreneur does not live on a desert island. He has to sign contracts with other individuals, both for exchanging the products of his labour and in order to create a state where formally no one could infringe upon the rights of others. This is why man's personal responsibility for his actions and the need for endurance in overcoming hardships were stressed in capitalist culture from the very start.

To a great degree, the Enlightenment had a serious effect on Western social consciousness and culture during the 18th and early 19th centuries. The Enlightenment thinkers saw the broad use of human reason for furthering social progress as the most vital task. Many remnants of medieval mentality in such varied spheres as law, the judicial system, religion, art, morality and politics were abolished during this period. The Enlightenment fostered the gradual democratisation of society, since more and more people took advantage of their legal rights, acquiring the opportunity to participate in civic life and gaining access to the achievements of high culture.

A significant development occurred in Western culture in the 19th century, when the principle of Realism was adopted by ideology, art and philosophy. Realism replaced illusory, mythological worldviews, man admitted the existence of a reality which was independent of the human consciousness. Utilitarianism, closely linked with the demands imposed by real life, began to take shape.

At the same time, the mature capitalist society of the 19th century became aware of its grave social and intellectual contradictions. This gave rise not only to criticism by social scientists, but also to broad political movements, aimed at the restructuring of society.

However, capitalism was not able to cleanse itself of its inherent contradictions even in the 20th century. They simply changed their character. The new structure of production, industrial growth, the dynamic progression of the scientific and technological revolution all affected the intellectual sphere. The socio-cultural context changes in a matter of decades, which only reaffirms that modern capitalism is capable of rapid change. This situation, more than ever, is laden with contradictions. On the theoretical level, this signifies that the formulation of any general thesis must be accompanied by an appropriate antithesis. This makes a general systematic conceptualisation of capitalism exceedingly difficult. However, let us attempt to outline the trends apparent in material culture.

The singular rate of development of productive forces had a variety of results. First of all, the role of technology in the economy changed. The scientific and technological resources of production were forced into permanent development and improvement and the cultural prestige of natural science and engineering increased accordingly. However, while automatisation was a blessing for culture, it was also an enormous tragedy for the individual. The number of unemloyed rose, which resulted in a dual attitude towards technology.

The changes in the position and role of technology in everyday life were extremely important for the development of culture in the 20th century. Even though technology was developing quite rapidly in Europe during the 19th century, it did not seriously affect people's everyday mentality. However, in the early 20th century the individual was bombarded with a multitude of new inventions in a mere 15-20 years. These included electricity, trams and cars, lifts, vacuum cleaners and refrigerators, radio, telephone, sound recording and so on. The mass press and photography were also highly important. The rate of technological progress continued to increase as more and more achievements were made.

As technology transcended the bounds of production and got into direct contact with man, it attracted attention in and of itself. Now it was the physical embodiment of such important human values as order, reliability, effectiveness and power. In the 19th century technological form as such was not truly significant. Increased effectiveness was associated mostly with quantitative parameters, i.e., large size, increased consumption of energy, and so on, but not with changed form. Exterior design began to play an important technological and aesthetic role only with the appearance of modern machines, such as cars and planes, where it was not a secondary factor, but the object of special effort. The people who did this work, — the designers — gradually formed a separate profession, and soon began to design the exterior of all manufactured goods, whether meant for production purposes or everyday use. Thus, technology acquired aesthetic form and became the object of cultural, as well as purely practical, interest.

All of these factors, which completely overthrew many established stereotypes, had an enormous socio-psychological impact. Knowledge of the most recent technological achievements gained by the general public, and especially intellectuals, changed the attitudes towards this strictly rational and extremely dynamic sphere, as well as the very worldview, of 20th-century man. A space which as recently as the 19th century was still an absolutely neutral and homogeneous receptacle for things has now become so condensed that the dependence of its characteristics on processes occurring within it, previously comprehended only theoretically, began to manifest itself in daily life too.

The sense of time has also changed dramatically. The strained tempo of life caused by modern technology abolished the perception of time as a homogeneous and impartial continuity. History, which was previously viewed as the distant past, has now become a vital element of everyday existence. Orientation amidst objects and processes now strictly requires that account be taken of the "fourth dimension", an inner dynamism and complex correlation with other objects and processes in time. No matter how paradoxical the world unveiled by relativist physics is it still corresponds as much to the world of the "second nature" created by modern technology, as it does, to, let's say, the medieval teachings about the eternity and the heavenly hierarchy of the socio-objective reality.

Culture and Technology

Technology significantly affected human perceptions of the world, both with its results and its methodology, i.e., the active forms of interaction of man with nature. The more long-lasting achievements of mechanisation lay not in the machines, which turned obsolete very rapidly, nor in the goods produced, which were consumed rapidly, but in the forms of activity which became possible due to the machines. The main feature of these forms is the drastic increase of the proportion of experimentation within the overall volume of production. Now the actual product, manufactured on a mass scale, and for the most part by machines, instead of by hand, was not as important as the first sample, which is an embodiment of an idea developed during the course of long experimentation. New technology devaluated the uniqueness of each single product, its sentimental ornateness and the skills of its maker (take for instance, *style moderne*). Integrity, plainness, and clarity formed a new ideal of perfection and beauty. All of these important and essentially positive changes had a direct effect on the bourgeois culture of the 20th century.

However, in general, the intrusion of the newest technology into culture gave rise to sharp contradictions in capitalist society, with its inherent class antagonism and pursuit of profits. As advanced technology penetrated into yet more spheres of human activity, it gave rise to new socio-psychological imperatives, as well as very specific socio-technological forms of organising this activity, restructuring it according to the models of large capitalist industry. Passenger transport, retail trade, the service industry, daily leisure and entertainment, tourism and even various hobbies all turned into branches of mass production, aimed at earning a profit and operating on the principles of strictly rational, industrial mechanisms.

This process affected intellectual culture as well. Intellectual activity metamorphosed from a process where the producer was (or at least thought he was) an independent creator, into the industry of mass consciousness. The intellectual was drawn into a commercially orientated industrial-type mass intellectual production, and thus virtually lost his freedom. He became a hired part-time worker, which is illustrated by the history of capitalist industry.

The intellectual culture which arose on this basis was naturally different in character as well. People realised that intellect in all its manifestations is bound by rigid fetters and that there is no longer any play of free intellectual potential, but merely the "product" of a gigantic rationalised machine. This realisation primarily led to the increased influence of technology on people's notions, which reflected the contradictions inherent in capitalism between the increasing rationalisation of various spheres of society's activity and the total unpredictability of its results. There arose a kind of cult of technology, faith in its decisive role both in social history and culture, as well as the improvement of human existence.

Of course, this was the direct descendant of 19th century classical positivism. However, it had inherited but few of its predecessor's liberal evolutionary illusions and instead showed a tendency for anti-democratic technocracy and the ability to integrate ideas of social manipulation. At the same time, it became to a great degree universalised by metamorphosing into scientism.

This faith in the omnipotence of the exact sciences became the opposite of the arts, morality, religion and intellectual values on the whole, all of which were viewed as being somewhat inferior and archaic. This is what the English writer C. P. Snow meant when he spoke of the split of the previously whole body of capitalist culture into two cultures. Therefore, scientism can be viewed as the ideological nucleus of the belief in the supremacy of technology, which penetrated most spheres of human activity, even those unrelated to science. This belief is reflected in unscrupulous conformism, as well as ritualism, which became the behavioural norm for the so-called silent majority, for whom consciousness deprived of any inner nucleus and focused only on the passive absorption of guiding principles, gained the status of common sense. It also lies at the base of cynical modern capitalist politicking — a sophisticated technology of manipulating public opinion — and various formalistic tendencies of modern art, which portrays man and his inner world as an assemblage of mechanisms produced with dispassionate virtuosity. It also clearly manifests itself in the principles of ethical formalism, which are abstracted from man and his values and amount to the codification of impersonal forms of behaviour. What about sociologists? They treat the individual as a multi-functional machine designed to perform social roles. And last but not least, it gave rise to the pan-gnosiological principle in contemporary philosophy, which dismisses traditional philosophical problems, as being unscientific and instead focuses wholly on the problems of methodology.

Yet, despite the fact that all these ideas seem to be the universal guiding principles of modern Western culture, they have never been generally accepted. Some strata of bourgeois intellectuals always resisted their spread, both during the pre-war years, when technology first penetrated into culture, and in the post-war era, especially during the industrial boom of the 1950's and 1960's. The more the influence of technology increased, the more fierce and destructive the opposition to it became. This individualistic counter-culture is the modern version of classical 19th-century Romanticism. However, the power of pro-technological ideology makes the opposition somewhat dependent on it, as the opposition takes shape and functions only as its antithesis.

The oppositional intellectual movements vary greatly in their positions. They range from subjectivism and individualistic anarchy to religion and mysticism, which strive to resurrect some sort of spiritualistic consciousness. The irrationality of these ideas is reflected in Freudian and neo-Freudian interpretations of the human psyche and human behaviour, existentialist or personalist abstract humanitarianism and the resurrection of various models of feudal utopian socialism. Its socio-psychological premisses are also contradictory. It is a naïve, groundlessly optimistic view of future, combined with fatalistic pessimism and disbelief in the possibility of the salvation of civilisation or even the continuation of man's existence on Earth.

The above transformation of the Romantic worldview in the mid-twentieth century and the ensuing change in its significance for bourgeois culture does not negate the assertion that the antagonism between pro-technological ideology and the counter-culture, which absorbed the previous opposition of the Romantic and Positivist types of social consciousness is at the heart of modern bourgeois culture.

Even in the 20th century, the ruling classes of capitalist society opposed the overall cultural development of the masses. However, there was a whole series of reasons why they could no longer prevent the access of the masses to culture. The resolution of this contradiction involved the establishment of the multifaceted system of so-called mass culture, whose main social function consists of channelling mass cultural demands aroused by the scientific, technological and social progress in a direction which suited the ruling classes. This was achieved by creating illusory forms of cultural consumption.

Such quasi-cultural processes do not lead to the true development and inner enrichment of the individual, even though they do make him use his socially significant potential. What comes into the foreground here is the primitive commonplace varieties of the attitude towards technology, namely, petty materialism. Consumer goods are perceived not as means of satisfying basic human needs, but as proofs of individual success and embodiments of the individual's primary social qualities. Moreover, the turbulent battle of competition casts the individual into the chaotic world of consumer goods, while the caprices of the artificial innovations of fashion time and again devaluate items which only yesterday were either trustworthy or prestigious. The consumer is often the victim of advertisements, which dramatise the world of consumer goods, skilfully exaggerate their actual significance in his daily life and fan his natural desire to get some of them into an overwhelming passion. Thereby, petty materialism not only needlessly exaggerates the significance of material and physical needs at the expense of intellectual and creative ones, but also transforms the basic needs of people into a semblance of highly emotional and intellectual tensity, turning genuine values into something vapid, dull or simply superfluous.

The Social Aspects of Mass Culture

Mass culture entails the production of intellectual values, forms, images and styles tailored for mass consumption. Mass culture is culture suitable for a maximally broad segment of the population, even though social disparity and levels of cultural development noticeably vary its volume of consumption in concrete environments. At the same time, efforts are made to ensure the permanent daily presence of mass culture through the mass media.

The producers of mass culture (those who control the mass media, including cinema, television, video, etc.) usually justify their production as being "what the public wants". Quite often, success is measured by box office receipts or popularity, which in the long run is also judged by the income. The apologists of mass culture view it as a positive phenomenon, which reflects higher living and education standards and also as a factor in the democratisation of society.

However, many criticise mass culture as being a camouflaged means of manipulating social consciousness and the state of the masses. This culture is built into the system of consumer orientations, which resolve subjective conflicts among the masses, thus ensuring the functioning of capitalism as a type of social organisation.

The adherents of elitist culture also criticise mass culture. They perceive mass culture as the distinct consciousness of a narrow-minded self-satisfied, aggressive and ignorant mass, which seeks to force its own primitive cultural attitudes onto society, thus diminishing the quality of intellectual life in general. They describe mass culture as "demonic" in order to explain its ubiquitous ability to bring genuine cultural values down to the level of the least developed tastes.

The mass media is an extremely powerful means of spreading culture. It has fundamentally changed the production, maintenance, dissemination and absorption of culture. Some sociologists believe that this changes the basic character of culture, too.

As far back as 1964, the Canadian sociologist, Marshall McLuhan, described the world, which is controlled by modern mass media, in paradoxical form, as a "global village" with a single culture. According to his conception, the network of electronic means of information is rapidly being spread to the entire planet, creating a common denominator for the world's cultural environment, eroding the boundaries between ideologies, religions, nations and social groups.

The French sociologist, Abraham Moles concurs. He believes that the emergence of mass media nullified the significance of the previous cultural heritages of both society and the individual. Even the basic system of education, accepted by society, also loses its previous role. The average person places much more significance on what he hears on the radio, sees on TV or in the cinema, reads on posters or in the papers or finds out from conversations with colleagues or neighbours, than on the knowledge he acquires in his family, school or college. As a result, the previous more or less uniform system of knowledge and values which made up man's worldview and the structure of his personality is replaced by a set of changing standpoints, subject to the constant influence of the mass media. This process inevitably preserves and widens the gap between the elite and the general public, which becomes the object of manipulation.

This approach, which mirrors the principles of the technocratic circles in the modern Western world, encounters serious opposition. The problem is that not only have both national cultures and the structure of individual human personality proved to be perfectly able to withstand the torrent of information, but also that the mass media themselves are subject to tremendous pressure on the part of the more active segments of society, which demand that they conform to humanitarian principles.

Western sociologists continually debate over the essence of mass culture and its role in society. Is it an evil, is it a harmless sedative, or does it free the mind?

In the past, mass culture was usually defined as pseudo-culture, as a low-standard intellectual ersatz intended for mass consumption. However, its evolution over the past two decades has proved this approach to be too shallow. Mass culture is not a homogeneous phenomenon, but one that possesses a complicated and changing structure.

Kitsch is one component of this phenomenon. It dominates cinema, concert stages, and other forms of mass media. Today, *kitsch* leaves not only the intellectuals, and the middle class in general dissatisfied, but also skilled workers. It now satisfies a minority of the population, people with little education, unskilled workers, and immigrants. And mass culture adapts to the new situation by turning to elite culture and borrowing themes and styles from it.

During the 1970's and 1980's middle culture became the dominant form of Western culture. Television, and radio programmes and magazines corresponding to that level of culture combine elements of *kitsch* and high culture. For instance, the plays by great playwrights, such as Shakespeare and Chekhov, performed by outstanding actors are interrupted by toothpaste ads and astrological forecasts. And serious films by such directors as Federico Fellini and Michelangelo Antonioni are shown side by side with entertaining flicks such as *The Exorcist* or *King Kong*. Middle culture has brought into fashion some works of genuine value (for instance, the intellectual novels of Albert Camus or William Faulkner), popular science, sport, or styles of several decades ago. It is more varied and representative than *kitsch* both in terms of genres and themes.

New forms of mass culture seek to imitate elite culture. For instance, extremely low-quality imitations of Leonardo da Vinci's *Gioconda* adorn perfume bottles and candy boxes. Traditional genres of elite culture mingle with mass culture. Pocket books originated as cheap reading matter of the lowest quality (mostly detective and pornography novels). Today, this form of publication includes serious works, such as literary classics, sociology, and psychology, while modern pop music, including rock operas is increasingly turning to serious social problems.

Various factors have allowed mass culture to rise to a new level and mutate, all the while remaining unchanged in essence. The most important one is the "scientification", which is reflected in different spheres. This includes the introduction of sociological and psychological methods for determining the efficiency of the mass media, and the elaboration on their basis of an effective system of manipulating mass consciousness. It also includes the general dependence of mass culture on technical means of mass interaction and the knowledge required to make them. According to McLuhan, new technology transforms the human psyche, while the social process depends on the nature of technology. Scientification also means certain changes in the character of mass culture brought about by scientific progress and increased interest in science among the general public. Mass culture now includes scientific subjects, ranging from information about scientific discoveries and technological advances to science fiction. Mass culture widely disseminates science, even if sometimes at a level which borders on profanation. Under the guise of science, mass culture spreads many pseudo-scientific, usually very conservative, myths.

In the 1970's and 1980's many attempts were made to raise the moral standards of mass culture. The corrupting influence of mass culture is well known. The glorification of violence, pornography and drugs has turned into one of its attributes. Advocates of mass culture, believing that it is a necessary element of the modern world with its technology, began to call for a higher moral level. This is largely the result of the growing influence of intellectuals on the establishment, and of state interference in culture.

Mass media reports about public and political events resemble entertainment programmes. Their subjects have included student unrest and protest demonstrations, the sexual revolution and the hippie movement.

Sensationalism is the only criterion for the selection of information.

There are those who advocate certain minimum standards in mass culture, because they recognise the need of the individual to be socially active and the lack of opportunities for him to do so. Art happenings — such is the intention behind the new mass culture — are to make art part of everyday life, directly incorporating some forms of social experience into the sphere of artistic endeavour. Art is presented as a form of political activity, while political events are seen in aesthetic terms.

Contemporary sociologists, such as the American Daniel Bell and the Frenchman Abraham Moles, interpret the convergence of elite and mass cultures as the transfer of style and information from the elite to the masses. Television and film have become a form of passing on good taste, habits and lifestyle to the masses. In the United States, mass culture advertises the American dream, i.e., getting rich and joining the elite. Mass culture pressurises people into copying the elite without actually belonging to it. It encourages self-realisation through the consumption of goods which stand for a certain status.

Counterculture

This trend either discards West European culture in favour of something radically different, or rejects intellectual values altogether. Some of its advocates call for a return to nature, i.e., they disavow the principles of utilitarianism and scientific rationality characteristic of bourgeois culture.

The adherents of counterculture are mostly young people from the upper middle class who reject the cultural aspects of a Western lifestyle. In the 1950's and 1960's many of them opted for peaceful escapism, forming the hippie movement. This entailed rejection of regular work, idealisation of vagrancy and self-isolation from society at large. In concrete terms this included:

1) utopian communes whose members put their money into a single pool, rejected the nuclear family and brought up their children collectively; 2) groups professing various Eastern beliefs (Zen Buddhism, transcendent-

al meditation, the Hari Krishna movement, followers of Rajneesh, etc.) and 3) movements adulating pop music.

Sociologists take different views of these trends. Some criticise them, accusing the younger generation of seeking to extend their childhood existence indefinitely and refusing to take on adult responsibilities and commitments. This view is in line with neo-conservative efforts to resurrect outlooks which lost considerable ground when the counterculture was at its height. Others note that positive trends have also appeared within the counterculture. These include environmental groups (the Greens), campaigns for the demilitarisation and debureaucratisation of society and endeavours to promote interpersonal relations based on humanitarian principles.

It would be an exaggeration to claim that the commodity-money relations forming the basis of capitalism dominate the circulation of items which embody cultural values. Capitalist society has developed stable mechanisms to protect art from the repercussions of the market. Various government, public and private institutions support and subsidise the arts, finance museums, pay for the restoration of cultural monuments, and so forth. Nevertheless, one can always tell the difference between commercial and genuine art.

Works of high culture, whose authors are almost always known, are, in one way or another, related to the basic human values and principles.

Mass culture is sometimes called ersatz culture or the dream industry, because it is aimed at the manipulation of individuals, their subordination to existing conditions and the encouragement of human passions, weaknesses and self-deception. However, the cause of it all is the division of labour between the capitalist producer of culture and its consumer, who is impersonalised and cannot see himself as an independent and active member of society.

In spite of the ability of mass culture to lure followers from various social strata, it is only a part of modern bourgeois culture. It is complemented by its opposite, the so-called elite culture. While the product of mass culture function as market goods meant for everybody, the products of elite culture are conspicuously intellectual and meant only for the "initiated". The former are simply entertaining and do not bring up any problems, while the latter are serious and conceptual. Whereas mass culture is marked by shallow optimism and vogue is more important in it than anything else, elite culture deals with such problems as the meaning of human existence and the future of the world, and is usually very pessimistic. The opposition of mass and elite cultures as different aspects of modern bourgeois culture is only relative. There are many intermediary and mixed forms, and instances of mutual influence.

Thus, in capitalist societies, the increased complexity of socio-cultural activity leads to an increasing disparity between the cultural and production spheres. During the second half of the 20th century, capitalism has been characterised by the fact that labour and even property have been losing their significance as means of satisfying human needs as such. Such former principles as diligence, hard work and the priority of one's business career become less and less of a pivotal component of the intellectual life of the individual.

These principles are increasingly replaced by the emphasis on consumption for the sake of sensual pleasure, raising one's status or improving one's living standards. This process is accompanied by moral dissoluteness. The search for new forms of sensuality is destroying the old way of life and the old forms of art. Yet these tendencies successfully fit in with the system of capitalist production. Capitalist production binds the individual to market dynamics as a consumer, leaving him the freedom of choosing the goods and thus making him an organic component of its structure.

And yet, the antagonistic contradictions inherent in capitalist society result in increasing numbers of people experiencing personal alienation, both in production and in consumption. Counterculture is the protest of the individual against the dominant values system.

The phenomena and processes described in this chapter are typical of the culture of the developed Western capitalist countries. During the last decades, these tendencies have also spread to some of the developed nations of the East (Japan and others), even though there they have their own unique characteristics. It is necessary to examine the general character and structure of Eastern civilisations and the African region, in order to understand the nature of intellectual life in those countries. They evolved in the course of historical development within the framework of basic civilisations, and still affect their socio-cultural essence.

If you wish to study the subject in depth:

1. *Khudozhestvennaya kultura v kapitalisticheskom obschestve* (The Arts in Capitalist Society), Iskusstvo, Leningrad, 1966.

2. Ashin, G.K., *Sovremenniye teorii elity: kriticheskii ocherk* (Contemporary Theories of the Elite: a Critical Essay), Mezhdunarodniye otnosheniya, Moscow, 1985.

3. Davydov, Yu. N. and Rodnyanskaya, I. E., *Sotsiologiya Kontrkultury* (The Sociology of Counterculture), Nauka, Moscow, 1981.

4. Kukarkin, A. V., *Burzhuaznaya massovaya kultura. Teorii. Idei. Raznovidnosti. Obraztsy* (Bourgeois Mass Culture. Theories. Ideas. Varieties. Examples), Iskusstvo, Moscow, 1978.

5. Bell, D., *The Cultural Contradictions of Capitalism*, Basic Books, New York, 1976.

6. *Cultural Industries. A Challenge for the Future*, UNESCO, Paris, 1982.

7. *Culture, Society and the Media*. Methuen, London-New York, 1982.

8. Moles, A., *Sociodynamique de la culture*. Mouton, La Haye, Paris, 1967.

10

Eastern Cultures and the Major World Religions

In this chapter, consideration should be given to the following:

1. What were the basic factors in Hegel's and Weber's views of the spiritual systems of the East?
2. What prompted Weber to conclude that Eastern cultures were unsuited to industrial development?
3. How do Eastern religions relate to everyday economic activities?
4. How, in the East, did the powers temporal relate to the powers spiritual?
5. How does religion affect a society's intellectual and moral life?
6. What are the principal characteristics of a sect?
7. How does a religion help to integrate a society?
8. How do the major traditions in Eastern religions interrelate with any minor ones?

In Chapter 6, we considered the more general links between culture and religion, and we saw how religion may play a significant and at times a dominant cultural role. This happens because religion can sanctify and thus uplift the status of those norms, values, understandings, and goals which determine the basic socio-cultural processes within any civilisation. Religions promote a broadening of society's cultural horizons and thus its spiritual life; and brings in common values, blurring ethnic boundaries. Despite striking contrasts between different peoples' religious values, symbolisms, and institutions, their general functions as a means of social control are clearly quite similar.

In the previous chapter, we discussed the particular characteristics of Christianity, the latter's social role in Western civilisation, and the way these factors and the very substance of Christianity underwent considerable changes during the Reformation (of the church) and the modernisation of society. In Eastern spiritual systems, associated as most of them are with pre-capitalist societies, it is altogether a different story. In traditional communities, inter-personal relationships are dominant, and these need religion, firstly to facilitate the way various social, ethnic and cultural groups interact, and secondly, to determine how the powers that be shall rule. What's more, in setting the norms for the spiritual life of society, religion exercises great influence upon its economy as well.

To carry out a sociological analysis of these various differences, a special theoretical approach was required. And over the years, social scientists world-wide have worked out a comparative study of East and West.

A Sociological Study of Culture, East and West

In the 19th century, one of the most important cultural problems in this social science concerned different cultural values and dynamics in various societies. By this time, Western capitalist culture had already formed and matured; its expansionist tendencies were becoming more and more obvious; but in other countries and amongst other peoples, it was coming up against fundamentally different intellectual systems. This became the general basis for a comparative study of East and West.

In the West, the study of Eastern civilisations has long been firmly established. By the beginning of the 20th century, this had led to an accumulation of significant academic achievements, these became both a basis for a more profound study of non-European cultures, and a source of "anthropological" recommendations for use in colonial administration. Western sociological and cultural-cum-anthropological theories appeared in the most varied forms: from racist ones to those marked by refined liberalism which have been a part of a broad spectrum of ideological thinking in the West during the past two centuries.

Euro-centric ideas caused many to contrast the intellectual and hence religious values of the East with those of the West. Thus Eastern societies were described as undeveloped; they were still a part of nature, yet to find their internal dynamism. This, it was felt, determined their religious and philosophical ideas, the character of the individual and certain peculiarities of their state structures.

Such was Hegel's view of the history and social structures of the East. His ideas on world history, of which the history of the East is an inherent part, are especially valuable. He suggested the latter was still at a stage which the West had come through. This theory greatly influenced the development of 19th-century social philosophy.

Weber, meanwhile, was one of the first to carry out an extensive sociological analysis of the basic religious systems of the East: Buddhism, Hinduism, Confucianism and Islam; all continue to play a major role in the life of the newly independent nations of Asia and Africa.

With but a few exceptions, the theological and philosophical teachings of Asia were accessible not to the lay, but only to the enlightened clerics. Knowledge, whether it was gleaned from written scientific sources or gained by mystical intuition, was in the long run the only "straight and narrow" path to the perfect holiness in this world and the next.

Weber suggested that the mystical nature of Eastern teachings and wisdoms has two important social consequences. Firstly, there's the idea that only the chosen few have been blessed with a special quality or charisma, and only they will be able to comprehend mystical knowledge — this is far from being accessible to all. Secondly, such mystical knowledge is held incommunicado — that is, it cannot be passed on to others by simple rational means, and the comprehension thereof is of an especially individual, apolitical and asocial nature. Any rational interpretation of such mystical experiences will lead to inner discord: on the one hand, there is a tranquillity with God representing real, eternal values; on the other, a restlessness confined by time and space, is but a passing phenomenon, an illusion with no divine values. This irrational world of universal magic pervades all walks of life and exercises considerable influence on the overall economy.

Weber presented positivism and rationalism as two mutually exclusive philosophical ideas. This extreme definition of the two phenomena was a clear antithesis of the interpretations of Sir James Frazer, the English classicist of religious studies. He suggested that magic is very much a part of contemporary science, and based his findings on the following: the fundamental premise of both magic and science is a firm belief in the natural order of things.

Weber considered the main difference in the development of the two parts of "the Old World" lay in the specific features of their cultures and religions, with emphasis on the latter. In the West, the Protestant varieties of Christianity have been able to create an ethic of rationalism, and this has become the main prerequisite for a great historical transformation. In the East, meanwhile, because of the dominant role of magic and the specific features of their various religions — Hinduism, Buddhism, Confucianism, Islam and so on — none of these beliefs have been able to rationalise either the way of life or indeed the individual himself. The foundations of traditionalism were therefore in no way undermined. And accordingly, the new industrial civilisation, capitalism, appeared in the West. This led to a progressive and dynamic development of Western society, while Asian societies stagnated in traditionalism.

The question of how Western societies differ from their Eastern counterparts has been a topic of sociological interest throughout the 20th century.

One of the most important contributions to Western thought in this century has been a falling emphasis on the concept of human evolutionary progress and a greater stress on the variety of life, both in regard to the existence of the individual on the unconscious level, and as concerns national cultures, as well as that of the world. A major achievement of cultural anthropology has been the recognition of the co-existence of different cultures; maybe they're at different levels, but each nevertheless has its own character.

People then started to study the values and spiritual components of traditional societies in a much more profound way. This mainly involved the study of religion as a broad amalgam of spiritual, social and political factors. Comprehensive investigations of religions and intellectual cultures were based on the theories of Weber, Durkheim, and then of Toynbee and Sorokin, as well as Western research into Buddhism, Hinduism and Islam. Subsequent findings became a major factor in the multi-faceted studies of the Afro-Asian countries. And although all these estimations of Eastern intellectual values remain the subject of much dispute, it is obvious that religion influences the economic and political life of every society.

In academic literature, we often come across the idea that Eastern religions are socio-cultural combinations which bring together not only sacred concepts, faiths and rituals as such, but also moral codes, legal systems, aesthetic values and social doctrines. These religions also involve various corresponding institutions—some less sacred, some more so—and they regulate the way believers interrelate on a spiritual plane.

Nowhere, however, does religion have the prerogative on every sphere of intellectual life, no matter how influential it may be. Secular cultures played a significant role in a number of the functions mentioned above, sometimes making their contribution in the religious sphere, sometimes acting beyond the latter's framework. In any civilisation, a separate secular culture is bound to emerge.

Religion is one of the factors determining the character of any civilisation, but the latter exercises its own influence upon religion, determining the ways of its evolution and giving it its final shape.

Religion and the Economy

A religious institution was never society's substitute for socio-political or economic factors. Religion simply placed the latter within a definite framework, to a certain extent smoothing out any contradictions which might have been created thereby, if only by re-directing society to the achievement of more heavenly goals. Religion allowed for the necessity of material production, but such was allotted a rather low status. In pointing out the frail and temporary nature of such production—subject as it is to the whims of nature and the vicissitudes of fate, and hence to decay and destruction—the church * insisted on the permanence of moral and spiritual values—

* The word "church" is here used in its broadest sense, meaning the religious establishment, be it based in a mosque, synagogue, temple or whatever.

truth, charity and justice; these, it said, will outlive all our troubled times.

The religious hierarchies cared little for the material well-being of society. Such was the responsibility of the Christian kings, Buddhist emperors and Islamic caliphs or emirs. They also had to provide for the care and welfare of the people who could then seek personal and spiritual perfection. In Islam under the first caliphs, a time not beset by the hungry or the needy, every imam received hand-outs from the general social fund made up by the people living in the area he administered. Buddhist monarchs had the title of "chakravartin" or "wheel-turners", and they were recognised by society as the truth- or dharma-bearers.

In India, one of the most popular characters in literature and folklore was the King Vicrama the perfect. A ruler of exceptional generosity, he defended the oppressed and humiliated, and provided for the good of all. His influence was so great that many kings in India then took on the title of Vicramaditya, (Vikramaditya), just as the emperors of Rome had called themselves Caesars.

In the way they related to material wealth, both clerical and lay were basically of one mind: riches should not be accumulated. In *The Life of Vicrama,* a collection of medieval short stories, we find a typical phrase: "Those possessed of plenty should either give it away or spend it in fun, for there's no point in burying it." This advice was presented in the form of a secular call, rather like the sayings of the numerous characters in the fairy tales of *The Thousand and One Nights* and other literary relics of the Middle Ages. In bringing the individual to spiritual values devoid of all worldly passions, the major religions condemn the excessive pursuit of wealth. In so doing, they also condemn an attachment to enjoyment if such leads either to moral breakdown and disappointment, or to deceit, immorality, theft, cruelty, murder and so on.

In ancient Chinese or Indian traditions, they say a human society starts to collapse when some start to accumulate more food than is required for their immediate needs, for this is then associated with the acquisition of personal property, and this in turn is accompanied by lies, violence and every other vice. Thus they emaciate nature, the source of all human subsistence.

Islam is more lenient in this respect, for it gives direct encouragement to commercial activities, but it condemns excessive accumulations of wealth if they are for personal gain rather than for the greater glory of religion.

The world's major religions do not insist on a direct redistribution of wealth. They do, however, welcome any form of "a fair share" as a means of contributing a laid-down quota to the religious social fund (the *"zakyat"* in Islam, the giving of gifts to the monks in Buddhism, and so on). The personal accumulation of wealth, if it's just for new investments and excessive consumption, is sinful and irrational; wealth should instead be subject to the principles of sharing with others via presents, and the redistribution of resources, and used for prestigious expenditures or charitable works, such as will increase the donor's authority and his chances of personal salvation, while at the same time easing the lot of the faithful. But even when a religion was able to smooth over the consequences of social division, it was never capable of eliminating the causes thereof.

World Religions and the State

Relationships between the powers temporal and spiritual took many forms: in Islam and Mahayana Buddhism, the two were indissolubly united while in Hinduism and another sect of Buddhism, the Theravada school, the powers were to a large extent separated from each other. The pious caliphs of Islam were simply doing the work of Allah, and this theocratic ideal has survived right up to the present day. In Buddhist tradition, King Ashoka was praised for his moral renunciation of personal success (though this did not stop him preserving Kalinga's conquered kingdom).

Nevertheless, relations between the two power structures were to a large extent similar. Although the Buddhist sangha maintained the principle of not interfering in the affairs of state, it nevertheless made great demands thereon, and more so than Islam. On the other hand, the political passivity of the imams at times reached the stage when the political establishment included a lot of those who professed a different faith, simply hirelings and slaves; such was the case in Egypt under the Mamelukes in the 13th to 15th centuries, as too in the classical period of the Ottoman Empire (16th-18th centuries).

The difference between the way Hinduism and Islam relate to the state, is a purely theoretical one, although adherents often make reference thereto. It seems that, unlike Islam, Hinduism separates the powers spiritual and temporal. A close analysis of the reality, however, suggests the difference is considerably smaller and of little import. Gustav E. von Grunebaum, is one of America's leading experts on Islamic studies, and he has noted a merging with traditional Persian forms of government, which promoted the spread of Islam. This allowed for certain political principles to be incorporated into the overall ideological system of the Muslim world such as could be applied independently of religion. In India, though, society was aware that the state is invariably linked to dharma, the law of general order and stability, for it is this which must be the basis of any just form of government.

Religious leaders used to insist the spiritual powers were superior to the temporal, but in times of stability, there was a formal or an implied delegation of functions between the two. The religious establishment invariably played the role of the guardian of the general interest in its utopian-cum-illusory forms, forever keeping an eye on the activities of government. The legitimacy of power was invariably conditioned by the state's relationships to the religious establishment and by the way the latter's requirements were fulfilled thereby.

Sometimes, however, the state sought to protect religion from its own shortcomings. Accumulations of church wealth or the clergy's departure from their original vows led to a moral collapse and a violation of the behavioural norms of all — both clergy and lay. This caused a breakdown of social harmony in the country. A favourite way of maintaining the external appearances of the church was to confiscate church lands and property, and this inevitably led to the separation of functions between church and state.

The absence of any precise demarcation between the temporal and spiritual powers often led the political establishment to appropriate for itself an almost divine prerogatives. State-cum-ethnic cults were continually cropping up, depending on the zeal of the given dynasty or ruler; this was the case especially in Buddhism, even though in practice such a logic might well appear paradoxical. The rulers in Burma (now called Myanma) and Ceylon (Sri Lanka) not only declared themselves to be boddhisattvas, they also made themselves into Buddha's descendants.

In contrast to previous cults, the major world religions allowed for criticism of the civil order, of abuses of power and so on. Such criticisms, however, might then turn into a sanction of the civil order, as when via religion a social evil acquires a cosmic status and becomes a part of a divine predestination; to get out of this evil, the only answer is to leave the world of politics and enter a purely religious sphere. It's clear that Buddhism in its original form resolved this matter in a most radical manner, even though it was then able to co-exist in an amazingly intimate way with a deification of its earthly monarchs. There again, Confucianism and Islam persistently emphasised the social significance of the state. In China, the public was aware of a spiritual need to be at a distance from the political powers. This caused Confucianism, which had always been closely associated with the political establishment, to shift a little, so to allow room both for an imported Buddhism and for their own, indigenous Taoism; thus the above need was fu filled.

"The permanent drama of Islam" has been a dilemma between (a), the ideal of an indissoluble unity, which has been maintained throughout its history, and (b), the reality. The divergence between religious and political needs was getting bigger and bigger, and the actual demarcation between the two caused the faithful to cease to hope for the setting up of a just power; instead they became politically indifferent and passive, although there were occasional outbursts of religious-cum-political utopianism.

Thus a relationship between the state and the religious hierarchy should not be seen as the mere use of the latter as a means of strengthening the former. A world religion has its own means of controlling both society and the state itself. Religion is without doubt a very general societal influence. The state can give expression to such only on certain, definite conditions, and mainly if it supports religion. The temporal power is always presented with certain theocratic requirements, which must, at least to a certain extent, be satisfied if it's not to be confronted by powerful religious forces. Earlier attempts to limit the powers of the church, so to facilitate a more liberal interpretation of religious dogma — such was the case when the caliph Al-Mamoun expressed a certain sympathy for the Mutazilites (Mutazalites) in the ninth century — met with only temporary success. What's more, they were accompanied by a return to an even more extreme variety of the old regime and the introduction of additional religious guarantees against any other new ideas. The defeat of the powers behind the Mutazilites; the anathema traditionally pronounced on the Chinese despot Qin Shi huang-di, in the 2nd century B.C.; and the triumph of Brahmanism in India, all led to a formal victory for the forces of conservative orthodoxy and a defeat for those involved with social innovations and experiments. Such really great state reforms, East and West, were rare. The power and might of the religious establishment deprived the political one of any initiative, even when the latter tried to initiate albeit just a partial renewal of society.

At the same time, a society having only a religious establishment was incapable of giving any effective opposition to any self- ssertion or profit-orientated claims from the powers of state. For as long as the church was not affected thereby, the clergy generally did nothing to oppose even the most despotic power, whether it was engaged in a relentless struggle for power, a cruel exploitation of the people, a senseless killing of the population in a series of successful and unsuccessful wars, personal caprice or unbridled profit. No matter what the abuses and disorders in society, the spiritual powers reconciled themselves with the temporal, so to avoid the even greater evil of total chaos and anarchy.

Religious leaders were even able to come to terms with foreign conquerors, if the temporal powers were unable to throw them back. The right to dissent, even though it's a part of Islam and Confucianism, was almost never put into practice; it was consistently repudiated in the name of a severe self-discipline. Any form of dissent was a problem for the Buddhist faith, for a tolerant attitude towards the political establishment was one of its principles. In Islam, there's a very strong activist and egalitarian principle, and this was a more effective stimulus for popular movements than were any Buddhist utopian ideas of renunciation. Later on, however, Islam clearly became more conciliatory; the difference between the ideal and the ignominious reality was submerged in obedience.

Indian sociologists frequently note a similar tendency in the Indian sub-continent: there was hardly a single legal institution which would preclude the violation of the dharma by a monarch. Justice was enshrined in moral-cum-religious precepts which held no political legality. However, the preservation of the dharma was inconceivable without a monarchy; if such was not to be, there'd be a state of anarchy and the law of the jungle.

In times of political upheaval, religious ideals of just rule used to be a motivating force and a basis for the popular masses. Such movements were usually prompted by a social unrest fermenting to the point of popular, grass-root revolt; they had quite a large effect on the workings of the religious establishment. The Islamic movement to re-instate the "legitimate caliphate", which continued up to the 1900s, is a case in point; so too were the struggles by the followers of Confucianism for a "just government"—these took place during severe social confrontations in China, Vietnam and Korea.

Ideals of justice inspired the concepts of the "legitimate caliphate" in Islam, the "rule of Maitreya" in Buddhism, the "great unity" ("Datun") and the "great concord" ("Taipin") in Confucianism. These ideals co-existed both with extremes of wealth and poverty, and with a system of rule and subjugation; they compensated for the fact that the people were actually very deprived.

The historical limitations of these ideals lay not only in that they suggested that no progress could be achieved by improving the organisation of work or by developing the material means of production. As history clearly shows, socio-ethical solidarity was both theoretical and unobtainable, for it was undermined by different forms of social conflict. The need for such solidarity was so great, however, that throughout the ages, though the utopian ideal was forever being infringed... it was always, later on, re-instated. In various times in the history of Eastern societies, there have arisen broad-based movements inspired by the ideals of a united society wherein would flourish the principles of equality, justice and prosperity.

The Spiritual Mechanism of a World Religion

The religious principle of any social organisation is linked with an appeal to our communocratic relationships, which, in pre-capitalist societies, served as a basis of social control. In contrast to state or ethnic cults in world religions, these relationships were not connected to some worldly object — a temporal power, unable to overcome its own transitory nature; rather, they were associated with a super-object taken beyond the framework of human society, beyond the confines of time and space. That which brings the believers together is a desire for a certain all-embracing entity, which belongs to no one individual in particular, but which is raised above all and linked with them all, only via spiritual threads.

A world religion offers an overall ideological system wherein lie ethics and the law. This presents the believer with a choice of behavioural patterns somewhat removed from his everyday activities, but it also firmly directs his conduct. A world religion lays down certain moral commandments to cover the general, idealised principles of behaviour. These are extensions of, amendments to, or sometimes substitutions for, the norms of the previous social order. Religion in its various forms serves to introduce general ethical standards and uniform behavioural patterns for the faithful, regardless of their basic social groups. To enforce its universal ethical commandments with unquestionable authority, it creates a "visible body" — dogma, a cult and its own formal establishment.

Laying down such universal criteria turned society's entire spiritual life into a dynamism held between the following poles: the ordinary and transcendental, the particular and universal, the empirical and ontological, the finite and eternal. All religious ideologists have said our human weaknesses—our short lives and limited consciousness—are a proof of the need for religion and of the existence of an all-knowing and almighty God, the laws of whom are beyond our human ken.

Every world religion tries to introduce a profound reorganisation of the natural order and of everyone's immediate endeavours. Such involves the following:

1. There is a violation of the unity of the subjective and objective, the material and intellectual sides of our human activities and of the interests of the individual and the community. A world religion shall undermine this unity by countering the ordinary with the transcendental, the common with the sacred, and the political with the divine.

2. The link between the individual and his particular natural and social milieu shall be weakened or (in extreme cases of mysticism) overcome. Then shall a single "superior being" be used to help all believers come together in a universal fraternity.

3. Religion shall diminish the significance of the people's immediate emotional relationships and their appreciation for each other. Instead, the principle of a common communion with God (or sacred, higher law) shall be introduced.

4. To various degrees, religions shall contain an historical dimension. Sure enough, within the framework of Eastern religions, historicism is to a large extent limited by cycles or by the ideal of the "golden age" which existed long ago which, one day, must return. And

5. It shall be so arranged that the individual's possession of, and faith in, his sensual relationships with the outside world shall be overcome. Such feelings shall be redirected to a transcendental object, which shall be beyond the compass of human understanding. Changing a person's inner state shall also diminish the importance of his own worldly passions on account of their sinful, erroneous or illusory nature; and no longer, therefore, shall he believe in them.

A world religion will cause these earlier values either to acquire a straight negative sense, or to fade into the background, there to be subjected to new principles.

Physical strength and powers of endurance are not good in themselves, but only when directed in the service of God or of some ascetic goal. The flesh shall be an object of flagellation and mortification (if only when fasting). Thus, some Hindus will subject themselves to certain forms of self-denial with various degrees of yoga. While the popular Muslim notions of sensual paradise are transformed by Sufism, a mystical trend in Islam, into several stages of self-purification. The super-sensual values of religion lie beyond this finite world of our human existence; rather, they signify the triumph of the spirit over the flesh, the victory of eternal life over earthly death.

In studying spiritual life as it has emerged over the ages, sociologists make a distinction between the most important, definitive values affecting social relationships, the economy and the state. Weber tried to define these forms as ideals, but these attempts were criticised as a biased systemisation both of the actual multiplicity of spiritual factors which exist in every society, and as a reduction of a contradictory and mobile structure to a single type. Furthermore, this predominance was basically only a form of religious ideology and was far from being descriptive of the realities of the situation.

Weber and other sociologists tried to set up comparative models for each religion, based on some artificially chosen concepts. It was therefore almost impossible to suggest (a) that the only psychological type characteristic of China in the Middle Ages was the *shenshi*, an extrovert interested in other people and his social milieu and (b) that his Indian counterpart was an ascetic who had ceased to be interested in the people and in all material things generally, even in worldly illusions. In the classical Indian poem, the *Bhagavad-Gita,* the main hero, Arjuna, first vacillates and then becomes convinced by the God Krishna of the finiteness of his own moral sufferings and of the fact that he cannot escape his duty. He therefore goes into battle, so to fulfil the behest of the caste principles, to kill his own kin. Such are the behests of the dharma, and they apply to all members of society and to all castes. Only a few ascetics can move to another plane, so to stop thinking of these worldly illusions, and there they may seek their own personal salvations. They enjoy general respect but they are not examples to follow for those who must fulfil their dharma, specifically for those realistic folk who are to use the instructions of the *Arthashastra* in their own political work, business or handicrafts. (This is discussed in greater detail in Chapter 17.)

Every religion has several sets of values, orientations and goals. Such are combined into a certain system which lays down some more or less prestigious ways of relating to society and of behaving therein. An examination of the world's major religions from a historical and structural point of view allows us to draw up the following sub-divisions based on their various forms of personal inter-relationships and social behaviour, even though such may be typical of different religions to varying degrees. A religion may:

1) accept a given social order and way of life so that the individual must bear the burden of earthly chores, finding therein his own justification before God. Generally speaking, this principle was the dominant basis of religious orthodoxy;

2) await the divine kingdom on earth, wherein all social conflicts shall be resolved. This was typical of many millenarian and sectarian movements, which represented the utopian and egalitarian ideals of the popular masses;

3) assert that all worldly activities pleasing to God may help the individual attain a higher status in society. Such ideas have encouraged the powerful to be rather enterprising; and finally,

4) accept various types of asceticism as a means of getting closer to God or of attaining a higher order. Such involve a certain distancing from society with the acquisition therein of a special status. And such may be expressed in Sufism, yoga, Zen Buddhism, and various forms of monasticism.

However, within the framework of each religion, these forms of social conduct led to the emergence of a number of different beliefs, still within the one religion. Both Islam and Buddhism split into two great but separate traditions, whereas Hinduism is typified by an internal pluralism of faith. Meanwhile, the four *mazhabs* (or *mezhebs*), the religious-cum-legal schools of Islam — the Hanifites, Malikites, Shafi'ites, and Hanbalites — established a basis for the admissibility of a certain (though still strictly controlled) variation of the orthodox faith.

Spiritual Values and Work in the Community

Every major religion states that the most important principle in our spiritual lives concerns our religious salvation, and it is this which governs the entire system of personal behaviour. But in the theory of culture, what actually does the word "salvation" mean? It is one's greatest desire, and it's epitomised:

(a) by one's avoidance of any evil, be it moral (as when one is ensnared by sin) or physical (as in suffering or death); and

(b) by the total victory over one's alienation and enslavement. Salvation is the goal to which all one's endeavours are directed, and it's God's greatest gift to humankind.

In primitive religions, salvation was associated with a particular situation and a particular sense, limited in time and in its final goals. Either the deceased continued to live amongst his own gens as one of the ancestors, or he returned to life, born again into his own likeness. Salvation was seen in a high, moral context, beyond the confines of one's own tribe or province; indeed, it was identified with the salvation of the entire nation.

Both in the Middle Ages and in modern times, there was and is a constant renewal of the particular means by which a society may avoid a calamity, be it a natural disaster, invasion or war. Such a salvation is held partly in the hands of the country's leaders and political activists. So too in mythology, such trends are usually shown in the cult of leaders.

Religious salvation is the ultimate goal of one's life and work, the ultimate and all-embracing state, achieved either on an individual basis, or in a religious grouping, or again within the whole community.

Religious salvation involves and stipulates various types of secular activities, albeit on a conditional basis and to a limited degree. Typical goals of one's earthly life may include wealth, power, love, longevity, the gift of many children, or the strengthening of one's family or community links. To a greater or lesser extent, these are admissible and recognised by every religion (even if at a very low level). And every secular culture has always been involved in working out just which values, thoughts and cognitive processes are to apply.

On the basis partly of Protestantism and partly on the Eastern religions of Hinduism, Buddhism and Confucianism, Weber evolved a methodology for the cultural and sociological analyses of the principles of a religious salvation. This methodology — which is still very significant, even today — has had a huge influence on research into the interaction of economic and spiritual factors in the modernisation process of newly independent nations.

Weber showed salvation to be the believer's systematised, practical behaviour, via which he aims to achieve the final goal as determined by his attitude towards a God or transcendental law. In such conduct, the believer gains justification and reason for his chosen way of life.

Any form of salvation needs a critical side to reject the ways of the world, as well as a more positive approach. Salvation can be obtained only if the individual concentrates all his efforts and thoughts, both on avoiding any negative factors in life, and on achieving the only goal that matters from the religious point of view. He needs to overcome not only any desires for any worldly goods he may encounter, but also his natural, physical and psychological functions. This he can do by limiting his appetite, restraining his sexual desires, self-purification and suppressing any negative social feelings (self-interest, malice, hatred, envy and so on). Meanwhile, his physical and psychological training should go along with a methodical control of thought and deed, aimed at an inner perfection. This is done by the introduction of prohibitions and commandments as prerequisites of salvation. Thus Buddhism bans the sins of the body (murder, theft and carnal enjoyments), of the word (lies, rudeness and idle chatter), and of the mind (greed, malice and hatred). The commandments include righteous thoughts, intentions and deeds, generosity, a willingness to suffer for righteousness, a sense of duty, moral stoicism, patience, and so on.

Ideally, the believer must re-create his entire life. In fact, of course, this can more or less be achieved only in monasteries or religious orders. The rest of the population can only be involved in religious activities from time to time, and mainly in the performance of rituals. Nevertheless, the extensive and popular introduction of various forms of religious rules into society has affected the whole spiritual milieu.

Moral perfection is regarded not only as a precondition, but also as an important form of behaviour on the path to eternal salvation. As the believer thus proceeds, he may sense within that he's approaching the required standard; meanwhile, he gains more and more social prestige as an example to be greeted, respected and followed. Every religion has evolved different levels of holiness corresponding to these final values.

Numerous are the descriptions of humankind's moral virtues, not only those which arouse respect amongst one's neighbours, but also those which one is told are absolutely essential.

Ritualism has always been one of the important paths to salvation, for thereby emerges a way of life, well worked out in every detail, capable of broad application, and firmly opposed to the everyday world. In a fully developed system of rituals, the chaos of life is overcome, while everyday happenings are viewed as only transient and shallow. Thus may one obtain the sense of being in communion with the supernatural. And although this may seem strange, rituals eliminate any motives for magical influences which may be aimed at improving our human lot in this world. Indirectly of course, rituals should also be to our eventual benefit, improving our prosperity in this world via an impersonal transcendental mechanism. A well known social consequence of such a form of salvation is the separation of the sacred sphere from the social one, and thus spiritual deeds become a formal burden.

Faith is usually defined as follows: a believer is said to have faith when, both philosophically and psychologically, he accepts the basic tenets of the given religion. Thus to greater or lesser extent he opposes faithlessness. Despite the opinions of many one meets, faith is far from being just a blind conviction, for it's based on certain teachings. Such usually concern the supposed existence of particular beings and principles, and these form the fundamental dogma of the given religion or (its version of) the truth. Of such is its education and propaganda. Faith is not only a conviction in the truth of the religion's laid down principles and supernatural laws; it is also the resolve to adhere to these commandments, and this shall be a guarantee of salvation, despite all doubts and temptations. The words "faith" and "faithfulness", as well as "faithful" and "the faithful" (the believers), are common to all theistic religions.

Every religion is rich with its own varieties of faith and service in God, and such have often arisen in an emotional way. To counter the rational extremes of Vedanta — the ancient Indian religious and philosophical system — Hinduism experienced a powerful development of *bhakti* or pious love, linked to the worship of the God Krishna. This became very widespread in the Middle Ages and also in more recent times.

To do one's duty. A person can reach a high level of moral perfection if the dominant principle in all his works is that of duty. This is understood to be the carrying out of all necessary functions as stipulated either by society's aspirations, or by supernatural (-cum-"super-social") law.

The *dharma* of Hinduism takes a number of different forms — the law, moral righteousness, charity — and they include the clear recognition of duty as one of the most important commandments given unto all castes (*jati-dharma*) and every individual (*sva-dharma*). The *Bhagavad-Gita* lays down precise instructions as to how each should fulfil his duty... not by doing that in which he has some practical, vested interest and/or that wherein there lies a chance of success; but by doing that which is directed unto some higher goal, i.e., the service of God. In this, God is the personification of that higher law on which the universe is founded. The Hindu's interpretations of dharma may be very varied; they all depend on the ethics of his caste. Little wonder then that the commandments laid down in the *dharmashastras (dharmasastras)* make up a complex of social roles.

In a word, socially significant deeds have their spiritual justification. Depending on how he carries out this higher law or the commandments of God, the Hindu may receive the gift of faith. To a large measure, each should perceive his external duty as an internal personal responsibility, according to the extent to which he depends, not on his own position in society and the respect he enjoys in his community, not on the commands of some temporal or spiritual power, or on the laws of that society. In fulfilling his duties, therefore, there's the danger that his thoughts and deeds will differ from the laid down social norms established by worldly forces.

Both in Islam and Confucianism, the idea that administrative work was a duty was highly developed. Everyone was duty bound, that was indisputable; such might even involve administering to the "vicious"—usurpers and rebels—yet thus could one remain faithful to one's basic principles. Similarly, a profound understanding of his own personal mission helped the follower of Confucianism to oppose any abuses of power and to stand up to any persecution. As in any other religion, he who maintained the principles of a sacred duty despite all the vicissitudes of fate, would be the recipient of great honour.

The Principles of Religious Salvation

In established religions, the final means of salvation were not primarily seen to be individual strengths or sectarian teachings. Instead, all could be saved via the church, the established church founded and blessed by a God or His prophet. Between religions there were considerable differences on the principles of spiritual guidance. Weber describes three characteristics of such a salvation:

1. Salvation shall be given only to members of the church, and it alone is entitled to administer the gift of grace.
2. The gift of grace is not the result of the priest's charisma, but of his office.
3. The personal religious qualities of he who is in need of salvation are of no interest to the priest of God who, on account of his holy office, is to administer the gift of grace.

Disseminating the principles of salvation enabled (a) the broad masses to be attracted to a single religion, and

(b) the average behaviour pattern to be established. A religious establishment makes salvation more or less accessible to all, albeit in the distant future. On the one hand, it makes grace accessible to more people; on the other, it distributes the deserts of the more virtuous, using the latter's spiritual and material contributions to help the others. Hence the mutual relationships: the religious establishment helps the believer who cannot gain salvation by his own efforts to progress towards the final goal; and in return, the lay give various forms of support to the church.

In the Theravada sect of Buddhism, there are two institutionalised systems of religious salvation, one for the monks and one for the lay. The *sangha* consists of about 10 per cent of the male population, and they achieve their salvation by first renouncing the world, social contacts, family ties and property, so to receive grace and personal perfection. This grace they then pass on to the laity. The latter, meanwhile, can improve their *karma* by achieving merits large and small, and these shall be judged primarily by the size of their contribution to the *sangha*—building holy places, arranging religious festivals, donating real estate and other properties for a holy cause, and so forth.

The Religious Sect as a Separate Path to Salvation

Throughout the ages and within the confines of every religion, there have emerged trends or movements with different goals and ideas. The question of how a social and political protest forms into a religious movement or sect has been well researched. Most of the political movements were of a temporary nature. Either they were crushed, or played out in clashes with the existing order. The structure of the world's major religions has come to be a complex affair comprising as "minor traditions", certain heterogeneous variations as well. On the whole, however, only those movements or sects which involve a particular type of religious salvation,—one, not for all the followers of the parent religion, but just for a limited number thereof—have survived the test of time.

One may define a sect's spiritual role, either as the setting up of separate ways for the fulfilment of the religion's spiritual goals, or as the initiation of special tasks not shared by the great mass of the believers. From a sociological viewpoint, a sect is usually determined by its relationships to the church concerned, and the former attracts a limited number of believers in a combined effort for a special form of salvation. This is the basic difference between the sect and the church as a general organisation, and the latter is not so strict with its rules of entry. The faithful include all who carry out the rituals, obey the commandments or simply regard themselves as followers. A sect presents its members with more demands than does the orthodox religion, even if only because a separate existence makes additional demands. The essence of a sect, however, consists mainly of the fact that it offers its adherents a special and more effective form of salvation. Religions differ from each other both on the spiritual plane and on the organisational level. We should all, therefore, either refrain from using such negative terms as "heresy" and "sects", or treat them as neutral for methodological reasons. However, in researching such phenomena, it's better to use the words "heterodoxy" and "dissidence".

Differences in social, political and cultural factors found expression in a pluralism of spiritual goals, and these were now seen in a religious sphere, now in a secular one. The extent of these differences and attitudes thereto depends mainly on two factors: the structural peculiarities of the religions and the state of their overall dynamics.

The work of different types of spiritual or psychological movements which may even clash with each other, are as follows:

1) the transformation of people's inner selves by the use of psychological and physical training, supplemented by some special deeds. The world is a pernicious place, and a person is usually subject to its perniciousness. However, having changed psychologically, he'll be able to counter this external evil and find new ways of communicating with his fellow creatures;

2) the attempted destruction of the existing social order in the name of human salvation, and the proclamation of a new, just society. Such higher thoughts are

usually to be expected from the supernatural being who bears them, the saviour of a suffering humanity (the Buddha Maitreya, the hidden Imam). Active movements required their members to take part in setting up new social orders which will, it is suggested, very quickly emerge after the change-over (radical Shi'ites);

3) a rejection of the world and any changes thereto. Salvation is only possible via a fulsome piety in limited, isolated groups;

4) self-adjustment to this world by improving one's relationships and by working expediently in this world for such temporal goals as wealth, health, success, happiness, prestige, and lots of children. In some ways, these goals were essentially very close to those which existed at pre-civilisation levels of spirituality. In the new milieu, these movements have acquired the ability of using the achievements of any developed society;

5) the alteration of existing church rituals and commandments, with the aim of gradually improving the lot of the members and of increasing, later on perhaps, the number of believers; and

6) the radical rearrangement of social relationships within the confines of the local community. These shall be based on the working principles of solidarity and co-operation amongst the faithful in setting up these relationships. The actual achievement of such was often reflected in the "chosen few", moving elsewhere to build a different society with the necessary special means for controlling the sect.

One must draw a distinction between movements seeking to separate the spiritual life even further from the social sphere, and from those egalitarian and utopian pressure groups which reflected the aspirations of the peasants uprooted as a result of new ways of life, and which demanded a return to natural simplicity and justice.

The state and church joined their efforts to eliminate various sects or impose restrictions upon them. If the first took on a mainly administrative coercive approach, the second would favour or even bless this work, with an idealised crushing defeat of any dissidents.

Mysticism

There arose in every religion movements to bring a person into direct contact with the supernatural being. Such groups had relevant teachings to devise, justify and regulate these practices. Depending on religious or social conditions, philosophical arguments in favour of mysticism differed remarkably. In theistic religions—Christianity, Islam and so on—the individual is united with his God. In the non-theistic faiths, the supreme being is of an impersonal, transcendental nature—the tao of Taoism, the *shunyata* of Buddhism and the Brahman of Hinduism. All these mystical teachings, however, have their common characteristics: they gravitate towards irrationality and intuitionism, and they are expressed not so much in understandings, more by symbols which destroy the developed structures of consciousness.

The practice of mysticism suggests a system of psychological-cum-physical exercises to regulate the physical and spiritual state: yoga in Hinduism, and the *tantra* in Buddhism. Much consideration is given to an inner concentration gained by meditating on certain images or word-symbols—*manṭras*. In so far as mystcism involves progressing via unusual moods, the role of the master must be stressed—the guru of Hinduism, the monk of Buddhism and the *pir* of Sufism.

Mystical experiences are not necessarily achieved on one's own. They're usually witnessed by groups, communities or orders of mystics. Such groups developed especially quickly in times of crisis. In certain conditions, mystical movements turned into a form of protest against social oppression and/or the clerical hierarchy.

Religion and Spiritual Integration

In addition to introducing variety into the intellectual life of society, civilisation also creates the conditions for its unity thereby overcoming any class, elitist, ethnic and/or parochial barriers. Furthermore, it develops overall cultural forms. Differences in the intellectual production of a society dependent on class or any other social criteria—town or country, centre or periphery, and so on—do not eliminate the unity of a civilisation, if the latter has acquired its own means of establishing its common nature. And one of the most important and most widely deployed means of integrating a society is religion.

Religion has always provided social stability in the event of internal conflicts or foreign invasion. No matter what the political fates of those societies which had taken to one of the world's major religions, no matter how cruel the internal shocks or how severe the onslaughts of an external aggressor, the final advantage has always been on the side of that society which was capable of maintaining a unity and continuity despite the collapse of a dynasty and its political structures.

Though religion as such is unable to save a country from domestic disorders and crushing invasions, it has often been the source of a nation's regeneration, in that it has re-established society's earlier structures and cultural traditions. Even when the government was weak, paralysed or destroyed in times of political decay, conquest and fragmentation, religion displayed great survival abilities and often accepted a large share of the duties of social integration and the maintenance of law and order. Such was the case, for example, of Islam during the collapse of the caliphate under the onslaught of the Turkish nomads. The same was true—and very significant—during many an anti-colonial struggle.

In certain conditions, a world religion may even carry out a particular civilising mission. In various sections of society, it creates an understanding of the "higher" norms of culture, morals and behaviour. And it attracts into this culture the populations of outlying districts and border countries, and eliminates within its own sphere of influence the dichotomy of civilisation-versus-barbarianism, even at the price of setting up new hierarchical principles. Despite the occasional emergence of strong states in various parts of Asia most of which, included several civilisations—such as the empires of Genghis Khan, Tamerlane, the Great Moghuls, and the Ottoman Empire—the crushing invasions of China by the Mongols and Manchurians, and constant wars between various kingdoms in South-East Asia, each civilisation preserved and fortified its own socio-cultural unity, either driving out any nomadic elements, or by absorbing them. Withdrawing to their own homelands these warriors agreed to accept missionaries and educators and to then renounce the use of force, so to gain spiritual salvation. And although the subsequent economic-cum-political relationships were those of the colonialist and the subjugated, on the cultural side everything was associated with the more developed centres. The international character of its religion allowed a society to move beyond its state borders, and to develop its own cultural contacts; so too it facilitated the formation of wider political grouping of those countries which happened to be within the religion's sphere of influence.

The Major and Minor Traditions in Religion

No matter how extensive the sphere of religion or its effects on other aspects of human life, it has never been the overriding influence; sometimes, indeed, religion itself has been subject to other external effects. Thus may sociologists, who deal not only with general religious factors, have sufficient grounds for describing pre-capitalist societies as disparate and particularist, for all too easily did they disintegrate into communal, caste, ethnic, professional and other social groupings. At times, these were loosely connected by commercial ties; more often than not, however, they were on mutually antagonistic terms. The settlement of initial conflicts of interest (between different ethnic groups or peoples, between the urban and rural, the central and peripheral, and so on), did not eliminate the causes. In any civilised society, such conflicts would be subject to a certain higher understanding or relationship.

Various components maintained their strength and merged into macro-systems. Both in town and country, various ethnic and social groups controlled their own existence, according to their own principles, these being compatible with more general ones. Weber suggests that the world's major religions usually preferred the town. If urban pretensions, which led to greater differences between spheres became extreme, however, these were invariably met with a rebuff from the religious establishment, and the latter would then call for assistance from its half-civilised peripheral neighbours. In the Arab world, the collapse of dynasties under the corruptive influences of urbanisation is only one example of this tendency.

In his day, the celebrated Arab scientist Ibn Khâldun (d. 1406) did a lot of ground work on these matters. His basic historical contribution to the science of sociology was a deep analysis of the socio-cultural nature of Islamic societies; this included the power structures in, and the inter-relationships of, towns and their nomadic peripheries.

The word civilisation is taken to contain two basic levels of socio-cultural heritage:

1. The major or the great, tradition; this comprises the classic legacy, expressed in sacred texts and ancient literary works, and it stipulates the basic spiritual principles, the various social and political structures, and the established forms of historical consciousness.

2. The minor or folk, tradition; this relates to local variations of social and spiritual control. This form of tradition became the favourite research project for Western social anthropologists, for in local micro-structures they found a realistic base for some empirical recearch into the ways traditions affect whole societies.

In every religion, general forms of social integration have led to various interpretations of its main beliefs. Both Islam and Buddhism divided into two, separate, great traditions, while Hinduism is renowned for its pluralism of faith. The establishment of the four *mazhabs* in Islam caused slight yet strictly formalised differences in orthodoxy and religious law. Indeed, the antagonism between the Sunnis and the Shi'ites has often been the cause of war.

Criteria for identifying a minor tradition are difficult to formulate. In no way can a minor tradition be treated as merely comprising oral folklore, peasant cultures, or local faiths. The concept should also comprise urban culture with its literature, which in every developed society is created and spread by professional people. It's almost impossible to separate the two traditions, they rather represent a gradual change-over from a popular (or grass-roots) to an elite (or upper, intellectual) echelon, involving some common elements. It is at times, therefore, very difficult to explain the differences between an object of strictly anthropological research, and one of classical orientalism.

The degree to which both traditions co-exist varies enormously. It depends not so much on the nature of the religion itself as on the particular situation in society at the time. Sometimes there's a severe persecution of the lower echelon of culture, resolute attempts at driving it out forever and/or campaigns against vulgarisation; and at other times, these are exchanged for policies of tolerance and peaceful co-existence.

Co-existence was sometimes permitted, even when the sect maintained values directly opposed to those of the parent religion. This was emphasised, for example, by many writers on Hinduism and Buddhism, wherein such values were not condemned as sinful and evil, but were simply treated as belonging to their own, "lower" sphere. In such religious structures devoid of any synthesis, there was room for both good and evil, both spiritual impassivity and self-interested magic, both monasticism and witchcraft, both transcendental meditation and dances of ecstasy.

The lower strata of society have not only retained previous beliefs: the highest principles and symbols of a religion were often subject to profound transformations too. Although The Buddha has entered a state of nirvana, the average Buddhist can still pray to him in the hope of then being favoured. Sacred texts were used for the taking of oaths and divination. Every religion has had to carry out the occasional campaigns against "reduced standards" of spirituality, superstitutions and false ideas, infringements of cult and monastical precepts, and so on. And at times, these purification functions had to be carried out by the powers temporal.

Some researchers (the American Marcus George Singer, for example), on the basis of the achievements of anthropological science, proposed another principle for investigating the integrative potential of, say, Indian society. Civilisation appears as an uninterrupted network of various groups, cells and elements, all interlinked by forms of such spiritual activities as cult rituals, festivals, ceremonies, art and so on, each taking place in their own locations, in temples, memorial buildings, pilgrimage sites, centres of learning, etc. And for creating a socio-cultural entity, a written language and literature were very important.

The actual relationships between major and minor traditions varied from one civilisation to another. A major tradition created an originality for each civilisation. On the whole differences between minor traditions were less obvious, because most people felt their beliefs to be rather similar, as too their everyday life styles.

Social Mechanisms of Integration

The most important means of bringing the believers together into one societal unit is the institution of the church itself. Whereas for the priests and monks, the church was mainly a means of salvation, for the lay it fulfilled two functions: helping the work of salvation, and promoting the unity of the believers. Putting these functions together into an overall description suggests the church "gathers in" the spiritual deserts of individual believers, and then "shares them out" again, among everybody. On the spiritual side, this was expressed in the reverence of the saints and those teachers helping the faithful attain their salvation; and on the material side, the collection of donations and dues was very important, both for maintaining the church and for redistribution among the less fortunate members of society.

The church made very few demands on the spiritual lives of its flock. As one of Dostoyevsky's characters put it, the church shall accept the weak, too, for it shall satisfy their "need for a *universal* worship". * All it required was that they should believe, and not hope to be saved just by their own efforts and in their own, individual ways. There were looser demands and all of them were acceptable, although the church then set up a general scale of merits and honour in the community, and awards thereof depended both on a person's degree of piety and, more importantly, on his donations.

---

* *The Brothers Karamazov*, Vol. I, Penguin Books, London, 1958, pp. 297, 298.

Indian Civilisation

The uniform yet multifaceted nature of Indian civilisation is a matter of great theoretical dispute. It's very difficult to draw up a picture of Indian society; this is due to the enormous spectrum of religious, regional, social, caste, age, sex, educational and other differences. And such variety is inevitably compounded by contemporary processes of modernisation.

Hinduism is defined as an inclusive system. This means it consists of various and at times contradictory elements. Hinduism is renowned for its religious tolerance, and over the years it has absorbed various magical and mythological elements, influencing them but little in the process of assimilation. In addition, the priests used to keep lots of teachings secret, while the lay were not meant to be enlightened thereby. The principles of the absolute formed in the Vedanta (one of the six classical systems of Indian philosophy) were abstract and speculative ideas of religious philosophy, and thus they remained.

Rituals varied according to castes, subcastes and regions. Society was doubtless generally aware of the principles of dharma, but not too much emphasis was laid thereon. The work of salvation was more strictly subdivided than in other religions, and there was no concept of a "general salvation", for such would have violated the natural order of things.

The absence of a general creed was compounded by the absence of any overall religious organisation. The sacred teachings were all held by the Brahmans. And society was divided into castes according to the traditional means of distinction which have formed over the centuries and been passed down from one generation unto the next.

It is still impossible to summarise Hinduism as a conglomerate of different sects, the only purpose of which is "salvation", or as an inclusive spiritual way of life. Yes, it's difficult to give a theoretical definition of the uniformity of Indian civilisation, but it exists alright, even if only as our perception thereof. This uniformity depends (i) on certain general spiritual and cult principles, even of an abstract and speculative nature, and (ii) on the one set of cultural activities. In comparison with other religions, Hinduism is a polytheistic amalgam of beliefs and cults but it is essentially monistic. This is embodied in religious-cum-philosophical principles of a higher level, and these may be acquired by recognising the authority of the ancient Indian holy scriptures—the Vedas, and common rituals and customs.

The Indian sociologist, M. N. Srinivas, and the American, Marcus George Singer, developed the concept of the uniformity of Indian civilisation as a system of socio-cultural links. On the one hand, they regarded it in a horizontal (or territorial) dispersal of various rituals typical of each caste and, above all, of the Brahmans; and on the other hand, it was a vertical (or social) dissemination of prestigious ritualistic norms achieved via the use of Sanskrit. Thus could new groups join into the one system of Hinduism, while those groups already within its milieu are able to display a certain mobility. An important prerequisite for such an approach is as follows: Hinduism has to be regarded as a flexible system, both monistic and pantheistic, hierarchical and egalitarian. Thus was it possible to maintain albeit a relative but firm and systematic uniformity.

Srinivas' initial prerequisite that the overall Indian Hinduism was identical to Sanskrit Hinduism was undermined in subsequent, more detailed research. A recognition of the undoubted value of this Sanskrit Hinduism was not obligatory on all castes; furthermore, it was subject to some doubt, for it didn't correspond to current practice. Indeed, the business activities of the *banya,* a caste of merchant traders, could be much more attractive and it might even serve as a model for the emergent strata of traders. Thus forms a certain pluralism, in which Sanskrit Hinduism is but one variety.

Having carried out an empirical analysis of Hinduism as it is in practice, Singer made the following sociological discovery: the uniformity of Hinduism is not contained in a recognition of the sacred texts, nor by the prestige of "twice-born" Brahmans, and nor again by the one set of approved norms; rather, it's all a part of an interaction between different groups and levels which creates an uninterrupted network of relationships. This consists of the following:

1) customs and traditions: wedding ceremonies, religious pilgrimages to holy places, festivities and so on;
2) trade;
3) the system of government;
4) places of worship, temples and religious centres;
5) folk art; and
6) a cultural elite: the clergy, pundits and gurus.

Such a structure provides for the one cultural cloth, the one set of inter-relationships which makes up a cultural unity of town and countryside, different ethnic groups, social classes and strata, and regions. *

In the seventh century lands of Arabia, before the emergence of the nation-state, there was a need for unity; Islamic civilisation emerged in answer thereto. Islam has never recognised a separation of spiritual and temporal power. It was clearly conceived as a religion for one ethnic group to belong to, namely the Arab population, in unity with the state,—the caliphate. One of the main problems which had to be resolved in the early days of Islam was that of power ... not just *a* power (because the unstable princedoms which had existed prior to the prophet Muhammad had failed to be the cohesive force in such a tribal democracy and thus these princedoms had collapsed); but *the* power, the power of righteousness, i.e., that which might care for the general interests of all the Arab population in accordance with the laws of God.

Islamic theological teachings always supported the idea of a caliphate—a sacred state order under the protection of God and ruled on the basis of a holy law. "The way of Khosrow and Caesar" for ever served as a negative model, and throughout the full fourteen centuries of its existence, Islamic ideology has maintained a mistrust of any authority which opposed its God-given laws.

The political realities of the world were dramatically confirmed even in the reigns of the first four pious caliphs, for three of them were assassinated by various malcontents. The so-called *kharijits* were a form of utopian extremists campaigning for communal power. The movement was quelled, and the caliphate then developed a huge military and bureaucratic machine, which

* A more detailed analysis of the spiritual and social structures of Hindu civilisation is given in Chapter 17.

became less and less religious and more and more secular as early as the ninth century. It came to be essentially the same as the rule of those two hated monarchs: the Persian King Khosrow and the Byzantine Caesar.

The Sunnis formally recognised that the caliph should be chosen on merit. Real power, however, was no longer in the hands of the "holy rulers". Thus caliphs were replaced and even killed, according to the arbitrary will of the military. The Shi'ites, meanwhile, remained steadfast adherents of theocracy, especially the radical sects of Ismailis, who demanded all should be the unconditional subjects of the Imam. He alone was the embodiment of all divine emanations, and the indisputable authority in affairs both religious and secular. The basic difficulty for the Shi'ites was the fact that the person who was actually the ruler was not "the he" they wanted him to be. They found a way out of this problem by using the assistance of the "hidden Imam" or the awaited Mahdi.

The Islamic state was often the scene of a power struggle, and this was sometimes between a weak caliph on the one hand, and on the other, strong sultans and emirs, who had usurped it. The way the ideals differed from the realities of power became Islam's permanent drama. Both for the Sunnis and the Shi'ites, the one in power was not "the he" he should have been, and only with great difficulty did the temporal powers — the emirs and kings — separate from the spiritual. In the 18th and 19th centuries, the idea of sharing power once more gained ground. This was because the Ottoman sultans, having acquired the power of the caliphate, then put this idea into practice, as too did some popular movements: the Wahabis were campaigning for restoration of the communal principle of power; while the Mahdiists declared the power of their rulers to be sacred.

In this chapter, we've examined the way various integrating tendencies in a religion nevertheless create additional differences. Setting up a united faith considerably reduces the possibility of having spiritual and/or everyday differences, for only the constructive and stabilising ones were recognised. Any contradiction in these tendencies caused by the natural laws of civilisation in their entirety, used to exert permanent influence on a religion's evolution and appearance.

The fact that a religious establishment could not be broken up disguised the fact that here lay a profound antagonism. Society was largely unaware of this. But an intensive struggle between these two elements and outlooks often resulted in an exacerbated ideological argument or the emergence of strong social or political movements, which took a religious form.

If you wish to study the subject in depth:

1. Erasov, B. S. *Sotsialno-kulturniye traditsii i obshchestvennoye soznaniye v razvivayushchikhsya stranakh Azii i Afriki* (Socio-cultural Traditions and Public Awareness in the Developing Countries of Asia and Africa), Chapter III, Nauka, Moscow, 1982.

2. Bongard-Levin, G. M., Ilyin, G. F., *Indiya v drevnosti* (India in Ancient Times), Nauka, Moscow, 1985.

3. Vasilyev, L. S., Istoriya religii Vostoka" (A History of Eastern Religions), Nauka, Moscow, 1989.

4. Levada, Yu. A., *Sotsialnaya priroda religii* (The Sociology of Religion), Nauka, Moscow, 1965.

5. Ugrinovich, D. M. *Vvedeniye v teoreticheskoye religiovedeniye* (An Introduction into the Theoretical Analysis of Religion), Mysl, Moscow, 1973.

6. Grunebaum, G. von, *Classical Islam. A History of 600-1258,* Allen and Unwin, London, 1970.

7. Needham, J. *The Shorter Science and Civilisation in China,* Vol. 1, Cambridge University Press, Cambridge, 1978.

8. *The Origins and Diversity of Axial Age Civilizations,* Ed. by S. N. Eisenstadt, State University of New York, Albany (N. Y.), 1986.

9. *Orthodoxy, Heterodoxy and Dissent in India,* Ed. by S. N. Eisenstadt, Mouton, Berlin and New York, 1984.

10. Singer, M., *When a Great Tradition Modernizes. An Anthropological Approach to Indian Civilization,* Pall Mall, London, 1972.

11. Weber, M. *Sociology of Religion,* Introduction by T. Parsons, Methuen, London, 1965.

11

Secular Cultures in Eastern Civilisations

In this chapter, consideration should be given to the following:

1. How do secular and spiritual values interrelate in different Eastern civilisations?
2. How did the temporal rulers influence cultural development?
3. What are the legal, scientific and artistic achievements of various Eastern cultures/civilisations?
4. How significant, today, is a developing country's cultural inheritance?
5. What sort of cultural dynamics are there, in the history of the East? And
6. What are the basic symptoms of a stagnation period, in the intellectual development of Eastern countries?

No matter how extensive the influences of each world religion, none affected the cultural side of life in its entirety. Isolated varieties of intellectual and artistic work cropped up here and there, and these created a wealth of literature, artistic productions, scientific achievements and philosophical teachings.

The development of secular cultures was conditioned by the necessity, not only of different forms of intellectual life, but also of its social variations (one culture for the elite, another for the masses; one for the privileged, one for the subjugated; one rural, and one urban). Secular forms of culture maintained a unified civilisation wherein the key spiritual principles were embodied in a religion.

A Secular Culture as One Part of a Civilisation

Civilisation first creates a basis for a significant intellectual growth; it then incorporates this wealth. Within the parameters of civilisation, a secular culture may develop independently.

When a civilisation first takes shape, great variety is possible, and there's room therein for a secular culture to develop. In the making of this civilisation, when a newly found form of organising social relationships facilitates an increase in society's productive forces, the intellectual side of life also enriches, and there's a corresponding increase in society's knowledge of nature, society and the individual. The significant achievements of the East in various scientific, technical, literary, artistic and philosophical fields, relate to this period. Today, they are the pride of the newly independent countries. A study of the history, literature, science, and philosophical thought of the East shows there was a wealth of cultural variety and originality in Eastern civilisations in their heyday.

The highest religious principles and doctrines were important sources in raising public awareness of morality, the law, aesthetics and philosophy. Thus a holy writ, an expression of the highest truth, included first a description of a truly righteous way of life, and then it stated the general principles for an aesthetic perception of the world and an intellectual discussion of the nature thereof. Accordingly there emerged an intimate link between those general principles which govern both religion and culture. And it was the former which initially created both the content and the style of art and literature. Art, therefore, was primarily determined by religious principles rather than by aesthetic ones. Nevertheless, art either depicted the real world, or it reflected an idealised form thereof in accordance with the principles of aesthetics.

Culture fills the spiritual gap between the ultimate landmarks of our existence and our everyday cares; it relates to the realities of life and the activities of people; and it was not always focused only on the question of salvation. The complex needs of the court as well as urban and rural requirements prompted an extensive ethical instructive and entertaining literature. The latter affected those who otherwise cared not for philosophical thought.

No matter how widespread the influence of religious teachings, both metaphysical and socio-ethical, there appread in every land a broad secular culture — belles-lettres, history, geography, astronomy (astrology), mathematics and philosophy.

In China, the golden age of the arts usually relates to the 6th-12th centuries. It was the period of the Dang and Xung dynasties, and it ended with the death of the leading philosopher Zhu Xi (d. 1200), who carried out a neo-Confucian philosophical synthesis.

Indian culture is considered to have enjoyed its culmination from the fourth to the mid-eighth centuries, when Brahmanism gained the upper hand over Buddhism and Jainism; the Brahmans then started to re-edit the ancient holy writings. This was the heyday of Indian architecture, art and philosophy, and many were the achievements of the natural and philological sciences. It was at this time that Kalidasa and other leading poets and mentors created their best works.

By the year 935, the Islamic lands had witnessed the political demise of the caliphate, and the area then returned to its previous status quo of separate, isolated states. But then the threads of civilisation brought it all together again. In the 10th-12th centuries, an Islamic form of social control was established with increasing rapidity on the basis of the *shariat*. The literature of the canons was set and sealed, and five basic schools of law were founded; little was added thereto in the years to come. At the same time, however, secular forms of culture were also being intensively developed. A significant number of differences emerged on the cultural side of life, and these facilitated the separation of the shariat and philosophy from the entire secular culture — *adab* (the latter includes philology, history and geography). Mutual interactions of orthodoxy and philosophy led to an enrichment of both. And various branches of learnings developed so that, in the 13th century, a number of detailed classifications had been set up. There were already about 150 different disciplines.

All the great civilisations were characterised by their ability to both unite and yet promote various, different branches. The existence of such a complex and large-scale organism required the maintenance of all its vital functions. At the height of a civilisation, there appeared an intellectual wealth, and many were the artistic and scientific achievements. These enlarged society's spiritual side, and thus did it co-operate with other civilisations in a way which led to their mutual enrichment. Co-operation was very fruitful when a maturing civilisation became aware of some inadequacy or other — the absence of a particular intellectual structural aspect — for it could then acquire same from without. One of the best examples of this was the Arabs' mastering of Greek and Roman philosophy and Persian political culture when Islamic civilisation was in the making; another was the absorption of Buddhism by the Chinese, the former with its eschatological beliefs and spiritual metaphysics, the latter with their well-established socio-ethical canons of Confucianism. India, meanwhile, forced Buddhism out of its own spiritual bosom, then to give this faith, along with its rich literature and art, a long life in East and South-East Asia.

Historical sociology suggests that the central powers in Eastern societies were rather prone to the destabilising consequences of ideological differences of opinion, of the accumulation of technical and other scientific knowledge, and these then affected the socio-cultural bases of such traditional societies. The result — unfavourable from the centre's point of view — was a redistribution of resources and functions from the centre back to the peripheries, and this was accompanied by a strengthening of the latter. To avoid same, a state might initiate various measures either to limit the development of the technical sciences, or to curtail any intellectual criticism of the existing social order.

There were undoubtedly some instances of such policies, but we can quote a considerable number of examples of how a ruling elite in various states initiated the development of the economy, urban craft industries and trade, as well as a military technology, so to protect its territory from aggression. Wise, mighty and wealthy rulers were interested, not only in wars, entertainments and ceremonies. History has preserved the names of many who jealously and sincerely protected the arts and sciences; some indeed even practised them. Sometimes, however, they only busied themselves with that which could bring additional prestige to their rule, or extra material strength. Back in ancient China, Qin Shihuangdi, the persecutor of the educated scribes, undertook large-scale economic development and thus encouraged the practical sciences, mainly those which promoted agriculture and prestigious projects.

Many great conquerors hastily built themselves capitals and castles, in addition, of course, to temples for the glory of religion. As a general rule, they came to an agreement with the spiritual leaders in all questions of state. Religion was to be the safeguard (of the state, in exchange for the latter's protection), to such an extent as would legitimise its retention of power; this could never have been achieved by some military success, let alone by an adjustment of the administrative system of government.

An important way of maintaining diversity within a unity was by limiting the spheres and channels for the dissemination of knowledge, both specific (its values and norms) and general. This was especially the case within a secular culture which was inevitably and permanently limited in its field of application, in those societies wherein there was no general level of education. To a large extent, literature, science and philosophy were the preserve of the "chosen few", who spoke their own special language.

Both secular culture and religious heterodoxy provided for various forms of salvation, not earmarked for everybody. Thus they set up means for the special selection of their followers and for handing over special knowledge and traditions involved in the creative arts. A student needed many years of study if he was ever to get fully acquainted with the wisdom of his mentor. Such a system was effective enough to provide for the use both of general principles and specific teachings. Knowledge public and secret, overt and covert, imposed and closeted, was disseminated as required. The education system did not have to satisfy any doubts and thus it maintained a synthesis with society's religious beliefs. At the same time, however, this facilitated heterodoxy, and this could lead to other forms of literature, art, science and philosophy.

In a study of different spheres of classical culture in the East, one can separate the sacred from the secular sphere only on a conventional basis. There was a constant flow from the former to the latter, and secular culture used to conduct religious searches for the complete answers to its own internal problems. Yet one can still identify a permanent conflict of the two spheres, such as demanded answers on the basic issues from the religious side, and a sensible limit to the secular.

The Law

By no means were all spheres of behaviour under the writ of a Holy law and predetermined norms of piety, via the observance of which a believer might approach the sacred ideal. For in addition to such, every developed society had another set of worked-out norms, both for controlling the way different social groups carry out their everyday activities, and for exercising government.

The Indian religio-legal texts were the *Dharmashastra*, and these gave detailed descriptions of the rules and regulations which guaranteed the privileged status of the Brahmans among the other castes, and of the protection thereof by the monarch. The latter was regarded as the expression of the dharma of the Brahmans, the compulsory laws of conduct sanctified by religion. The *Dharmashastra* included some of the traditional Indian laws: marital and family relationships, and the laws of inheritance. A second collection of texts, the *Arthashastra* came to light in 1909. With its rational pragmatism, it drew the attention of the scientific community to the revealed recognition of the priority of state interests and the admissibility of any means for the achievement of political ends.

The holy Islamic law, the *shariat*, includes a significant number not only of cult norms, but also of legal ones. A number of precedents—readings from the thoughts and deeds of the prophet and his disciples — became both the source of sanctioned norms of behaviour, and a basis from which to judge bad conduct. Thus the law was intrinsically bound with sacred tenets of faith. On the basis of various selected writings of the Khadiths (tales of the prophet), there emerged in the eighth and ninth centuries four recognised schools of canon law — the Mazhabs. In the Muslim world, there was no state codes of law until quite recently. In most countries, however, along with the *shariat* there was usually the *adat*, the norms laid down by traditional law. An especial part thereof was sometimes interpreted as a secular legal supplement to the *shariat* on those occasions when they had to make a decision based on the *ijtihad*, i. e., on an agreed legal judgement on matters not related to the canons.

For the purposes of government, many "sermons to the masters" were published: *A Book of Politics*, *The Nature of Kingship*, *A Book of Precepts*, *Adab of Emirate* and so on.

In China, the canons of Confucianism detail the rules and regulations for the work and conduct of society's main social groups. Thoroughly worked out ceremonial procedures were meant to inspire the lower classes to be obedient to the higher ones. At the very top of this bureaucratic hierarchy was the emperor; he was imparted to carry out certain ceremonies, as well as supervise the observance of moral-cum-ethical norms and the laid-down codes of behaviour. He himself had to follow existing canonical laws, the ones which dated back to the days when Confucianist dogmas were first founded. As the ruler of an administrative bureaucracy, however, he made use of secular legal principles to directly interfere in the economic and social spheres, so to try to promote the highest interests of his power.

Science

In discussing the existence of Eastern science, some disciplines of which are quite different from those of its Western counterpart, much evidence is given to the high level of the former's achievements. In recent decades, an important problem on which some of the world's leading scientists have devoted much time and effort concerns the role of science in the intellectual lives of these societies. In other words, it's a question of the cultural context of science, and this comprises not only the relationship between the intellectual particularities of each civilisation and the universal scientific code, but also the need of overcoming the Western emphasis in an understanding of science: European thought attaches little social or gnosiological significance to the sciences of the East.

A most important breakthrough on this question was contained in Joseph Needham's *The Shorter Science and Civilisation in China* (see No. 7 of the recommended reading list for Chapter 10). He set up a centre for the study of civilisation in Cambridge, and they now carried out some extensive research into the history and nature of scientific knowledge in China, and the way it related to the overall cultural system.

The history of Eastern science shows that every region at one time or another achieved considerable success in mathematics, medicine, chemistry, physics, astronomy, geography, optics and so on. There was also not a little success in the social sciences, of course: philology, philosophy, the science of law, literary theory and theory of the arts. The development of the science disciplines depended on experience, experiments and observations, though none of this was systematised and none became a leading field of scientific study.

The bibliography of the history of science and technology in India during the Middle Ages (from the eighth to the nineteenth centuries) contains about 10,000 titles; the majority of these are on medicine (about 5,000) and astronomy (approx. 3,000). The number of books grew from 26 in the eighth to 704 in the seventeenth century; but then, in the following hundred years, there was a rapid decline and at the same time, a greater penetration of Western scientific thought.

Right up to the most recent times (16th-17th centuries), Eastern science had always been well ahead of its Western equivalent. The study of science in China, India and Arab countries shows that up to the stated period, scientific, technical and philosophical teachings basically spread from East to West.

The Arts

There's more than just the one way of describing the interrelationships between religion and the arts at their mature stage. On the one hand, this particular culture had yet to really separate itself from a religious ideology, while on the other, literature and the arts in general largely avoided any dogmatism or ritualism. They—literature and the arts, that is—contain the power of human thought, the significance of the individual's sensual and psychological experiences and criticise the existing social order. However, such a contradiction frequently appears to be a part of the imagination, since a significant part of literature and the arts was or is linked to a form of religion not held in the canons. If we recall the above-mentioned two functions of religion—salvation and integration—we'll see how the former easily came to be an expression of the inner endeavours of the individual, himself a broad spectrum of ideas and feelings. Such was the basis of most of those religious movements which sometimes took on the nature of a sect—Sufism, Bhakti and Zen Buddhism. Their relative liberty allowed for free thinking and social criticism.

The integrative mechanism was also very significant. The extensive territorial scope of a culture using a common language and relying on a common system of images, facilitated an intensive intellectual exchange between the most distant centres. This allowed the philosopher and the artist to become acquainted with the intellectual treasures of a vast area, and for the successful to be widely recognised.

Meanwhile elsewhere, the need for a common language was why Arabic came to be supreme over such a huge area. Historic "accidents" and "God's will" caused all divine revelations to be spoken or written in Arabic, and thus there emerged a large literature of rules and holy laws. And it was Arabic that also became the official, literary, and scientific language of a vast civilisation. So when, in the early 11th century, the ruler Mahmud of Ghazni made Arabic instead of Persian the official language, it was met with enthusiasm. Sticking to a local language smacked of provincialism, hence the great scientist al-Biruni rejected the use of Persian in his scientific work, and wrote his treatises in Arabic. But he recognised the role of Persian in traditional literature, and compiled an Arabic-Persian dictionary.

The Dynamics of Eastern Cultures

Greater knowledge of the dynamics of cultural processes showed the limitations of previous conceptions of how cultures evolved and diversified. This forced the scientific community to devote more attention to why culture in various societies had developed slowly, stagnated or even regressed. Such has been the case at various times in every civilisation. The well-known Dark Ages of European civilisation came in the wake of the so very rich cultural achievements of the ancient world. And only with the greatest of efforts did Western Europe emerge therefrom, at the time of the Renaissance and the Reformation.

The cultural dynamics of the East were also rather complex. Some still feel the following played a significant role in the stagnation of Eastern societies: economic factors, such as the retarding effects of feudalism, external political causes — the presence of nomadic peoples in the peripheral lands, and destructive barbaric incursions; a despotic political system (or its opposite, the collapse of the unit state); and lastly, exacerbated tensions between a ruling class and the peasantry. All these phenomena influenced society, but their effects far from coincided with intellectual processes. We know full well that the collapse of the caliphate and the perpetual political instability in Islamic lands in the 10th-11th centuries did not disrupt the flourishing of their culture; and even nomadic onslaughts did not cause a collapse of the arts. Thus they survived, right into the 13th-14th centuries, when there was a significant upsurge with such poets and intellectuals as Rumi, Jami, Navoi and others. The political triumph of Islam came in 1453 with the fall of Constantinople. But this and the later splendour of the Porte took place on a background of a profound intellectual stagnation. The reinforcement of the unit state in India under the Moghuls was also marked by no great cultural upsurge.

Relying on the laws governing the emergence and development of a civilisation which were discussed in Chapter 8, we will try to define—albeit in a general way—both the processes which harboured the stagnation of Eastern societies, and their causes.

The main purposes, and therefore the main causes, of a civilisation are as follows:

1) the establishment of different socio-cultural lifestyles, according to the society's different levels of existence; and

2) the integration of these levels into one, socio-cultural system.

The two functions are inter-linked yet mutually contradictory. At a certain stage, this will lead to tensions and conflicts.

A civilisation establishes a link between the present, the past and the future; this then determines a socio-cultural continuity, a general direction and rhythm for the intellectual evolution of these societies. The more complex the variety of political and intellectual life in society, the more keenly felt is the need for unity. This can be achieved by laying down certain general principles and establishing a strict hierarchy. The processes by which a society achieves the above-mentioned variety—namely increasingly complex and higher levels of development, both intellectual and social (as in the growth of towns)—cannot spread to all spheres of the given civilisation. The general nature thereof was greatly transformed in accordance with its development. And as it emerged, there was a struggle for a consolidation of the various primitive tribal and separate and heterogeneous ethnic, cultural and governmental units. Later on, this turned into a tendency to submit the more developed and diverse structures to a common and universal unifying principle in a number of empires.

In answer to the growing need for civilisation to be a means both of integrating a society of different groups and curbing their different aspirations, and of protecting same from the excesses of a despotic government, the religious establishment increased its integrating role more and more, restricting the variety of intellectual life, so to affect the overall modus vivendi.

We can find a typical example of this in Islam. There were measures to preclude any attempts at overruling the *shariat*, and any other proposed alterations were also severely restricted. Indeed, the only amendments were those which had long been accepted and were now considered to be permanent. Even in the 10th century, the gates of the *ijtihad* had been closed to the Sunnis, who thus had been unable to judge or resolve important social and religious problems. This ban on any amendments survived up to modern times. The *shariat* was designed for the maximum good of the faithful; for their part, the latter had to adhere precisely to the rules of their faith, and maintain an unfailing belief in a God, the ways of Whom shall never be fully understood. The principle of the greatest possible good allows for the government of the community's entire life, and for the one true resolution of every problem.

They stifled the sciences in various ways; either they criticised, banned or even persecuted the intellectuals, or they simply ceased to recognise and support their work. Thus societies lost their creative potential. And thus empirical knowledge was restricted, and the road to new achievements closed. The principle of unconditional support for religious integration led to a severe limitation of any development which could only be seen as being a general or overall one. Any variations on, or departures from, the accepted dogma were excluded; the latter had acquired a certain harmony and definitiveness.

The orthodox always regarded science and philosophy as something to be mistrusted... for such thoughts allowed one to turn, not to the authority of the prophetic sacred texts, nor to traditions and nor again to the religious establishment, but to a different source of knowledge, one which would lead to free-thinking. In confirming the universal principle of life, the religious set forth a single philosophy to cover both local conditions and the realities of life. Thus they reduced all empirical values to a secondary level, for they felt any empirical knowledge should naturally enough be included in an overall code of conduct.

The clerics became the persecutors of any form of "unnecessary" and "pernicious" knowledge. They were clearly aware of their own vested interests, as well as their links with the socio-cultural bases of their civilisation; then they hastened to initiate if not a physical, then at least an intellectual (and at times anti-intellectual) suppression of that free thought which is essential for the growth of all empirical knowledge.

The strengthening of different forms of intellectual life was a feature of the growth and maturation of Eastern societies. Then, at a certain stage, this gave way to a tendency towards stabilisation and the preservation of the unity of various contradictory social structures. After a golden age of creation, a culture tends to concentrate on a bigoted conservatism. There now takes place a certain curtailment of both religious and secular cultures. Religious universalism will literally stifle culture, to leave only those functions which are necessary for maintaining the societal unit formed. The developed centre must adapt to the less developed periphery. As early as the 14th century, cultural stagnation was becoming more and more evident in the Arab world. And it was this which was the basis for the pessimistic theory of Ibn Khaldun: he suggested the most powerful and prosperous governments in the world of Islam will stagnate and collapse.

The vast area in which every civilisation existed, and the lengthy duration of each, makes it difficult to perceive their dynamics. In the lands of Islam, the intellectual centres were constantly changing... and Iraq, Spain, Persia, Central Asia and India took it in turns to become the centre of intense scientific and philosophical work. The change sometimes coincided with the migration of the intellectuals themselves, from one centre to another. In 1420, in the city of Samarkand, Ulug-Beg, Tamerlane's grandson, assembled the most famous astronomers and then built that which in its day was the world's best observatory. For the next 20 years, they produced the then best-ever catalogue of heavenly bodies. After his murder by religious fanatics in 1440, the observatory was destroyed and for many centuries cast into oblivion. Then came the Ottoman Empire, where a certain intellectual upsurge took place, once more to be replaced by total stagnation.

Similar though obviously asynchronous processes were also taking place in various other regions too. The English anthropologist Joseph Needham suggests the demise of Chinese civilisation took place in the years 1400-

1450 and that this was linked to the triumph of neo-Confucianism. Other sinologists are in agreement with him.

A major cause of a growing conservatism in Indian culture is often seen in a spiritual coming-together in opposition to the widespread dispersal of Islam. Although an interaction of the two great cultures led to a fruitful Hindu-Islamic synthesis, a profound conservatism emerged in Hinduism itself. The triumph of orthodox Vedantism reflected a similar spiritual conservatism.

At the dawn of the second millennium A. D. (and in Southern India a little later), Indian political-cum-legal literature began to decline. This refers to the *Arthashastras*, a practical guideline for a pragmatic state-run economy. (The book, alas, has not survived to the present day.) Meanwhile, there was a growing public awareness of the *Dharmashastras*, describing the ideal and sacred caste system. And although the only book of the *Arthashastras* which has survived — the *Kautilya*, written in the form of an encyclopaedia — showed a growing influence of orthodox principles, it nevertheless failed to stop its cultural decline. Those parts of it which repeated the *Dharmashastras* became superfluous and reflected the realities of life; and those which contradicted them were considered dangerous. Scholastic commenting of classic texts then became the intellectual's basic way of life. India's intellectual life fell into decline in the 12th century, and for the next 300-400 years was in a state of stagnation; such an analysis has been suggested by many an Indian thinker.

Every civilisation had an established spiritual basis. Teachings associated with the initial principle — faith — were systematised and included into a theoretical dogma. Searching for spiritual values was no longer required and was even dangerous sometimes. One only had to preserve and master that which one had already gathered... and then one got the impression that the system was a definitive one.

After a fairly long period of stagnation, every civilisation acquired a traditional air. Tradition stifled innovation. New lifestyles could be introduced to enrich the welfare and culture of society, but they couldn't affect the masses. In various fields of public life, traditionalism became entrenched, so to deal a blow at any novelty, for invariably the latter would be seen as a threat to the status quo of a united society.

This was the time when a certain type of personality evolved in various regions. Typical was his/her ability to be satisfied with a small guaranteed minimum, a simplicity, a rejection of excessive desires and a willingness both to submit to the whims of fate, and to see the importance, not of wealth or of energetic deeds, but of a "quiet wisdom", in observance with behests and laid down norms.

Changes in the cultural dynamics of the East did not always include a straightforward intellectual decline. Previous cultural zones to a greater or lesser extent declined, and there was then a formation of national cultures. Thus there emerged new ethnic communities with their own distinctive cultures.

The variety of cultural processes in the East was associated with the co-existence of very different tendencies: some, on the wane, were similar to those of the Renaissance; others were an imitation of earlier literature; and yet others the emergence of new national forms of the arts.

One of the most obvious indicators of a profound yet gradual spiritual change was first a declining influence of previously universal languages—Sanskrit, Pali, Arabic, Persian and Vanyan; and secondly, the emergence of new national languages and literatures, even if they were to a large extent a continuation of the former traditions. By the end of the first millennium and in the beginning of the second, literary works were being written in India, not only in Sanskrit, but also in the living languages of Bengali, Hindi, Punjabi, Marathi, Gujarati, Telugu and so on. Tamil shared this role and had done so from ancient times; Urdu is of more recent origins.

In the 12th century, Turkish literature began to stand apart. At the same time, Persian was once more taking over from Arabic in its native lands. The 14th century saw the advent of literature in Uzbek, Javanese, Malay, Burmese, Thai, Laotian and other languages. In the 14th-16th centuries, languages in the Far East which had been similar to spoken speech then became written languages: Baihua in China, Korean, Vietnamese and Japanese. Vanyan, however, a classic literary language, retained its significance throughout.

To a great extent, different forms of the arts—literature, poetry, theatre and the fine arts—all began to reflect the realities of secular life, with its intrinsic and continual flow of temporary, worldly interests.

All this led to a growth of both cultural and sociopolitical trends towards national self-determination, and these reached their apogee only in the 20th century. Prior to this time, they were still too weak; the growth of new productive forces, social relationships and various forms of intellectual life was slow and sluggish; and no new qualitative changes were taking place. Society in general was still weighed down in the past, and progressive ideas were stifled by religious conservatism.

Such was the state of Eastern societies, up to the 18th or 19th centuries... and then the growing colonial expansionism of the capitalist West led to rapid cultural and social change.

If you wish to study the subject in depth:

1. *Istoriya vsemirnoi literatury* (A History of World Literature), Vol. 3, Nauka, Moscow, 1985.
2. Mets, A., *Musulmansky renessans* (The Renaissance of Islam), Nauka, Moscow, 1966.
3. *Ocherki istorii arabskoi kultury V-XV vekov* (Essays on the History of Arab Culture in the 5th-15th Centuries), Nauka, Moscow, 1982.
4. *Etnograficheskiye issledovaniya razvitiya kultury* (Ethnographical Studies of the Development of Culture), Nauka, Moscow, 1985.
5. *The Cultural Heritage of India*, vols. 4-6, *Science and Technology*, Ramakrishna Mission Institute of Culture, Calcutta, 1978, 1983, 1986.
6. Goonatilake, S., *Aborted Discovery. Science and Creativity in a World Civilization*, University of Chicago Press, Chicago, 1974.
7. Hodgson, M. G. S., *The Venture of Islam. Conscience and History in a World Civilisation*, Vol. 3, University of Chicago Press, Chicago, 1974.

8. Jaggi, O. P., *History of Science and Technology in India*, Vol. 7, Ram, Delhi e. a., 1981.

9. Nasr, S. N., *Science and Civilization in Islam*, Cambridge (Mass.), 1968.

10. Needham, J., *The Shorter Science and Civilization in China*, Vol. 2, Cambridge University Press, Cambridge, 1978.

11. Needham, J., *The Grand Titration. Science and Society in East and West*, Allen and Unwin, London, 1968.

12. Toynbee, A., *A Study of History*, One-volume edition, Oxford University Press, Fair Lawn (N. Y.), 1972.

12

Colonialism and Culture

In this chapter, consideration should be given to the following:

1. In the period of Western colonial expansion, what criteria of civilised behaviour were used by the imperial powers in their relationships with the East?
2. What cultural methods did the Western Powers resort to in their efforts to secure control over a subjugated country?
3. In the Afro-Asian countries, what constituted the main enlightening and reforming trends in the early stages of national liberation?
4. How significant was the cultural aspect of the colonised peoples' struggles for freedom?

Colonial subjugation led to profound changes in the dependent countries. However, their irreversible economic and political inclusion into the world community of nations was insignificant and distorted.

The Ideological Basis of Colonialism

In their relationships with the West, colonies and dependent nations experienced mainly negative aspects of capitalism. And the colonialist and imperialist powers used intellectual influences both ideological and cultural in their policies of subjugation which were based on exploitation and the use of force.

Right up to the end of the 19th century, the West used mainly religious criteria in any intellectual exchange with other nations. Within an intellectual hierarchy, non-Christian races were regarded as being inferior to European ones. In his book *Asia and Western Dominance*, (see No. 5 on page 202) the Indian specialist Kavalam

Madhava Panikkar wrote that the work of the Christian missionaries was all a part of an expanding imperialism. "The sense of not only Christian but European superiority," he says, "which the missionaries perhaps unconsciously inculcated produced also its reaction..." They "not only preached the exclusive truth of the Christian religion, but made claims for the uniqueness of European culture... No Asian people accepted cultural superiority of the West."

The secularisation of society which swept through Europe in the 19th century asserted a racist principle, aimed against African and Asian peoples. This was founded on a pseudo-science of races. Rudyard Kipling and other European writers of the colonial era produced the necessary basis for the views of the colonial bourgeoisie, and this was the embodiment of the idea that the white man is superior to those of non-European stock.

In time, colonial regimes allowed those of a different race and creed — if they'd received a European education — to side with civilisation... and that meant the European variety. In contrast to other cultures of no matter what levels of development, European civilisation was considered to be the bearer of progress. Thus civilisation was not determined by the colour of one's skin; any race could become civilised if, in the course of its cultural development, it rejected its own national traditions. Such policies led to the setting up of a Westernised elite, an intellectual prisoner of the West.

Throughout the 19th century and in the first half of the 20th, right up to the destruction of the colonial regimes, a European understanding of the term "civilised" served the expansionist goals of the Western powers (which later included the USA and Japan), for the acquisition of trade concessions and other advantages in the political and cultural spheres.

It's important to note that such an understanding of the term "civilisation" contradicted the principles which had long been in existence in China, India, Japan and the Ottoman Empire. By the early 20th century, the following criteria determined whether or not a country belonged to the "civilised world":

1. The state must guarantee fundamental human rights to life, dignity, private property, freedom of move-

ment, free trade, and (that which was most important for those of European birth) freedom of conscience.

2. The state must rule its territory via a sufficiently effective administrative system.

3. The state must allow for normal diplomatic relations and the free flow of information.

4. A civilised society must establish humanitarian standards of public life, e. g., ban slavery, polygamy and the self-immolation of widows.

Free trade and the freedom of movement were the two most important principles. And in the colonial period, the European idea of "universalism" boiled down to these pragmatic considerations. As is well known, Western powers used all possible means (including war) to establish the need for opening up "barbaric" countries. By this they meant the provision therein of consumer goods, which also served to link the colony to the interests of the metropolitan power. Trade was the embodiment of a market-dominated civilisation.

The second most important criterion of principles was entailed by the above, and it boiled down to the maintenance of law and the provision of freedom and security, mainly for those involved in trade. This also applied to the missionaries who came in their wake to convert the barbarians to Christianity and to thus create a guaranteed demand for new goods.

The remaining criteria confirmed the universality of European norms, now dispersed as laws amongst all the "underdeveloped" races and peoples. The "uncivilised" had to gradually accept this new way of life and the principles thereof; this was the West's "civilising mission".

Countries were divided into three different criteria: the civilised, the barbaric and the wild. The first were defined by the measure of their community of interests and their norms of human interrelationships. Such were totally absent in barbaric and wild countries. Even in the first half of the 19th century, China, Japan, Persia, Siam and Abyssinia were regarded as only half-civilised; with such countries, one could conclude only an unequal treaty. (They themselves had no right to declare any international pretensions.) No such treaties could be concluded with wild and semi-wild countries; these could only be colonies or protectorates. In both instances, the

European power was the judge, and it defined how civilised or otherwise was the country concerned, and what measures had to be initiated. Failure to comply with these criteria was used as a pretext for the use of force, so to persuade the subject to recognise the orders of the "civilised" country.

In the early 20th century, Europe was considered to be the political and cultural centre of the world, and European standards of civilisation became the basis for admittance to the world community of nations. The gradual inclusion of certain non-European countries—Japan, Turkey and Siam—took place within an unquestionably European context. In their relationships with other countries, though, the European powers were apparently fully justified and well within the law to deploy armed intervention and to foist unfair treaties upon them. In a word, they thus justified the whole system of colonies and protectorates.

Colonial Influences on the Cultures of Subjugated Peoples

The proclaimed ideals of colonialism did not correspond to the actual deeds. They painted its external face with appeals for a conversion to Christianity and for the achievements of civilisation and the human brain. But behind this ideological cloud there were the crude vested interests of the colonial power. In its relationships with its subjugated peoples, the demagogue concealed greed, racial arrogance and the use of force. The reality of colonial mastery involved the suppression of freedom movements and a number of imperial wars; this turned the understanding of the word "civilisation" into a rhetorical anachronism and a diplomatic ritual.

The first generation of Asian and African nationalists of various political hues had one important task: to expose colonial rule as being in effect illegal. The more moderate aimed to overcome the negative aspects of colonialism and to establish a just civilisation; the more radical, meanwhile, led a decisive campaign not only against colonialism but also for national renewal.

In general, the colonial era had an extremely contradictory effect on all spheres of public life, and on public awareness. Although it directly or indirectly introduced certain contemporary reforms, colonialism led either to a destruction of the subjugated peoples' progressive social and intellectual principles in the colonies themselves or to open support of the colonies' traditionalism.

Thus in India from the end of the 18th century, the English colonial authorities used the *shariat* for the Muslims and the norms of the *Dharmashastra* for the Hindus. British academic circles were asked to help, and these then translated the Sanskrit *Laws of Manu* and other collections of Indian classical laws from the 11th and 12th centuries. The courts were run by the English. The judges surrounded themselves with ancient texts, selected a number of laws therefrom, and then foisted these on society, to the detriment of traditional law. Even when Hindu and Islamic theologians were flexible and ready for compromise, the English judges, on the basis of the Oxford dons of Islam and Hinduism, were held to be much more "logical". Only in the late 19th century did they note that *The Laws of Manu* did not correspond to the norms of the great mass of the people, and this led to a dangerous entrenchment of the traditional elite.

Later on, orientalists and anthropologists researched some isolated and previously untouched traditional communities, and recommended they should be left intact. Communities in the depths of Africa or the wilds of Asia as yet unaffected by the winds of change became a favourable area for such research. In the 1950's and '60's, there was a crisis in social anthropology as regards both the researchers' principles and conclusions, for the science was too intimately connected with the vested interests of the colonial regimes.

But apart from supporting traditionalism, intellectual influences of colonialism were exercised via the dissemination of contemporary ideals of Western culture which were supposedly superior to the retarded and stagnant cultures of the East. They mainly involved both a justification and the administration of the colonial system as such. Colonial ideology appeared to be associated with the intellectual development and achievements of Western civilisation. It was used to persuade if only the educated classes, during the earlier stages of colonial rule. Typical bourgeois cultural activities were aimed at industrial development and a more educated society. This was expected to lead to the demise of cumbersome traditional forms of behaviour and modes of thought, as well as of stagnating social structures, etc.

In these colonial conditions, however, there emerged an acute socio-cultural contradiction which is inherent in any bourgeois community: the people were alienated from the new forces of production. Values, highly approved of in a bourgeois society, were but a subterfuge to conceal the genuine state of affairs, and the destruction of the basic way of life. Overcoming these colonial ideals was a necessary pre-condition of any independence struggle.

Criticisms of the colonial powers were seen mainly as a denunciation of those Western stereotypes which were dominant in the apologetic bourgeois consciousness and became part and parcel of the colonial ideology. Such criticisms were sometimes a great force for the moral exposure of the hypocrisy and other negative aspects of bourgeois societies. The latter were mainly condemned for their exceptionally strong economic bias which supposedly led to social disarray, class struggle and the loss of basic humanitarian principles. This essentially moral criticism, however, was not strong enough. It was often regarded as an appeal to the false stereotypes of bourgeois consciousness—irrationalism, intuitionism, and various forms of subjective idealism. It was a criticism of utilitarian materialism and it set forth the significance of the ethical and intellectual sides of life. It tried to differentiate "its own" from "other" cultural values and social structures. But the real defects both of bourgeois society and of the colonial system were to a large extent beyond these critics' fields of vision.

Cultural Development and Social Reform

The movement for political and cultural modernisation was a major factor in the socio-political and intellectual development of the East in the late 19th and the 20th centuries. It was mainly reflected in social reform and the promotion of knowledge, and it formed the basis of a protracted and complex cultural renewal in Afro-Asian societies.

The overwhelming superiority of the West in technology, military affairs and political organisation forced public opinion in traditional societies to recognise the importance of these factors initially in international relations and then in their domestic policies.

The spread of knowledge was mainly the result of the influence of European enlightenment, and thus it was originally an elite trend of an apparently secular nature. Its supporters rejected traditional ways of life and campaigned (i) for the introduction and broad internal dissemination of Western public institutions, and (ii), for a direct assimilation of Western outlooks. Those who sought to achieve these aims, however, were unable to carry out two basic, closely interrelated socio-political tasks which confronted the East at this new stage of its development: national consolidation and national liberation. There was a basic contradiction in the socio-political character of their work, which manifested itself in their confrontations with a monarchy in which they continued to place their trust, and in their relationships with colonialism. This could only be resolved by moving beyond the framework of their ideology and programmes.

It would be wrong to suggest that these activities were off-stage. Such an orientation is perceived mainly as society's growing needs in its development of the sciences. Later on, it enters into a complex interaction with other cultural tendencies, mainly with those concerned with religious reforms.

The coming together of cultural and reformative ideas affected a wider cross-section of society and was an important stage in the development of new ideological currents. Teachers and reformers focused on the question of how to overcome feudal backwardness and how to eliminate caste, racial and religious discrimination, and other relics from the past. Educational developments, the dissemination of scientific knowledge and the setting up of a new literature in the modern languages helped enormously to awaken public self-awareness. Reformers tried to avoid any blind fanaticism in society and to extend both the rights of human reason and the individual's freedom to criticise his social and economic status.

For the reformers, ignorance and the common people's constraint and passivity were indisputable facts.

Many thinkers were afraid of the popular masses. According to the former, the state should be that force which can bring society out of its stagnation. If there's no supreme power controlling the lives of all subjects, the gulf between rich and poor will increase, differences will lead to fights, and the very basis of society will be undermined.

In practice, both reformers and teachers also had to carry out a protracted and onerous struggle with the traditional leaders in society, the clergy, monarchists, and feudal lords who still had reliable means of influencing both the people and the powers that be. Thus for a long time, reformers maintained there was a need for a strong but reasonable power, able to overcome local limitations. They were met by a stubborn opposition from traditional elements, and from the colonial regimes themselves, of course. Thus the reformers became more critical and more radical, soon to form movements of national renewal and self-determination. Then nationalism slowly began to take shape, not only as a counterforce to Western imperialism, but also as a movement for self-determination on both a cultural-cum-ethnic basis, and on a political one.

Nationalism brings a qualitatively new element into public awareness. This happens when monarchical or religious forms of social opposition and control lose their previous significance while at the same time there's a growing trend towards national integration.

In the cultural sphere, it's clear that colonialism thus caused some profound changes in the entire intellectual lives of the subjugated countries: for one, structural changes in the established order for controlling society's intellectual ways of life. The suppression and deformations of the previous ways were accompanied by a protest reaction against an alien rule and for the defence of an indigenous intellectual culture. However, self-determination did not only relate to religious and national communities; it was also based on a struggle for national unity and a genuine national culture.

The duplicity of colonial expansionism lay in that, along with political suppression and deformation of the society's intellectual life, colonialism led to an increasing

Western penetration into the cultural spheres of other civilisations. Thus Eastern society became more aware of such ideas, achievements and inventions as had been the preserve of Western civilisation.

In mastering the achievements of Western civilisations, Eastern countries underwent some profound cultural changes. However, the characteristics of Eastern culture did not fade into the past, to become known to historical sociologists alone. In describing the functions of culture in Chapter 5, we noted that it maintains a continuity throughout all changes taking place in society. To a large extent, it also provides for society's internal integration in its relations with other societies. The necessity of maintaining these functions throughout all these radical changes creates complex and conflicting processes taking place in the contemporary cultures of the newly-independent countries.

If you wish to study the subject in depth:

1. Yerasov, B. S., *Tropicheskaya Afrika: ideologiya i problemy kultury* (Tropical Africa: Ideology and Cultural Problems), Nauka, Moscow, 1972.

2. *Zarozhdeniye ideologii natsionalno-osvoboditelnogo dvizheniya (XIX—Nachalo XX v.). Ocherki po istorii obshchestvennoi mysli narodov Vostoka* (The Ideological Origins of National Liberation Movements (19th and Early 20th Centuries). Essays on the History of the Social Sciences of Eastern Peoples), Nauka, Moscow, 1973.

3. *Obshchestvenniye dvizheniya i ikh ideologiya v doburzhuaznykh obshchestvakh Azii* (Social Movements and Their Ideologies in Pre-bourgeois Asian Societies), Nauka, Moscow, 1988.

4. Gong, G. *The Standard of "Civilization" in International Society*, Clarendon, Oxford, 1984.

5. Panikkar, K. M., *Asia and Western Dominance*, Allen and Unwin, London, 1959.

PART III The Cultural Sociology of Developing Countries

13

The Formation of Cultural Sociology in Newly-Independent Countries

In this chapter, consideration should be given to the following:

1. What sort of contradictions emerge in the cultures of newly independent countries?
2. How did Western sociological evaluations of Eastern cultures develop?
3. What basic problems are currently being investigated by Western cultural sociologists studying the cultures of the East?
4. What is the general assessment of culture by sociologists in the newly independent countries?
5. How has an understanding of the word "tradition" developed among Eastern and Western sociologists?
6. What lies behind the concept of the "uniqueness of a society" in third world countries?

In chapter 9 we familiarised ourselves with the social characteristics of Western culture, and in Chapter 7, with the basic features of a socialist culture. In this section, we'll consider contemporary problems of cultural sociology in the newly independent countries.

It's no accident that in this textbook we find a certain asymmetry in the three basic socio-cultural worlds. The main need today is to understand the culture and its dynamics in those countries where the bulk of humankind lives and which play an increasingly significant role in current global processes.

The main changes in the newly independent countries are those relating to the profound and rapid alterations in their production processes. At the same time, traditional forms of public awareness are changing over to new. contemporary ones. A new perception of the realities is being created in these countries in an interaction between the legacies of colonialism and current world influences.

The Basic Problems of Sociology in the Newly Independent Countries

Contemporary development in various Afro-Asian countries started at different times from the mid-19th century to the mid-20th was and still is characterised by the following general contradictions, which also affect their cultural spheres:

1. Tradition clashes with the present. The national legacies of these countries, stagnant and burdened by obsolescent prejudices, dogmas and canons, hardly meet the demands of the present, and these clash with new ideas for a development programme to revive public life and rekindle knowledge, action, and a determination to change.
2. Society is aware of the mutually exclusive effects of East and West. To be more exact, society can sense its Eastern, cultural-cum-historical location, and the West is like the bearer of a pernicious and destructive power. Society's new ideas are still to be ratified, yet they are a basis for its survival and the guarantee of its sovereignty and uniqueness.
3. Various scales of local nationalistic trends—tribal, ethnic or national—are seen to counter universalist trends towards unification on a pan-national, political or cultural basis.
4. There are two diametrically opposed cultural levels corresponding to a certain extent to two definite social groups: a high cultural level to an elite, and a popular level to the masses. The main victims of this cultural gap are the intelligentsia.

The above contradictions unfold both in space, in different cultural-historical regions, and in time. Different trends oppose and yet influence one another, acquiring a temporary predominance over, substituting for, or supplementing one another. Thus they form either an autochthonous repulsion of everything and anything European, as if it is alien and pernicious or an introduction of Western values; the hope of a radical overthrow of imported Western institutions and values, or of their partial inclusion in indigenous equivalents in various forms of synthesis and symbiosis; and finally, the pursuit of a universalist pan-Islamic or pan-African, pan-Hindu or pan-Buddhist unity, or a defence of national and ethnic cultures.

Although these processes can be subdivided into certain stages, one can hardly see a finality or conclusiveness therein even today. The stability of same requires a careful and detailed estimate, taking account of the apparent repetition of certain stages and phenomena; and secondly, of the changes taking place in each of the opposing processes.

What have been the scientific interpretations of these trends? Two sets of conceptions have arisen: one in Western philosophy and sociology (see below), the other in the social sciences of the newly independent countries (see the next subsection). Together they represent two distinct separate approaches.

In the '50's and '60's, the cultural worth of Eastern societies was mainly determined by how much Islam, Hinduism, Buddhism or Confucianism could help or hinder a capitalist type of economic growth, with its corresponding social and political elements.

Weber had a rather negative approach, not only to Eastern religions, but also to the cultures and traditions of the region generally. They had to be overcome, he said, as quickly as possible, in the name of accelerated development.

In the '60's and '70's, Western researchers paid greater attention to the role of government power and social institutions. In similar fashion, sociologists from the developing countries insisted on the structural-cum-functional methods developed by the Western sociologists Marion Levi, Gabriel Almond, Lucian Pye, Fred Riggs, Emmanuel Sarkisyanz, David Apter and Schmuel Eisenstadt. They regarded culture as a function of the political and administrative spheres for influencing society. The failures and collapses of many political regimes among the newly independent countries forced certain academics to pay more attention to the role of culture as an important prerequisite of political deeds and administrative laws.

In so far as the suggested aims of socio-economic development appeared to be more and more unattainable, social scientists became aware of the unsatisfactory nature of previous attempts. Accumulated data showed more and more test-cases had to be regarded as exceptions. Both East and West, research was carried out on certain, separate processes, but the phenomenon of cultural life then failed to correspond to the concepts accepted by the academics. There were so many exceptions to the general theory that the famous Swedish scientist Gunnar Myrdal called for a radical reappraisal of previous conceptions of modernisation in his book *Asian Drama* (No. 2, page 215).

At the same time, Western researchers focused on the political and economic problems of the developing countries. And they reckoned the basic economic requirement was to speed up the change-over of the Asian and African economies to a Western style of production, i. e., to switch to the capitalist model. They regarded the state and the civil service as a means of rebuilding society in accordance with the needs of capitalist production. And industry, schools and mass communications were seen as an important way of attracting the citizens into this new style of work. They went on to suggest that this could be done without resorting to a traditional culture which was still archaic and which just did not correspond to contemporary needs.

Unsuccessful Western modernisation, however, led to a more fundamental approach to the cultural inheritance of the Afro-Asian countries. Despite the views of Weber, several specialists now feel the Eastern intellectual systems are perfectly capable of reform and bourgeois industrialisation. They stand for the inclusion of Islamic, Hindu or Buddhist beliefs and institutions into a modern industrialised society. And they therefore suggest that any intellectual reforms should be partial and structural, i. e., any objections to business enterprise from the religious community will thus be overcome, but the latter will continue to regulate all other spheres — family, social and ethnic — in accordance with traditional norms.

Thus the complexity both of the public way of life in the newly independent countries and of their cultural inheritance was taken to be more and more multifarious.

The evolutionary concept was therefore put further and further into the background; and instead, there was a growing recognition of the pluralism of world cultures.

Cultural research in the newly independent countries was restricted not just to the sphere of modernisation, for work was also being carried out into the role of culture in nationalist movements and in the emergence of nations. Culture and politics were seen therein as an expression of a unifying principle. It also became clear, however, that culture plays a contradictory role in national liberation movements. On the one hand, there's definitely the one national culture which brings together all social groups and classes, so to facilitate the self-determination of a nation. And on the other, certain attempts to define the essence of a national culture and a national character were theoretical and contradictory.

Western specialists on the unifying role of Eastern culture fall into two categories: left-wing radicals and conservatives. The former criticise the negative consequences of Western influences very severely; it was, they suggest, a cultural imperialism, and it undermined the former colony's internal unity and led to profound internal disorder. The latter, meanwhile, consider the interaction with an alien culture was a burden on the West; thus do they call for a demarcation of the cultural spheres of influence of both East and West.

In the last decade, there's been a growing criticism of Western influences by Asian and African ideologists and theoreticians. This has led to a serious reconsideration of earlier scientific studies of Western societies and especially of their cultures. (This is discussed by the American scientist Edward William Said in his book *Orientalism*—see No. 4 on p. 215.) He criticises the classical concept of the East as pure prejudice prompted by an affinity to the politico-economic goals and cultural ideas of the West; such a concept, he suggests, is just a belittlement of the achievements of Eastern cultures.

This criticism allows one to reject any cultural prejudice in the study of non-Western cultures, and this was a prerequisite for a new field of anthropological research: a study of the various ways different cultures influence and understand each other. Such work underwent a rapid growth from approximately the late '70's, and it is now devoted to a study, firstly, of the growing contradictions which occur in the course of a society's modernisation; and secondly, the increasing repulsion of a Western culture when in an alien milieu. The cultures of other countries and peoples were seen not only as an object of study but also as independent partners in a mutual interaction which could be successful only on a basis of mutual understanding and dialogue. (This is discussed in more detail in Chapter 18.)

Cultural Studies in the Newly Independent Countries

Public awareness in the above countries was initially focused on the problems of self-determination and development, and this influenced all aspects of public life. Many sociologists felt independence could not be achieved only on an economic basis, and this was because the economies of these countries were so multistructured and fragmented. Furthermore, they would still be dependent on the capitalist West. A society's self-determination, therefore, could not be based on its economy.

Public opinion in these countries regarded politics or culture as the basis of their self-determination. Third world countries attached great significance to the concept of political independence, and this made many specialists focus on the role of politics and government as the motivating force of development. Hence scientific achievements in the '70's were linked to political studies.

Even politics, though, is not all-powerful. Coups d'état, political reforms and the failures of authoritarian models of modernisation demonstrated the need of an interaction between political and other factors. Politics have to have a reliable link with the realities of life, i. e., they must be broadly recognised (legitimised). It would be quite impossible to evaluate a state's legitimacy, and hence stability and effectiveness, without a knowledge of its political culture.

Thus the enthusiasm for theories of modernisation in the newly independent countries is now being replaced by a critical reappraisal thereof. Even in the capitalist West, public opinion no longer holds dear those philosophies which are based only in science and technology. Instead it turns more and more to the religious teachings of the East or the mythologies of Africa.

As soon as the spirit of nationalism stirred in an Afro-Asian country, culture was regarded as the basis of its national way of life. This was reflected in the idea that theirs was a unique culture, for example. But it took a long time for public opinion to mature, so to progress from an ideological basis to a theoretical interpretation.

In searching for the essence of Afro-Asian society, many Afro-Asian specialists focused on a certain stable socio-cultural complex which they felt represented the initial realities of that society, its uniqueness, its parameters, and its potential for self-development. With this complex, culture was that sphere of overall characteristics, values, principles, aims, beliefs, codes of conduct, knowledge and skills which together make up the one corresponding entity — be it a subnational, national or pan-national one.

Third world specialists suggest their cultures often nullify socio-economic factors and any of society's inherent contradictions. The theory is that the self-determination and stability of a society depend on the maintenance of its vital cultural values and standards; and this has now been firmly stated in the resolutions of various UNESCO conferences which stress the need both to maintain and develop a society's cultural inheritance and to recognise the right of all peoples to their own, unique cultures.

In newly independent countries, the public is persistently trying to formulate the principles of that originality which may act as a basis for a nation's independent way of life. These searches far from always result in profound theoretical conclusions. Sometimes, an understanding of a society's uniqueness includes a certain existentialist idea which must then reflect the essence of that society's way of life.

No matter how varied the points of view or theoretical definitions, social scientists world-wide and authors on the third world are now of the opinion that culture is a broad sphere of values and norms, knowledge and philosophy. This coincides only partially with a narrower, more classical interpretation of culture as being of the arts and sciences. In a broad understanding, it's very much a part of a society's means of production and way of life; it also includes the motivations involved in production and consumption, as well as the norms of human behaviour, individual personality, etc.

UNESCO has published numerous definitions of the word culture, and the one which most interests us is contained in the programme called "To know so as to do" *(Comprendre pour agir*)*:

"Narrow, elitist definitions of culture, viewed as a system of fine arts and literature, a luxury reserved for the privileged few, must be superseded. Culture, in the full sense of the term, is a fundamental component of the vitality of any society; it is the sum total of a people's creative activities, its methods of production and of appropriation of material assets, its form of organisation, its beliefs and sufferings, its work and its leisure, its dreams and its successes." This definition gives a somewhat broader interpretation of the word; it seeks not to define culture as an elite field of the arts, but to include other aspects of society's way of life. Culture is now, therefore, represented in a general social sense as a system of values and understandings intimately linked with society's everyday needs and deeds.

Sociologists of non-Western countries have rejected various modernisation models emanating from a primacy of economic factors or from an assumption that bourgeois political structures play a key role. They also criticised at length the basic values of bourgeois culture, especially individualism and consumerism, which result in the pursuit of material goods and a loss of social justice and national unity.

Tradition or Uniqueness?

Sociologists were thus able to overcome the concept that traditionalism is in opposition to modernisation. Strictly speaking, they had set the two off one against the other, to then analyse the processes of development... but in so doing, they became more and more aware that such mutual exclusivity is just not on. Traditionalism in

---

* *Thinking ahead. Unesco and the Challenges of Today and Tomorrow*, Paris, Unesco, 1977, p. 19.

fact is not at odds with modernisation; rather, it helps to maintain vital aspects of the public way of life. Indeed, some of the more radical and critical sociologists have shown that traditionalism in developing countries gets even stronger in the course of modernisation, if such is dependent on Western capital. Furthermore, in turning to one's past and cultural inheritance, one can refute those arguments on the necessity of rejecting any archaic traditions. This led social scientists in the third world to think of tradition less and less frequently. Typically, some Western theoreticians still attach some prestige to this concept, despite severe criticism as to its inadequacy. Such a methodology tends to classify traditions as elements of stability—similar perhaps to the "Protestant work ethic"—in a process of bourgeois modernisation and look for Protestant-type ethic in Eastern religions.

Thus an understanding of the word "tradition", was far too wide, and sometimes its literal sense was taken to mean originality, unique character, cultural inheritance, cultural nucleus, cultural dynamics and/or powers of internal regeneration. The leading and most widespread understanding—uniqueness—is mainly used to describe a society's original nature, formed from its cultural characteristics and historical experience. Its uniqueness includes both objective and subjective aspects of its way of life, the internal and the external, the particular with the general, the deed with an awareness thereof, and a cultural stability with its dynamics.

An understanding of the word "uniqueness" was as one with a political understanding of the terms "independence" and "sovereignty". In 1982, UNESCO held a world conference on cultural policies in Mexico City, and cultural uniqueness was there stated to be one of the most important issues of our times. Thus they confirmed both the clearly distinctive meaning of the word, and the fact that it fully reflects the specific nature of that society's social development: ... not only a continuity between past and present, but also a sense of direction for the future. This was to ensure the unity of an individual and a people with the values of their civilisation.

In various conference documents, the uniqueness of a society was shown to be the vital nucleus of its culture. A society may rely on its past, draw strength from its own internal capabilities and master any necessary external values. Thus, via the dynamic principle of its uniqueness, it can realise a continual process of independent development.

The one drawback to the above definitions of the term "uniqueness" is as follows: the objective and subjective aspects thereof are so closely bound together that it's impossible to define the relationships between them. Such definitions often include a straight existentialist sense which should express the vital aspects of that society's way of life but it is too difficult to analyse as required by social theory.

Another important sense which emerges from an overloaded understanding of the word "tradition" involves those aspects which Afro-Asian societies have set up in difference to Western models. These, then, are their specific characteristics, a term for which it's rather difficult to give a theoretical definition. Such quite obviously would include a description of that society's norms, customs, values and codes of behaviour. The difficulty comes in defining its particular ethnic characteristics. In a general approach, there were quite vague types of national character or religious behaviour; but assessments thereof in more recent times have become more and more negative, for in comparison to non-Western and non-industrialised societies, they've been seen as rather exotic. This was because certain anthropologists used a prejudiced methodology, more suited to the needs of an expansionist West.

Eastern thinkers, however, tend to paint a different picture. The main factor of a non-Western society is the predominance of intellectual rather than economic values in life of the individual. In various forms of cultural uniqueness and of indigenous varieties of socialism, cultural values are intimately associated with social ones; indeed, the two condition each other in the one, unique entity. And we can find a number of definitions drawn up by indigenous Afro-Asian theoreticians, and these identify the uniqueness of a society with the principles of an ethical solidarity, regardless of whether or not these are based on actual communal-cum-religious structures.

Conceptions of the unique nature and specific characteristics of a society were often in the form of those principles and historical images which are inherent in a certain national or ethnic community or one of the world's major religions. Such conceptions, however, were rather similar to each other, mainly because they were based on an attitude to the rational-cum-industrial and individualistic West, and thus on a value judgement somewhat opposed thereto. Such theoretical generalisations neglected the differences between various non-Western civilisations and their cultural levels. The principles underlying a society's specific characteristics are very similar throughout Africa and Asia. Searches for other modes of life, those which differ from the ones the West has foisted abroad, concentrate on conceptions of the uniqueness or specific nature of a society, which have impeded the elaboration of a general theory.

At the same time, theoreticians had to try and identify the cause of underdevelopment in the countries of Africa and Asia, so as then to work out some recommendations for the elimination thereof. In protesting against the destructive effects of an alien form of modernisation, various ideologists have suggested a society's self-determination should be based on its uniqueness, but they did not propose an all-embracing programme for social reconstruction in accordance with modern fashions. Hence the opinion that excessive adherence to tradition hinders rapid modernisation.

The Development of Civilisation

Because the problems of cultural self-determination and development were insoluble (and this was due to a static understanding of the terms "unique nature" and "specific characteristics" of society), people tended to concentrate on historical factors, cultural inheritance, and the development dynamics of culture both past and in the future. Social scientists in Afro-Asian countries centred on an evaluation of their development potential; this was based on the achievements of the past and could facilitate their organic self-development.

An analytical examination of such problems relies on an evaluation of the historical dynamics of civilisations. Weber, Toynbee, Needham, Grunebaum, Redfield, Eisenstadt and Singer have established a general theory of civilisations. These scientists have studied the structures thereof, the interrelationship between their cultural and socio-political factors, and the growth dynamics and stagnation of Eastern civilisations. Their opinions are having an ever increasing influence on Afro-Asian sociologists. They criticise Western models of modernisation and suggest instead a theory of independent, self-regenerating development, one which by drawing on the nation's past and on the given civilisation's history, relies mainly on internal sources to activate society.

Without accepting the theocratic, philosophical pretensions of a total Islam (*Tawhid* *), many in the lands of Islam nevertheless see the resurgence of religion as a major turning point on a road to the self-determination of an Islamic civilisation. They regard the universal nature of Islam as the most important feature of this process. Hinduism and Buddhism may also be subjected to a similar interpretation. Instead of the one Western universalist civilisation, there's a complex coming together of all peoples and cultures based on their, mutual influences.

Social science may be enriched considerably by a focus on civilising factors. This is mainly by an understanding of a socio-cultural universalism which varies somewhat from the universalism of the West. The former is a basis not only of self-determination, but also of an independent historical dynamics.

Thus we have become acquainted with the basic sociological propositions on the culture of the newly independent countries. A scientific discipline has been established, East and West; this is a study, (i) of the general principles underlying the social significance of culture — its various aspects and functions, and its role in regulating society; and (ii), of different cultural forms in different social structures and different cultural-historical regions. An understanding of the specific nature of the culture of various ethnic groups, races and civilisa-

* *Tawhid* is the Islamic principle of the unique nature of the one and only God Who is represented in the multiplicity and diversity of this world. The dogma of *tawhid* declares everything to be subject to the will of the one God.

tions of the East requires an adequate theoretical approach.

Sociologists studying the cultures of developing countries tend to concentrate on different cultural forms and different levels of cultural development. The principle underlying societies' unique nature and their powers of internal self-regeneration are an important factor in determining those laws which govern the cultures of non-Western nations. The term "unique nature" of a society refers to its self-reliance, the specific characteristics of its culture, and its national integrity. A society's power of internal self-regeneration is the ability of its culture to be the internal motivating force of that society's development. In turning to the achievements of the past, contemporary ideologists, politicians and cultural activists of the newly independent countries suggest the possibility of modernising different spheres of society, while maintaining a continuity with the past. Their indigenous sociologists tend to criticise the negative influences of Western cultural expansionism; instead they favour a development of the principles of a mutual interaction between cultures, East and West.

The above methodological principles are helping us to identify the most important factors governing contemporary development in the third world.

If you wish to study the subject in depth:

1. *Obshchestvennaya mysl razvivayushchikhsya stran* (Public Opinion in Developing Countries), Nauka, Moscow, 1988.

2. Myrdal, G., *Asian Drama. An Inquiry into the Poverty of Nations,* vols. 1-3, Pantheon, A Division of Random House, N.Y., 1968.

3. Abdel-Malek, A., *Social Dialectics,* Vol. 1, *Civilization and Social Theory,* State University of New York, Albany, 1981.

4. Said, E., *Orientalism*, Routledge and Kegan Paul, London, 1978.

5. Singh, Y., *Image of Man. Ideology and Theory in Indian Sociology*, Chanakya, Delhi, 1983.

6. Shils, E., *Tradition*, University of Chicago Press, Chicago, 1981.
7. *World Conference on Cultural Policies*, Mexico, 26 July-6 August 1982, Final Report, UNESCO, Paris, 1982.

14

Present-Day Cultural Processes in the Developing Countries

In this chapter, consideration should be given to the following:

1. What is the essence of the theories of modernisation?
2. What are the main forms of interaction of tradition and modern trends in the developing countries' cultures?
3. How is the cultural synthesis of East and West manifested?
4. What are the expressions of the conflict of Western and Eastern cultures?
5. How do various social strata in the developing countries react to the modernisation processes in their cultures?

Colonial domination has brought about deep-going transformations in dependent societies. It has meant their involvement into world relations—both economic and political—although this was of a distorted character. From then on, these nations' entire traditional heritage experienced the influence of external factors.

No matter what the character and extent to which the cultural identity of Eastern and African societies has been preserved, today their involvement in global relations and also the changes taking place in various spheres of life are exerting a determining influence on their development.

Modernisation and Culture

The fact that the new elements introduced into the Eastern societies had a Western origin has prompted many sociologists to describe the process as Westernisation. The obviously contradictory character of the Western influence and the hatred of colonialism have prompted the majority of sociologists and ideologists to reject the term "Westernisation" in assessing the processes of renewal through borrowings from abroad. Instead, a broader term, "modernisation", gained currency, which was thoroughly developed in the 1950's and '60's.

Modernisation is the process of movement of premodern, or traditional, societies towards types of economic and political systems, and also mass culture, that are characteristic of present-day developed capitalist societies. Modernisation primarily implies increased opportunities for using modern science and technology in the main spheres of material and intellectual production and laying the groundwork (social, cultural, political and technological) for their application. Important parameters of such growth, which can be empirically measured by sociologists, are the population's mobility, its participation in social and political government, and the access of various social groups to modern culture.

Major factors of modernisation include the following: the character, rate and scale of socio-economic change, forms of a country's involvement in the international division of labour, the extent of economic and political dependence, the social character of government policy, industrialisation, urbanisation, social stratification, and changes in society's occupational structure.

On the cultural plane, however, of special importance are the following factors: the ethnic, religious, ideological, political, social and cultural situation in the country or in a specific territorial community; the level, extent and accessibility of the educational system; the level of the mass media; legal regulation of relations, etc.

Modernisation is a contradictory process. It includes a struggle between the old and the new, construction and destruction, and a clash between the interests of different social and political forces. These antagonisms are aggravated by the heterogeneous character of the given social environment.

Pluralism of economic forms in the developing countries, and the transitory character of their economies determine their main social and cultural features. From the sociological point of view, of special significance is the heterogeneous character of these societies, i. e., the coexistence and interaction within them of diverse social and ethno-cultural groups of the modern, transitional and traditional type. Heterogeneity also includes support of traditional cultural values and forms of social consciousness.

Forms of Interaction Between Traditional and Modern Phenomena

The complicated and contradictory character of modernisation gives rise to a number of different trends in society. Both on the socio-cultural and psycho-intellectual planes the processes of growth are peculiarly intermingled with trends of stagnation and disintegration and various forms of coexistence of traditional and modern features. Significant aspects of society's existence are increasingly becoming subject to new influences among which a special role belongs to industrial, professional, scientific, technological and political elements of culture that have come from the West.

Changes embrace not only relatively modernised groups of the population, but even broader sections of society which still stay aloof from new forms of labour and social relations. Accordingly, changes take place in the structure of people's consciousness and set of values, the character of interaction between ideology and everyday practice, etc. The spread of commodity-money relations undermines traditional forms of social stability, with the growth of industrial production, the formation of new political relations, the mounting of national liberation movements, and the socio-political restructuring of society.

Any attempt to single out the forms of interaction of traditional Eastern cultures with the modern Western culture is rather problematic, because of their vast differences. However, the following basic forms of this interaction are normally identified:

1) *Zero, or minimum, interaction,* in which traditional and modern features are relatively independent of each other and remain in isolated fields. This brings about the formation of enclaves of a modern way of life surrounded by an ocean of traditionalism, with old structures and corresponding cultural principles and mental stereotypes remaining intact. Conservative ruling groups intentionally encourage the majority of the population to keep to the archaic forms of social and intellectual existence. Parallel to this, there is a process of gradual modernisation in the way of life of the urban middle class. This is furthered by urbanisation, the development of education, the growth of employment in new occupations, political activity, and the spread of the mass media.

The social strata that are drawn into modern public life, considerably change their attitude to new means of production. They feel attracted to technology. However, these processes embrace only a tiny portion of the population, leaving behind the numerous peasantry and the urban lower classes, whose position hardly changes.

2) The second tendency is the *mutual adjustment of Western modernisation and local traditionalism*. Each side uses the other's possibilities for its own ends, which results in a synthesis. Traditional ties, standards and notions turn out to be quite viable, as tradition combines with the achievements of urbanisation and the scientific and technological revolution, at the same time retaining its original meaning.

In the most general sense, the structural adaptation of former consciousness to modern features consists in the fact that it still attaches great importance to solidarity relations. At the same time, the population adopts new forms of activity and consumption. As he enters a world of new, wider opportunities, the individual in the East brings into it his old principles. He seeks to use these new opportunities to strengthen the old solidarity, to consolidate his local group, to increase its consumption and build up its prestige in relation to other groups and at their expense.

Especially significant is the abidance by old values in new forms of economic activity. This phenomenon in modern Eastern and African societies is quite complex. It is definitely negative in the sense that it causes the destruction of the former principles of local solidarity and hierarchy. But it changes as soon as new consumption opportunities open up. The craving for new consumer goods ties a person to market relations, which disrupts former solidarity.

Nevertheless, traditionalism retards modern forms of activity as well, as clan, tribe, caste and ethnic relations, standards and considerations dominate over professional, class or national principles, giving rise to corruption and nepotism.

In this context, there is a growing influence of those forms of mass consciousness which religion tried in vain to eradicate or place under its control: magic, incantations, belief in various amulets which are supposed to bring success, health and happiness, etc. Witchcraft and anti-Vedic cultures are emerging, as well as numerous sects which produce strange combinations of religion and primitive beliefs.

A typical illustration of adaptation is the viability of ancestor worship in African and Asian societies and its spread to urban communities. This worship is viewed as the maintenance of cordial, intimate ties between the living and their deceased relatives and friends. The ancestors are human beings, who understand the problems of the living; moreover, they guide their descendants' actions and protect them from various perils, giving them advice and showing them the right way in life. It is assumed that observance of their behests and maintenance of proper relations with them will guarantee stability even under the new way of life. In a more developed cultural environment, mass consciousness seeks objects for such worship in one of the major world religions finding saints, martyrs and sages who become the counsellors, patrons and protectors of the living.

Traditional consciousness is often affected by new consumer goods and advertising. Old restrictions are lifted and new opportunities are viewed as a stimulus to increased consumption, which serves to raise the status and influence of the given primary group or individual. At the same time, the accumulation of material resources for production is alien to them. However, the striving to raise one's status within the traditional hierarchy brings about an acute struggle for greater access to welfare. Former solidarity increasingly relies on the consumption of goods manufactured outside the framework of traditional production.

The traditional privileged social groups—the tribal aristocracy, the higher clergy, and various echelons of bureaucrats—are the first to benefit by these tendencies. It is they, above all, who chase after prestigious forms of consumption (fashions, high-class goods, education, social status), which are usually inaccessible to the common people. In the long run, this has a damaging effect on society as a whole.

Activation of primary forms of solidarity (including ethnic and caste solidarity) enhances the pluralism of social and political structures which has proved to be one of the basic sources of instability in the young states. Competition for sources of living (including power) becomes more acute, which often brings about tensions and conflicts. Following the old principles, the individual and various solidarity groups find themselves in the power of forces which they cannot either understand or control. This results in a crisis of traditional attitudes and practices and intellectual orientations, which is viewed as a moral breakdown and the disintegration of society.

3) *Modernisation versus traditionalism*. No matter what the scale of the two above-mentioned tendencies is, the most influential, deep-going and dramatic is the third one: the disintegration of traditional standards of conduct and the crisis of culture under the impact of capitalist modernisation, which causes a protest reaction.

The penetration of capitalism into pre-industrial structures above all brings about a devaluation of the old productive forces. Their efficiency is obviously inferior to that of the new production methods. And it is not only a question of devaluation of traditional material production. Also distorted are the traditional relations of solidarity, which used to cement the entire social structure. The subordination of society to commodity-money relations and the transition from ethics to business deprives huge masses of the population of their traditional role;

they get no new role in return and become outcasts. The masses begin to see that the activity aimed at unlimited accumulation of capital is purely pragmatic and utilitarian, deprived of any human character and not conforming to any moral principles. The vast majority of society, still bound by pre-capitalist attitudes sees the advent of commodity-money relations as the cause of disruption of vital ties between people, even as the loss of the meaning of life.

The new situation is especially dismal in that, together with the loss of access to the means of production and of their place in the system of distribution, considerable sections of society lose all their property. The peasants, together with their land, lose their individuality and place in life. Likewise, the artisan cannot compete with factory machines.

On the whole, there emerges a deep qualitative variety of social structures associated with industrial and pre-industrial forms of production. The transition from one social system to another disrupts not only the "continuity of time", but the very fabric of society; society splits up into several groups associated with modern and traditional ways of life. The traditional mechanism of social regulation crumbles under the pressure of development imperatives; however, new mechanisms are slow in taking shape. The elimination or weakening of the traditional forms of solidarity brings to the surface conflicts that used to be hidden in the depth of society. Society is faced with a threat of splitting up into mutually hostile strata and groups, owing to the growth of ethnic, religious, class, and caste conflicts, those between town and country, and so forth.

Traditional principles formed by solidarist morality appear under the new conditions as gullibility and helplessness, becoming easy prey for "wicked" forces which use cunning and downright fraud to achieve their selfish ends. Traditional moral values and conduct standards which used to be seen as ideal and enjoyed sacred status are now used by hypocrites as a disguise for the seamy side of life. Thus, the caste system, which used to be seen as divine in origin, is now viewed as a self-seeking invention of the higher castes.

Political analysts and leaders in the developing countries point out the spread of discord and confusion there. This is above all typical of the towns, but the countryside has not avoided it either.

Social Aspects of the Culture of a Transitional Society

The complicated character of Asian and African societies has brought about the growth of diversity in their cultures and social consciousness. Generally speaking on the mass level, one can identify the cultural values and ways of life of various social groups: traditional peasant, new rural, those of the highly stratified urban population, including the working class, those of the privileged traditional, bourgeois, bourgeois-bureaucratic, and intellectual strata. Traditional factors have different effects on the attitudes of all these sections of society.

The working class, by virtue of its social and economic position, is not sufficiently involved in industrial production, is politically unripe, and is still tied down to traditional ways of life, all of which is sometimes manifested in the influence that ethnic, tribal, caste, and religious factors have on it.

In most developing countries, capitalist strata have taken shape, whose consciousness and principles are characterised by universal bourgeois stereotypes. The functioning of these strata is largely affected by their backward milieu, but on the whole the level of the bourgeoisie's development and its dependence on traditional ways of life are in inverse proportion (although this traditionality can be cultivated, as before, in secondary spheres of life or as a form of tourist attraction).

A much more substantial measure of traditionalism is characteristic of social strata which stay outside the new forms of production and consumption or are little involved in them. Peasant consciousness on the whole is less affected by the process of disintegration than that of the urban population. It retains for a longer period its traditional mythological attitudes and religious principles with strong egalitarian elements.

The Intelligentsia and Culture

Special attention has recently been devoted to the study of the so-called middle classes, which include the intelligentsia, civil servants, and military officers. This relative and unstable social conglomerate plays an important part in social relations and a still greater part in ideology even if by virtue of its direct bearing on intellectual production and management. The intelligentsia has a virtual monopoly on education and culture and therefore on the intellectual productive forces, too. In the context of the scientific and technological revolution, it constitutes one of the most developed modern elements of the social structure.

The intelligentsia plays the main role in the formulation of goals and principles for maintaining the cultural values, and in the attainment of requisite knowledge. By virtue of this role, it accelerates the development of society, providing for various advanced forms of interaction between traditional and present-day elements.

The need for intellectual work is visibly demonstrated by the experience of independent development gained by Third World countries. The demise of state resistance to change in Asian and African societies has often been accompanied by an end to furious, spontaneous popular protest. It took countless lives, prolonged oppression, and not a few setbacks, before these societies discovered that not only the traditional forms of social organisation, but also values and attitudes, had become obsolete and that they could not survive unless they took on new ideas and opposed the forces controlling them. Hence the need for intellectuals as a new culturally creative group and a source of ideas.

All this has weakened the social and cultural influence of the traditional intelligentsia. The set of values which it had formed and upheld proved inappropriate to the new conditions. The new leading status of the intelligentsia owed more to the value of knowledge and ideas than to any social factors. Certainly, considerable prestige always was attached to intellectual activity in these societies. Yet there are fundamental differences between culture past and culture present.

The intelligentsia used to be part of the system for regulating intellectual processes in society. This was an essential condition for maintaining the traditional order of things. Accordingly, its activities were geared to consolidating the existing way of life and social order as an embodiment of God's will on earth. Dogma, ritual and canon were the basic forms used by this intelligentsia (the ulema, Brahmins, Buddhist priests, Confucian mandarins, and others) in a system of culture which suppressed and eradicated any suspicion of innovation or individualism.

The difference between the traditional and new intelligentsia is, of course, rather relative. In recent history, there have been numerous examples of traditional scholars and people from a clerical background advocating a major departure from the existing cultural heritage; at the same time, the new educated elite has produced quite a number of figures seeking with all their might to preserve tradition in its most conservative aspects. Nonetheless, there is an evident divide between these two types of intellectual attitude which are determined not so much by the character and place of education as by the form of social relations they are connected with. There is a fundamental difference between a dogmatic and closed religious system, for which all knowledge merely serves to substantiate a pivotal divine idea, and the new worldview, which is open to global influences and geared to the future, recognises and supports change in the life of society.

The intelligentsia in the developing countries is a product and manifestation of society's transitional state, and this transitional state is unmistakably reflected in its position. It advances only when the past, resting on traditional religious culture, is in a process of disintegration, but the future — with its new forms of culture associated with modern types of public activity — has not yet taken shape. Thus it provides a link between past and future. Its potential derives from the disintegration of the traditional world based on the indiscriminate regulation of society through domination and submission, moral compulsion, dogma and ritual. The intellectual forces and cultural trends which had been fettered by tradition and colonialism in the old society are suddenly boosted and given extra scope for development.

The old world falls apart, and on its ruins there appear new values, ideas, knowledge, and forms of creative endeavour, all of which bring with them new potential types of human relations. As it establishes and disseminates these new elements of culture, the intelligentsia gains in strength and becomes aware of its important mission. It seeks to remould society. Through its new intelligentsia, society becomes capable of cultural and intellectual self-determination in the modern world and is transformed into a subject of history, rather than just an object at the mercy of outside forces. What is more, the new intelligentsia enables society to use its potential in order to join the modern world.

The intelligentsia invariably aspires to world standards, though with varying degrees of success. By virtue of its cultural involvement (an extension of political involvement) in world relations, the intelligentsia is able from the very outset to shake off the constraints not only of the social order, but also of national insularity as it joins in world cultural and political movements. In the ensuing period it expresses the interests of the nation as a whole. At the same time, the dependence of these societies' national self-determination on global factors imparts to the intelligentsia's activity an international dimension.

Just as on the political plane the intelligentsia had to go through a difficult period of re-orientation, disillusionment, adaptation and transformation, so on the cultural plane too its road was very difficult. That road was full of dramatic change, distress and search for a new identity, and for its goals, which, as it turned out, coincided with those of other classes. The point is that the intelligentsia's capacity for higher forms of intellectual production is by far not the determining factor in the overall existence of these societies. It must be fused with the material productive forces, with a social system corresponding to them, and also with political power which stimulates society's development. Knowledge, values and principles by themselves cannot change the character of society's activity. Likewise, the intelligentsia by itself cannot attain its ideals and therefore urgently needs to join other socio-political strata which could become the basis for society's self-determination and progress.

However, the intelligentsia can also represent the interests of the whole nation, primarily because it is motivated by the aspirations, notions and values characteristic of the entire nation and sets long-term aims, not temporary and transitory ones. Furthering the development of the national language, the educational system, ideology and culture, the intelligentsia strengthens the ties between all members of a nation and elevates the level of their interests to that of national interest.

Championing the interests of the nation in the face of all internal and external forces that retard its development and undermine the foundations of its existence, the intelligentsia at the same time represents it on the world scene in the interaction of various cultures.

Thus the developing countries face the need for modernisation. At the same time, however, they must retain social stability by eliminating the bitter antagonisms and conflicts which arose in the period of colonial dependence. These processes threaten the well-being of many people who cannot fit into capitalist forms of modernisation and find themselves outside civilised society. The crisis of traditional forms of social organisation threatens to shatter both social relations and world-view principles and causes much anguish. This gives rise to protest movements reflecting disillusionment, despair and hatred of the excesses of modernisation among broad sections of the population. All this causes an intensive search for a new social and cultural self-determination of society.

If you wish to study the subject in depth:

1. *Razvivayushchiyesya strany: ekonomichesky rost i sotsialny progress* (The Developing Countries: Economic Growth and Social Progress), Nauka, Moscow, 1983.

2. *Evolyutsiya vostochnykh obshchestv. Sintez traditsionnogo i sovremennogo* (Evolution of Eastern Societies: A Synthesis of Traditional and Modern Elements), Nauka, Moscow, 1984.

3. Constantino, R., *Neocolonial Identity and Counter-Consciousness. Essays on Cultural Decolonisation*, Merlin, London, 1978.
4. Eisenstadt, S. N., *Tradition, Change and Modernity*, John Wiley and Sons, New York, 1973.

15

Changes in the Religious Sphere

In this chapter, consideration should be given to the following:

1. What is the significance of reform trends in the religious thought of the developing countries?
2. What is religious fundamentalism?
3. What is the correlation of secular and religious components in the intellectual life of the developing countries nowadays?
4. How do Eastern religions affect socio-economic development?

Religion has played a contradictory role in the complex changes that have taken place in recent decades in the political and intellectual lives of the developing countries of Asia and Africa.

Undoubtedly, today we witness a weakening of religion's influence, the decrease of the activity of official and unofficial religious institutions, an increasing refusal to think in theological categories, and less importance being attached to religious ideals and to the once omnipotent symbolism. Despite the fact that in many countries Islam or Buddhism are still official religions, the sphere of their activity is limited. This is especially true of those countries where religion has never acquired the status of an official intellectual and political establishment.

Almost everywhere, the state and most political parties give priority to secular principles and goals in their official policies. Religion has had to give way to new nationalist or socialist trends in which religion plays a subordinate role or is supplanted altogether. It is gradually losing its grip on major spheres of social consciousness, the economy, politics and government.

At the same time, religion lives on in a number of spheres of society, in family and domestic relations, in the everyday conduct of broad sections of the population, in relations between and within social groups; moreover, in certain spheres its political and ideological influence is actually growing. In a number of Asian and African countries, its influence on official policy and ideology can be seen more clearly than before; religious principles of ethics and upbringing are more stubbornly asserting themselves. Religion becomes the medium for drawing considerable sections of society into political activity.

Islam, Hinduism, and Buddhism are not simply world religions. Each of them forms an important part of the given nation's social structure and culture; all of them reflect the history of many peoples. In Eastern religions, which, unlike Christianity, have not gone through any thorough reformation, rituals and secular activities are not separated. There is no clear-cut boundary between the transcendental and the earthly, between religious and legal precepts. Islam, Buddhism, and Hinduism have comprehensive systems of control of the believers' behaviour and consciousness, combining religious, educational and upbringing functions, regulating marital and family relations—in other words, leaving an imprint on society's entire way of life.

Basic Trends of Religious Thought

What is happening in religion itself in the course of the above-mentioned processes? Does it remain an immutable system of beliefs, rituals and relations, or is it changing too?

All the processes taking place in religion are usually divided into three basic groups in accordance with their ideological characters and socio-political orientations. These are conservative traditionalism (orthodoxy), reformism, and fundamentalism. Such division is, of course, very relative, and reflects the indistinctness and instability of the main social groups and the transitional character of society as a whole. Nor does it cover all the differences that exist on the world-view level and even less so on the mass consciousness level. But it enables us to identify the basic trends in the evolution of religious ideologies, and hence their influence on the ideological struggle.

For present-day religious consciousness, an important problem is to establish the necessary correlation between traditional and modern attitudes between the utilisation of new knowledge and of the heritage of the past. The processes taking place in religion reflect its complexity and diversity, with a constant interaction and struggle between different levels and types of consciousness and different values.

Religious traditionalism

Orthodox traditionalism is professed by stagnant privileged sections of society which oppose any change and seek to retain their privileges and keep the common people within their primary groups, whose isolation is consolidated by their internal religious ties. In a number of countries, traditionalism is actively used and fostered by the ruling classes in their attempts to hold down the people's growing dissatisfaction and activity.

Traditionalism invariably refuses to recognise the reality of change. Changes must be limited to the partial improvement of existing structures and the strengthening of existing principles, which in themselves have absolute value, and only the believers' "sloppiness" does not give them a chance to be realised. Orthodoxy tends to turn down any change or innovation rather than cast doubt on the "sacred principles", aimed at preserving the old "non-earthly" goals and notions. Traditionalists are particularly afraid of the atomisation of human relations, the disintegration of customary social groups and the devaluation of the old forms of conduct, all of which they view as a threat to the existence of society and its culture. Traditionalists ascribe all social ills and conflicts to "spiritual decay", i. e., the oblivion of orthodox standards and values and the abandonment of old religious structures.

Religious traditionalism largely proceeds from the baneful experience of contact with the capitalist West and seeks a solution in preserving the old pre-colonial order. At the same time, many theologians are bound to recognise that the imperialist West firmly supports traditionalism, encourages religion both overtly and covertly, in order to achieve its basic goals: exploitation of the developing countries.

It is a very typical feature of modern traditionalism that it gets on with technocratic and bureaucratic methods of government. The growing influence of religious circles on official policy turns them into one of the groups of the ruling bureaucracy. Hand in hand with the clerical circles, the government opposes any democratic change, steps up religious propaganda, especially the religious upbringing of young people. It gives religion the role of shock-absorber between its authoritarian rule and society, which it seeks to depoliticise. Religion virtually complements the political pragmatism of the ruling circles. Official propaganda calls on society to rely on science and religion. Thus religion becomes a means of controlling the masses which have been pushed away from public life; it acts as compensation for unrealised earthly hopes, a means of salvation or liberation from earthly troubles in the other world. In this capacity it is an essential part of the government mechanism of control over society.

Reformation

Reformation has become an important trend in changing the character and structure of religion in the Asian and African countries. Although it undoubtedly meets the interests of the national bourgeoisie, it is championed by broader strata of the middle class, especially in the towns, whose activity has undergone considerable modernisation. This trend can, therefore, be described as "modernisation".

In its traditional form, religion blocks the development of capitalism, imposing spiritual limitations on it. Such was, for example, the ban on *riba*—the exaction of loan interest in Islam (more precisely, in Koranic tradition). It was an attempt at the religious limitation of the functioning of capital in non-capitalist social structures and its subordination to the aims of religious salvation of all believers. In practice, however, this ban was circumvented in many ways. Otherwise, developed forms of trading capital could never have emerged in Muslim countries with their medieval customs and practices. This led the French scholar Maxime Rodinson to assert that Islam did not in itself contradict capitalism and its precepts virtually did not affect business enterprise. But history testifies to the contrary. The Koran's ban on loan interest held back the growth of business in the Muslim world. It is for that reason that the bourgeoisie actively supported reformed religion, above all, the lifting of restrictions on the functioning of capital.

The reformers of Islam, Buddhism, Hinduism and, of course, Christianity tried to give religious sanction to business. This was formulated as "worship of God through the use of His gifts", i. e., land and capital. The gifts were to serve noble ends: the prosperity and development of society. All the earth's resources and human faculties were to be used to glorify religion.

Reformation was above all aimed at establishing more active relations between man and the divine order. Instead of being an infinitely small particle before the Absolute, man gained the ability to exercise his will and achieve his goals. Worship of God as the supreme being remained, but man was no longer seen as a blind instrument in God's hands. Man was given right of choice, and he had to make right choice, striving to fulfil God's behest of self-imporovement. From now on, "reformed" God acted not by Himself, not as a transcendental being, but through man, through his will, reason and action.

Reformers choose those elements in religion which can be deprived of their sacred status, i. e. those which are not directly connected with God and do not constitute fundamental features of religion. Religious teaching was split up into spheres some of which applied to faith, and others to secular activities. The overcoming of fatalism sometimes required far-reaching changes in religion. Islamic reformers condemned the "atrophy of the soul" imposed by *taqlid* (devotion to stagnant tradition) and called for activity that would improve man's living standards, *taqlid* is replaced with *ijma* and *ijtihad* (man's ability for independent judgement) not only as a means of finding the rationale for certain precepts of Islam, but also as source of the individual's certainty that his actions are justified.

This major change in the original principles also encompassed a number of other important aspects of religion. The "methods" of relationship between God and man were revised. The main importance was attached to inner faith, and man could now have direct contact with God through reason, through intuition, and through activity pleasing to God. The role of intermediaries between God and man—priests, temples, effigies, sacrifices, rituals, etc.—was weakened.

Rational cognition began to play a more important role in substantiating faith and conduct, which helped overcome one's blind acceptance of dogma and precepts, revise one's attitude to the holy scriptures, and make broader interpretations of them. In Islam, this required an open or implicit lowering of the status of revelation, which led to bitter arguments over the relationship of revelation and reason. The problem was often solved by resorting to the doctrine of the duality of truth (i. e. justification of both science and divine revelation). The job of reason was here limited to supporting faith in its ultimate fundamentals.

Reformation consisted in the weakening of the dogmatic and institutional aspects of religion, and in its interpretation as mainly a set of ethical standards providing a basis for recognizing various forms of secular activity useful for society. Religion's aim from now on was not the maintenance of the existing order of things as created by God, but the moral improvement of man and society. In Hinduism, for example, the law of cosmic dharma became an expression of primarily ethical principles.

The increasing striving to reform religion is connected with the development of new forms of activity which involved broad sections of society. Fulfilment of one's obligations, no matter how unpleasant or sinful, for the benefit of society is an important principle of reformation. Reformist tendencies were also expressed in calls to lift bans which fettered certain forms of activity (for example, the Buddhist ban on touching money, which had to be circumvented by complex casuistry; the ban on killing living creatures, etc.). Individual performance of daily ritual became simpler and more accessible, and ritual norms were eased. Even the very important Buddhist principle of non-violence was reinterpreted—it was not to apply to those who threatened the existence of society.

After the achievement of national independence, reformist tendencies gained new strength, fuelled by the bourgeoisie's growing desire to acquire religious principles which did not contradict its interests. However, reformation still embraces only a fairly small part of society, that which is drawn into new relations. Big business frankly switches to a philosophy of bourgeois pragmatism and utilitarianism, while the petty bourgeoisie, feeling the instability of its position, usually adopts orthodox or fundamentalist varieties of religion.

Fundamentalism

In the context of social crisis, society increasingly turns to the religious trend often called fundamentalism, or revivalism, since it proclaims the revival of the true religion which resolves all social conflicts and embodies the ideals of universal happiness, unity, and equality. In actual fact, however, it was a question of reviving only one variety of religion—that which in the past fuelled chiliastic, messianic, and sectarian movements, and which today sometimes gains a tremendous persuasive force.

Rejecting reformist calls for adjusting religion to modern requirements, revivalists insist that the world must rise to the height of the religious principles proclaimed many centuries ago—principles which so far have not been properly understood or fulfilled.

Revivalism goes back to the old idea of "golden age", the ideal social order. In Islam it is the rule of the Four Righteous Caliphs and Companions of the Prophet; in Hinduism, the period of creation of the early Vedas; in Buddhism, the period of the early Buddhist states, especially under King Ashoka. It is assumed that one only needs to return to those time-honoured models, overcoming the delusions caused by the self-seeking of the privileged classes, government officials and clerics who have departed from the original ideal. The ideologues of fundamentalism put most of the blame for social decay on dynasties which had wilfully breached the sacred laws, thereby undermining the foundations of society.

Fundamentalist leaders often make far-reaching attempts to revise the whole history of their nations, interpreting it as a constant struggle to implement the original principles of their religion. Islam, Buddhism and Hinduism are presented as the most important heritage of society, while the essence of history is viewed as protection of this heritage against apostasy and Western influences. Much more vehemently than reformists, revivalists condemn the Western bourgeois attitudes, extending their criticism to the West as a whole, and contrasting their own religious purity to the West's spiritual and moral disintegration, thereby rejecting its socio-economic principles along with its religion and culture.

The social creed of fundamentalism is the omnipotence of faith, democracy and justice. Democracy and justice are interpreted as embodiments of equality, for they eliminate both extreme wealth and extreme poverty, put an end to exploitation, and make means of subsistence available to all. These principles have a powerful appeal, attracting the common people and rallying them for active struggle against social and national oppression. This ability to attract the masses to this day makes revivalism an influential ideological and political force, a powerful means of shaping broadly-based movements against imperialist expansion in Asia and Africa.

An example of this movement, characteristic of the recent past, is Gandhiism. The impetus which Mohandas Karamchand Gandhi gave the Indian national liberation movement helped unite various sections of society, turning it into a truly mass movement. He called upon people to have moral fortitude and be ready to give up their lives for their nation's freedom. Gandhi succeeded in mobilising the moral readiness, the wrath, protest and readiness for struggle which had built up in the Indian people.

Revivalism found fertile ground in Islam, with its well-developed teaching about the establishment of a just society (the Islamic state) on earth and the strong appeal of spiritual principles expressed in the Koran and Tradition. This is well demonstrated by the role played by Islam in the 1979 anti-monarchist revolution in Iran.

The revivalist movement assumed a similarly large

scale in Buddhist countries, also spreading to its country of origin, India. In India, neo-Buddhism primarily inspired members of the lower castes, attracted by its ideals of equality and social justice. Neo-Buddhism levelled criticism at the *sanghas* (monastic communes), calling upon them to return to the original behests of Buddhism and undertake the task of improving the social system. Revivalist trends offer to the ordinary believer new spiritual principles in the face of the crumbling old foundations of society.

The following ways can be identified in which revivalist principles correspond to the basic needs of the people:

1) the standards of group solidarity are not rejected but broadened to unite all members of a religious community cemented by joint participation not only in ritual acts (prayer, pilgrimage) but also in a common political cause;

2) equal rights are demanded for all the members of a religious community. This is promoted by collective actions involving members of all social strata. The unity and closeness of high-ranking officials and the common people is emphasised in every way. An important role in asserting egalitarian principles belongs to the redistribution of wealth through the taxation of property, donations, the renunciation of loan interest, the elimination of prestigious and ostentatious luxury, etc.;

3) in relation to material comfort, revivalism views consumption merely as a means of satisfying one's immediate needs, in many respects limiting and condemning the accumulation of wealth (inlcuding excessive private property). The aim of the economy is seen, not in development and prosperity, but in bringing man closer to God. A harmonious society must maintain a balance between economic achievements and morality;

4) Revivalism voices the aspirations of the masses as expressed in demands for a just system of government with no interests of its own apart from those of the people. Such government is usually associated with a charismatic individual endowed with special qualities and an ability to express the people's interests. At the same time, there is a need for an indisputable God-given body of law which cannot be altered at man's will;

5) Revivalism uses popular attitudes as a basis to set

forth a rigid moral catalogue of rights and duties for all members of the community. Attaching little value to the human personality revivalism resorts, not only to moral censure of sinners, but also to physical punishment for anti-social acts (stoning, cutting off the hand, etc.);

6) popular egalitarian views are also expressed in calls to eliminate discrepancies in consumption, social status and cultural standards. This leads to attempts to dispose of technology and any form of academic endeavour and to simplify cultural life;

7) the contradiction between solidarity and the accumulation of wealth is turned by revivalist ideology into an all-out confrontation between the lofty Spirit and the vile mercenary Matter. The former is expressed in religion and the latter in capitalism (or, in the eyes of the petty bourgeois, big business). The moralistic condemnation of capitalism is accompanied by a programme for the spiritual purification of society;

8) the obvious fact that modernisation is an effect of Western capitalist influence gives revivalist ideology a powerful anti-imperialist thrust. As they fall on religious soil, these ideas often assume a sharply anti-Western complexion. The West as a whole is branded as the carrier of pernicious materialism, while its culture is associated with expansionism having been resisted for centuries by Islam, Hinduism and Buddhism. The result is the zealous eradication of all evident Western presence in the life of a religious community, including a return to non-Western fashions, manners, moral standards, languages, etc.

Constrained by popular attitudes, religious revivalism, keeps its contradictions and limitations. On the one hand, it stimulates the masses to take part in socio-political action capable of radicalising the political situation. Revivalism expresses the anti-imperialist and anti-capitalist sentiments of both the working people and those bourgeois sections which feel the crippling effects of world capitalist expansion. On the other hand, the strong reaction to the growing socio-economic antagonisms enhances spontaneous protest in society, undermining the possibility of constructive social reform and accelerated development. This reaction can result in backward movement, be accompanied by a decline in social development, loss of social achievements, and the restoration of elements of the past. Such ideological principles are based on subjective factors, exalted faith, emotional symbolism, and verbal hypnotism, rather than on the rational understanding of reality or the consideration of objective historical patterns.

Thus we witness the various processes going on in religion which as well as culture reflect their deep-going transformations under the impact of the new spiritual situation taking shape today in all developing countries. These processes take on local complexion in each particular country and depend on the social environment, the socio-psychological condition of the masses, etc. Nonetheless, it is the long-term factors acting within a given civilisation and global processes that in the long run determine character of the changes in intellectual life.

If you wish to study the subject in depth:

1. *Zarubezhny Vostok i sovremennost* (The Foreign Countries of the East and the Present Day), Vol. 3, Nauka, Moscow, 1981.

2. Rybakov, R. B., *Burzhuaznaya reformatsiya induizma (XIX - nachalo XX v.)* (The Bourgeois Reformation of Hinduism, 19th and Early 20th Centuries), Nauka, Moscow, 1981.

3. *Islam v sovremennoi politike stran Vostoka* (Islam in the Present-Day Policies of Eastern Countries), Nauka, Moscow, 1986.

4. *Obshchestvennaya mysl Indii. Proshloye i nastoyashcheye* (Social Sciences in India: Past and Present), Nauka, Moscow, 1989.

5. Arkoun, M., Gardet, L., *L'Islam: Hier, demain*, Buchet/Chastel, Paris, 1978.

6. Laroui, A., *Islam et modernité*, Découverte, Paris, 1987.

7. Naipaul, V. S., *India: A Wounded Civilization*, Deutsch, London, 1977.

8. Nasr, S. H., *Islam and the Plight of Modern Man*, Longman, London-New York, 1975.

16

The Principles and Problems of Cultural Development in the Newly-Independent Countries

In this chapter, consideration should be given to the following:

1. What is the role of the state in regulating cultural life in the newly-independent countries?
2. What are the main objectives of the government's cultural policies in these countries?
3. What is the structure of cultural management in these countries?
4. What is the cultural character of the educational system in these countries?
5. What is the significance of the mass media in society's cultural life? How do they use cultural traditions?

In the preceding chapters we spoke of the contradictions that the newly-independent countries come up against in the course of developing cultures meeting the demands of the new times, and of the complex character of the cultural processes in those countries. What are the means and principles by which cultural processes are regulated? What measures do the developing countries take to reform their cultures?

Cultural Policy

Underlying the development of culture is not only its inner logic. As part of society's intellectual life, it is also regulated by the state. The newly-free countries' desire to consolidate their independence and carry out their self-determination as soon as possible, and speed up their overall development requires systematic government regulation of these processes.

The character of such regulation is determined by the following factors:

1) The ruling classes' policy of encouraging or limiting private enterprise, ensuring the nation's independent development or attracting foreign capital;

2) The level of a country's development and the character of its economic and cultural relations with the outside world: isolation and peripheral location (as certain African states), or the influence of several cultures on it (as in the case of Egypt and Indonesia).

The fact that in the newly-liberated countries, the state plays an important role, often the determining one, makes them view cultural policy, too, as a function of government. However, the regulation of culture is not only carried out by the state. This process also involves public organisations, which give state policy in the cultural field a social dimension. But this entails complex problems in the correlation of official and public activity.

Cultural policy can reflect both national interests and the narrow interests of the ruling classes. In cases where it is guided by the interests of the ruling classes, there is growing opposition to it from democratic sections of society. Defending the principle of freedom of artistic endeavour, they oppose the official propaganda of one-sided views, misconceptions and restrictions that stand in the way of society's cultural development.

Despite all the differences between the regimes in the Asian and African countries, we can identify the following common basic elements of cultural policy:

1) Efforts to preserve the distinct cultural identity of a given country as an important factor of national unity and solidarity;

2) Propaganda of the principle of cultural continuity, i. e., the link between past and present, the preservation of the nation's traditions and cultural heritage;

3) Knowledge and protection of the cultural heritage, which implies that it must be studied, disseminated and used in modern life;

4) Emphasis on the cultural features common to the entire nation which implies the obliteration of differences between urban and rural communities and between tribes and ethnic groups;

5) Co-ordination of cultural and socio-economic development, and concern for the correspondence of all the aspects of national development to the basic cultural values;

6) Democratisation of culture, i. e., drawing all social strata into cultural life;

7) Encouragement of dialogue between the intelligentsia and the rest of society;

8) Assistance to all forms of cultural endeavour and efforts to raise the standards of art;

9) Training of professional staff in various forms of cultural activity;

10) Encouragement of the integration of science in national culture on the basis of studying the influence of science and technology on society's cultural processes;

11) Literacy programmes;

12) Expansion of the network of cultural establishments;

13) Assistance to the demonstration of the nation's cultural achievements abroad.

In African and Asian countries which comprise several ethnic groups with their different religions and languages, the main principle of cultural policy is "unity in diversity", which implies centralisation of cultural life while preserving its pluralism. Such, for example, is the situation in many African countries with fairly high ethnic disunity. The pursuit of such a policy in India, with its highly developed culture, for example, does not rule out the pluralism of the numerous castes and subcastes, ethnic and religious groups and subgroups. Apart from ethnic and linguistic differences, many countries have a pluralism of "high" cultures and world religions. For example, the interaction of Islam, Hinduism, Sikhism and Jainism in India, and of Catholicism and Islam in the Philippines, creates complex problems in these countries' cultural life.

All cultural programmes in the developing countries without exception emphasise the need to support various forms of artistic endeavour, both individual and collective. The state provides assistance to traditional music and dancing, and supports handicrafts, setting up artisan co-operatives. It takes part in organising various kinds of festivals. The social, aesthetic and ritual character of art is seen as an important factor in maintaining national identity.

Institutions of Cultural Policy

Each country has its own administrative structures designed to assist cultural development. In the 1960's and '70's, many countries set up ministries of culture, whose activity, however, was mostly restricted to a certain narrow field. In India, for example, responsibility for cultural development is divided between the Ministry of Education (which has a Cultural Bureau), the ministries of Information and Radio Broadcasting, Tourism, Public Works, Housing Construction, Agriculture (with its Department of Communal Development), Trade, and Handicrafts.

A broad understanding of culture adopted by many governments includes: education, the mass media, tourism, social policies, and rearing of the youth. Obviously, such diverse and broad fields of culture must be controlled by different government departments. Therefore, interdepartmental committees or parliamentary commissions are set up to co-ordinate their activity.

No matter how great the role of government institutions, an important part in cultural life belongs to non-governmental organisations, both national and international. Various associations, writers' and journalists' unions, diverse theatrical, dancing and music groups, private publishing houses, film studios, museums, etc., constitute a broad network which maintains the country's cultural life.

The cultural process often experiences a clash between two trends: state centralisation of cultural activity, on the one hand, and its democratisation by non-governmental organisations, on the other. Government interference in the work of cultural organisations and groups is often necessary, since without government support they could run into financial and other difficulties and be forced to close down. At the same time, government interference often makes cultural activity dependent on the ruling classes, resulting in serious distortions of cultural life as a whole.

Cultural planning is usually included in overall social development planning or is connected with the government planning of education and the mass media. A serious obstacle in cultural planning is the absence of adequate data on the results of cultural development and the scantiness of available statistics. The latter are usually limited to only some figures (the number of libraries, museums, newspapers, etc.) while no information is given on the cultural needs of various social groups, no analysis is made of various forms of cultural activity, or of cultural budgets and expenditures.

Methods of financing in Asia and Africa differ from country to country. It is often hard to determine the actual expenditure on culture and education. Only rich countries can afford to allocate large funds on public education, the establishment of a network of cultural centres, and so on. The poorer countries more often rely on support from public organisations, foreign aid, and cultural agencies and religious missions from other countries. Nevertheless, these sources fall short of these countries' needs.

Education and Culture

Education is one of the basic fields of culture. A major role in it belongs to the state. While shaping education policy that would meet the country's needs as a whole, the state, at the same time, takes into account the interests of the ruling class.

The newly-independent countries' urgent need to develop all forms of education is dictated by the necessity to introduce up-to-date forms of production, social relations, and political structures. Through education, the young generations learn about cultural achievements and acquire the knowledge and principles essential for them to become useful to society. Thus public education promotes the socialisation of each individual.

The young sovereign states of Asia and Africa have inherited education systems established by the colonial regimes along Western lines — systems fundamentally antagonistic to the new socio-economic environment and incapable of training personnel in the interests of national development. A utilitarian approach to education as merely an instrument of economic progress and the overemphasis on vocational and professional training and the general cultural characteristics with no regard for the actual situation in a given country, have had a negative social impact.

The Western model of education has increased the social and cultural stratification of society. Education was viewed primarily as a channel for leaving the traditional cultural environment and abandoning the unprestigious sphere of manual labour, as a means of gaining access to an almost magical, and in any case more prestigious, sphere of knowledge and concepts which promised to change an individual's status in the existing social hierarchy.

The shaping of an educated elite solely on the basis of Western cultural values disorientated large sections of the young intelligentsia. Much too often education was aimed not so much at giving knowledge and teaching skills essential to improving production and the people's living standards as at introducing ideas and standards far removed from reality. Young people often lost their sense of identity with their social milieu and became disillusioned in life, which resulted in the disintegration of the family, alcoholism, and a growing crime rate.

This education system came under heavy criticism. Not only its social orientation was condemned, but the drawbacks in teaching methods under which curricula took no account of the general comprehension level shaped by ethnic stereotypes, and the existing gap between school and everyday life. The refusal to broaden education in the national languages, which has resulted in the poor development of modern disciplines, has received no support, either.

Gradually, with great difficulty, did the young states' national educational systems cast off the burden of the colonial past. New models were developed, intended better to meet the countries' social and cultural needs. In many newly-independent countries, the entire network of educational establishments—from elementary school to university—is currently undergoing a radical restructuring. This is reflected primarily in the broader education in the national and local languages, in greater emphasis on one's own national history, culture, folklore, and handicrafts. Attempts are being made to return to traditional education systems. Universities are gradually transformed into cultural centres that correspond to the local socio-cultural environment and seek to train personnel in the interests of national development.

Textbooks are written by national authors and based on the findings of research and field studies done by national scientists. Efforts are made to re-establish traditional values and re-awaken national pride. In arts classes, emphasis is placed on the study of folklore, mythology, legends, and local architectural monuments. This helps not only to understand one's own history, but to find one's bearings in the present socio-political situation in Asia and Africa as a whole. Natural science and technical departments of universities also build their curricula in such a way as to direct the students' research at raising their nation's prosperity.

In shaping the young people's political culture, schools in many newly-independent countries devote much attention to problems of national unity. This is achieved above all by teaching the single official language and by putting emphasis on historical facts of co-operation and rapprochement of different ethnic groups inhabiting the country and their common interest in maintaining a united state.

On a world-view level, however, young people from developing countries are much more influenced by their study in industrialised countries, where they are exposed to a variety of ideologies ranging from the extreme right and left to truly progressive and scientific ones. From all this variety of theories, young people usually absorb those which reflect the world-view dominant in that particular industrialised country, especially if their basic principles correspond to the reality they see around them. To be successfully absorbed, such theories must not essentially contradict an individual's original views and principles, which are normally determined by his social background and the micro-milieu in which he lived before leaving his native country. This mainly explains why the West constantly seeks to attract as many young people from the developing countries to its universities as possible. In doing this, the West also pursues purely pragmatic—economic and political—aims. But its main aim is to have future leaders in the Third World countries who would have essentially Western attitudes.

The Mass Media and Culture

The mass media play an ever increasing role in the lives of the developing countries. They are not only the most important source of information about current events, but also a major factor in shaping public opinion, spreading knowledge, and formulating basic sets of values. Of special significance is the mass media's role in ideological processes, for they are crucial in developing national culture and protecting it from foreign influences.

In solving cultural problems, the developing countries use both modern and traditional forms of communication: the oral tradition, musical folklore, rituals and customs. These endogenous means of communication include various performing arts (folk drama, songs, dancing, ballads and epics), on the one hand, and personal channels of communication at various gatherings, fairs, religious centres, traditional clubs (such as the *banjar* in Indonesia, mothers' clubs in Korea, mutual assistance clubs in China, and so on), on the other.

The traditional system of communication differs from the system of mass media in at least three parameters: the size of the audience, flexibility of content, and its deep roots in the local culture. While the news media are aimed, as a rule, at a broad, general audience, traditional means of communication are most often meant for an audience limited in size and geographical location. The folk puppet theatre, for example, cannot perform to more than a hundred people at a time, while traditional clubs provide communication opportunities to only a restricted category of people in a given village (an Indonesian *banjar*, for example, is open only to married men). Therefore, people forming part of a traditional system of communication are almost always homogeneous ethnically and linguistically.

Cultural continuity and interaction between traditional systems of communication and the modern mass media are characteristic of communication systems in any society, but in the developing countries this combination is vital. The use of traditional communication systems plays an important part in the cultural development of the young states which lack the material, technical, and financial resources and facilities sufficient to compete with Western news agencies.

One cannot fail to see the real danger for the developing countries' cultural sovereignty from the gigantic disproportions in the mass media field between these countries and the leading Western nations. Western news agencies produce the lion's share of TV and radio programmes, and they own dozens of permanently operating communications satellites. Western news agencies control 80 to 90 per cent of information disseminated in the world. The four major news agencies alone—Associated Press, UPI, France Presse, and Reuter—churn out a total of more than 35 million words daily. This is a thousand times more than is disseminated by the press agencies of the non-aligned countries uniting about 100 national information services.

All the developing countries put together have fewer radio and television sets than the United States alone. Asia, Africa and Latin America combined have only about a quarter of the world's radio stations and about seven per cent of TV stations. Many developing countries do not have national information agencies or TV centres. At the same time, it should be borne in mind that radio and television are the fastest developing news media in those countries. The number of people who regularly listen to the radio exceeds the number of literate people. For example, whereas in the past decade the ratio between the circulation of newspapers in the developing countries and their aggregate population has remained practically unchanged, the number of radio sets in the same period has grown by some 50 per cent and TV sets by about 80 per cent.

The number of radio and television sets, in the developing countries has reached, and in many has greatly exceeded, the UNESCO minimum of five radio and two television sets per 100 population. By contrast, the number of newspapers even in the most developed region of the Third World—Latin America—has so far failed to reach the required minimum of ten copies per 100 population.

The developing countries' lag in terms of mass media, given their financial, technical and personnel shortages compels them to turn for assistance to the industrialised, most often Western, countries, on which they are economically dependent. The developing countries as a rule lack the facilities needed to supply enough information to fill the entire space of their newspapers and magazines, and the broadcasting time of their radio and television stations.

Western information and propaganda centres literally flood the developing countries with their radio and television programmes, records, audio and video cassettes, and films. The profits from their exports are huge despite the fact they are sometimes sold at dumping prices. Of all the latest devices, video technology is most active today in promoting mass culture. Millions of video cassettes inundate many developing countries. This video invasion is to a large extent changing the character of mass culture in those countries.

The propaganda of mass culture in those countries is aimed at conditioning their population to consumerist values, thereby preparing the ground for the marketing of Western goods and services there.

With the growth of their national, political, and class awareness, Asian, African and Latin American peoples also struggle against intellectual and cultural expansion, for national sovereignty in the information and cultural field and for restructuring international cultural and information exchange.

Since each nation wishes to keep its independence, the developing countries are forced to take active steps to protect themselves against Western information expansion. Each country does all it can to develop its own mass media network; regional and continental information associations are set up in order to weaken the dependence of national mass media on Western corporations.

Of crucial importance for the developing countries is the part played by the mass media in raising the status of their own languages, literature and art. By performing this function, the press, radio and television help to find ways to enhance national awareness and unity and help the masses get better access to their cultural heritage. In many former colonies where for decades the mass media mostly used the languages of their metropolises, today a large proportion of the national radio and television programmes is broadcast in the national languages and attempts are made to publish periodicals in them as well. In certain countries, the national languages have already supplanted the European ones and are now the basic languages in the mass media. This is easier where the majority of the population speaks one local language. However, in many countries of Asia and Africa which have a multitude of local languages and dialects, it is often difficult to decide which language is the common one, since such attempts often spark off intertribal and intercommunal antagonism. In such cases, national radio and television networks use several languages of the major tribes or ethnic groups, while in certain areas with monolingual population, newspapers are also published in that language. In most developing countries, however, the mass media use the European and local languages in parallel.

Of all the mass media, radio makes the broadest use of the local languages. Comprehension of radio broadcasts in these languages does not require any level of literacy from the listener. Such broadcasts are received in the remotest part of any country and, considering the comparatively low prices of simple transistor radios are easily accessible to the population. All this makes the radio the most wide-spread and effective information and propaganda medium. It is not an accident that the major world radio stations also make considerable use of local languages for their broadcasts beamed at the developing countries.

Such broadcasts in the local languages are, of course, meant for the mostly illiterate rural population and, therefore, require special structuring of programmes and selection of information about facts and events that would be of interest to a given audience.

The leaders of the developing countries take into account the growing role of the mass media in shaping their cultural policies.

Effective co-ordination and management of cultural activity can only be ensured on the basis of sufficient information about its state. However, this information will be useful only if it is received and processed in accordance with the principles of cultural sociology. Concrete sociological research can reveal the state of various aspects of cultural life:

1) The material base of culture (number of cinemas and libraries, the level of the mass media, etc.);

2) The amount of cultural available facilities;

3) Characteristics of the cultural infrastructure (attendance of theatres, libraries, etc., and the population's interest in, and response to, culture);

4) The level and character of cultural activity of the intelligentsia and the common people (including the number of amateur groups, their ethnic variety, etc,);

5) The population's literacy and educational standards and the degree to which school and university education satisfies society's cultural needs.

Sociological research helps not only gauge the actual state of a society's cultural life (in contrast to ideologised and therefore incomplete concepts). They also show the effectiveness of methods used by political or administrative institutions in pursuing their cultural policy.

If you wish to study the subject in depth:

1. *Kultura i politika v stranakh Azii i Afriki* (Culture and Politics in Asian and African Countries), Nauka, Moscow, 1986.
2. *Kultura v stranakh Azii i Afriki. Voprosy teorii i praktiki* (Culture in Asian and African Countries: Theory and Practice), Nauka, Moscow, 1989.
3. *Intelligentsiya i sotsialny progress v razvivayushchikhsya stranakh Azii i Afriki* (The Intelligentsia and Social Progress in the Developing Countries of Asia and Africa), Nauka, Moscow, 1984.
4. *Cultural Development: Some Regional Experiences,* UNESCO, Paris, 1981.
5. *Science économique et développement endogène,* UNESCO, Paris, 1986.

17

Social and Cultural Change in India

In this chapter, consideration should be given to the following:

1. What are the basic principles of the Great Tradition of Indian culture?
2. How does the caste system fit in the scale of cultural values?
3. How does the concept of karma explain an individual's destiny?
4. What changes took place in Indian culture in the past?
5. What is the essence of Sanskritisation?
6. What effect did the West have on Indian culture?
7. What factors contribute to India's cultural modernisation?

Tradition and modernity as heuristic concepts are easy to formulate, but to separate them at substantive level is rather difficult. The modern seldom comes to traditional society in the same form or brings about identical cultural consequences in every society that it comes in contact with. Modernisation as a process, has more elasticity of form than tradition. It implies an open world-view which like science undergoes perpetual change in its value-structure and postulates.

Comparative studies on modernisation in the new states have shown that contrary to stereotyped beliefs, old traditions are not completely displaced by modernisation; what follows is an accretion and transmutation of forms. Similarly, tradition does not necessarily retard the process of modernisation. In India, caste associations, which are otherwise typical symbols of tradition, have increasingly been found to serve the ends of modernisation. Lloyd I. Rudolph calls this phenomenon "modernity of tradition" [1] and concludes with Edward Shils that "modernity has entered into Indian character and society but it has done so through assimilation and not replacement".[2] Other studies in Indian social sciences also provide evidence that traditional institutions like joint family, kin-based entrepreneurial functions continue to coexist with and support modern values and forms of social action. From the advancement in modern means of transport and communication not only the cultural diffusion of modernisation but also that of traditionalism is accelerated.

These processes in the institutional realm of modernisation are also in harmony with the historical growth of this phenomenon in India. The rise of the nationalistic movement, which later changed into a movement for political, cultural and economic modernisation was itself never bereft of the consciousness of the past tradition of India. It is fair to assume that as forces of cultural modernisation grow there will also simultaneously grow the feeling of national identity and the identification with the nation's past tradition. Cultural modernisation will under this process assume a syncretic form and persist along with traditional values. Modernity will never completely supplant tradition in India.

The Great and Little Traditions of Indian Culture

The cultural tradition of Hinduism, its religio-ethical values and aesthetic patterns, the lifestyles and conduct norms were crystallised about 1 000 B. C. in Vedic literature and were subsequently formalised in the Epics. The forms of Vedic Hinduism, especially its manifestation during the period of the Epics, laid the foundation of a system of beliefs, ritual patterns and cultural practices which may be treated not only as distinct from other world religions and cultural traditions but also as being autochthonous or primordial in nature.

---

[1] L. I. Rudolph, "The Modernity of Tradition: The Democratic Incarnation of Caste in India", *American Political Science Review*, Vol. LIX, No. 4, December, 1965, pp. 975-89.

[2] Ibid., p. 983.

Some of the basic attributes of the Hindu Great tradition are capable of being formulated in spite of the complexities and contradictions apparent in this tradition. Behind the extreme degree of permissiveness and liberalism in beliefs and variety in ritual practices as admitted by Hindu canonical system, there exists a strictly logical view of phenomena in terms of which the principles of *order* and *change, being* and *becoming, creation* and *destruction, hedonism utilitarianism* and *spiritual transcendence* can be meaningfully explained. Implicit in this system of logic and metaphysics is a theory of society and culture which admits little confusion and has been formulated with extraordinary clarity. The twin basic concepts of this system are *order* and *change*. Order is conceptualised through the principle of hierarchy and change, which is assumed to be the immanent nature of all phenomena, and is thought of to be cyclical. Most of the cultural themes of the Great tradition may be integrated around these twin concepts of *order* and *change*, and the principles of *hierarchy, holism* and *continuity* are the necessary ingredients of this tradition.

The principle of hierarchy could easily be called the ethos of the Hindu traditional cultural pattern. It permeates most of the cultural categories, and it may be seen as governing the cultural structure at many points. A few of such areas where this principle may be found in manifest form are: role institutionalisation and its legitimation in terms of *varna* and *jati*, the realms of goal-orientation or the theory of *purushartha*, the classification of the levels of charisma and, finally, the changing cultural cycles.

Hierarchy through role institutionalisation and its legitimation provides us with the cultural counterpart of the social structure of the caste system which still persists in India. The Brahmins, the Kshatriyas, the Vaisyas, the Sudras, and the untouchables as social groups based on differential commitment to standards have existed from the time of the Vedas. During the time of the Epics and the Dharmashastras the caste system underwent changes which rendered its values internally more rigid and subject to greater non-equalitarian sanctions. The caste system emerged as a cultural system based on institutionalised inequality. The earlier notion of distance between one caste and another, which was mostly based on functional criteria was accorded a ritual complexion; intercaste distantiation thus became a ground for elaborate distinctions and rationalisations about pollution-purity relationships. Thus hierarchy which was a functional principle became a religious phenomenon.

The charismatic qualities of individuals are conceived on the principle of levels, the highest and the most virtuous being the quality of *sattva*, of brightness and virtue, associated with the sages and the Brahmins. Next in hierarchy comes *rajas*, the charismatic quality of passionate commitment to action, to power, the attribute of the Kshatriyas and the kings; the last and the lowest in hierarchy is *tamas*, a charismatic endowment to dullness, to profane inclinations and to servitude, which is the endowment of the low castes. This theory in Hindu cultural tradition provides a systematic formulation of the principle of charismatic legitimation not only of the caste hierarchy but also of the order of power or kinship.

The third major hierarch in the Hindu cultural tradition is that of values regarding goal-orientation patterns. Life goals have been arranged with increasing merit into the pursuit of *kama*, or sex and other material goals of sensual enjoyment, *artha*, or the economic-utilitarian goals, the *dharma*, or the goals of moral obligations, and finally *moksha*, or the pursuit of salvation from the chain of birth and rebirth.

Hinduism does not deny the pursuit of any of these goals because of being at a lower level of merit. *Kama* or biological gratification is as laudable as that of *dharma* or moral obligation. But each level of goal-orientation is to be pursued at the appropriate stages of social life-cycle. These stages are defined through division of Hindu life into another hierarchy of four stages, called *ashramas*. These are *brahmacharya*, the stage of learning and strict celibacy, *grahastha*, the stage of householder's life, *vanaprastha*, the stage of relative withdrawal to exclusive pursuit of moral and spiritual goals without leaving the family, and finally *sanyasa*, the stage of complete withdrawal from affective social obligations, and devotion to pursuit of spiritual values and its propagation in society. If we compare the hierarchy of goal orientations with the hierarchy of life-stages the specific and diffuse meanings of *dharma* as moral obligation would be clear. For example, the pursuit of *kama* as sensual gratification is a legitimate goal for a householder but a deviation or sin for a person who has not crossed the stage of *brahmacharya* or education. Similarly, attempt for *moksha* or salvation is a laudable objective but only at the stage of *vanaprastha* or *sanyasa*. It should, therefore, be clear that commitment to ascetic other-worldliness in Hinduism is not absolute and all-pervasive, as generally conceived. Most of these values of life-stages being parts of the Great Tradition, conformity to them was only expected from the upper castes. The rest of the population had greater permissiveness in this regard. Most of these values found only ideological expression but were not materialised in the institutional framework of society. A great deal of flexibility was allowed in the expectation of conformity to the prescribed values of goal-orientation.

As evident, all hierarchical levels of the cultural structures fit together into a logical pattern and develop into a holistic view of culture and society. But these components relate to the synchronic and structural dimension of the cultural Great tradition of Hinduism. A diachronic view of the human condition does nevertheless exist although it may not be the same as in the Western sense. The persistent hierarchical way of things would have been very tormenting for the majority of the population and threatening to the existence of stable social and cultural systems but for another counter-balancing cultural category which has occupied an equally important place in the Hindu Great tradition. This is the notion of *continuity* and its chief institutional manifestation has been the theory of karma or predestination through one's actions. Its allied category is the theory of transmigration of souls.

The theory of karma is based on the assumption that the soul being immortal, its rebirth, its social placement after birth and its accompanying happiness and sufferings are due to the accumulation of deeds (karma) in the previous lives and the nature of commitment to the prescribed norms of action in the present life. These also hold the key to one's future after death. Final liberation from this cycle of birth and action (karma) could only be attained through salvation (moksha), which liberates man from birth either by means of the right conduct (dharma) or through devotion (bhakti) or accumulation of knowledge (jnana) or finally through the mastery of one's self (yoga). The concept of action (karma) and rebirth (transmigration) provide a rationale for the hierarchical view in Hinduism in regard to various cultural dimensions, such as goal orientation and role institutionalisation. In time dimension these provide orientation in human life not only to one's present but also to one's past and future.

The principle of hierarchy amounts to a denial of the principle of the individual in the Hindu cultural tradition in the Western sense of the term. The concept of the individual does not exist in the ideal-typical structure of traditional Hindu culture.

Hinduism constitutes the basis of a primary, or endogenous cultural tradition in India. In contradistinction, all other religio-cultural patterns existing in India parallel to it provide instances of heterogenetic or exogenous growth in its cultural traditions. Hinduism, as repeatedly emphasised by many scholars, may not be viewed as a religious system alone but more than that, it represents a way of life. It constitutes a distinctive world-view and a cultural complex, in the background of which endogenous transformations in culture may be analysed.

As in other civilisations two levels are distinguished in the Indian cultural system: first, that of common people or unlettered peasants, and second, that of the elite or the "reflective few". The cultural processes in the former comprise the Little tradition and those in the latter constitute the Great tradition. There is, however, a constant interaction between the two levels of traditions.

Patterns of Change of the Indian Cultural System

All cultures start from a primary or indigenous type of organisation and in the course of time evolve and become diversified not only through internal growth, but more important through contact with other civilisations in a heterogenetic process. This refers both to the Little and Great traditions.

In the past the internal reorganisation of the Hindu cultural tradition from the post-Vedic times to the era of Gandhiji has been marked by various changes, including decline and renaissance, a growth of devotional trends as represented by Guru Nanak in Punjab, Kabir and Tulsida in Uttar Pradesh, Chaitanya in Bengal, Ramdas in Maharashtra, etc. Another kind of change in this tradition is revealed in the formation of new autonomous traditions through differentiation. Buddhism, Jainism and Sikhism are three major examples of such changes. Out of these, Buddhism and Jainism have been purely indigenous in nature. Sikhism though fundamentally based on the general tenets of the Hindu tradition had also been influenced by the heterogenetic tradition of Islam.

In modern India in spite of many changes the Hindu Great and Little traditions are still alive. But they undergo significant changes. The Western impact has gradually led to acculturative and innovatory changes in the cultural pattern of India. It not only brought modernising acculturation, but also reinforced the endogenous tendencies for change. The two important aspects of the whole process relate to the process of cultural synthesis and the cultual identity.

Endogenous Change through Sanskritisation

The term Sanskritisation was used first by M. N. Srinivas to describe the process of cultural mobility in the traditional social structure of India. He found in his studies that lower castes, in order to raise their position in the caste hierarchy, adopted some customs of the Brahmins and gave up some of their own, considered to be impure by the higher castes. For instance, they gave up meat-eating, consumption of liquor and animal sacrifice to their deities; they imitated the Brahmins in matters of dress, food and rituals. By doing this, within a generation or so they could claim higher position in the hierarchy of castes. In many cases these higher castes were non-Brahmins; they were Kshatriyas, Jats, Vaisyas, etc., in various regions of the country. The crucial idea, however, was that of hierarchy in the caste system theoretically represented by *Varna*.

Sanskritisation has been throughout Indian history

a channel of cultural and social mobility during the periods of relative closure of the Hindu social system. It is a culturally specific case of the universal motivation toward the adaptation to the culture of a higher group in the hope of gaining its status in future.

Westernisation within the Context of Indian Culture

The contact of the Indian (Hindu) tradition with the West was of radical sociological significance. Historically, it was a contact between a premodern and a modernising cultural systems. Gradually, the Western impact has led to acculturative and innovatory changes in the cultural patterns of India. This process brings to light not only how far the modernising acculturation has taken place in the Indian tradition, but also the extent to which such acculturation reinforces the endogenous tendencies for change and modernisation, and how far these changes do or do not pose a threat to the cultural identity. The two aspects of the problem are in a way interrelated: the first relates to the process of cultural synthesis and the second to the phenomenon of cultural identity. However, the two processes are disparate. The question remains: can there be a point of convergence for these processes?

We can use the term "Primary westernisation" for changes induced by the Western impact on the Indian Little tradition. This includes the subculture represented by those Indian intellectuals who not only adopted many Western mental patterns and styles of life, but also supported their rapid expansion. Sub-cultural westernisation of this kind has always been characterised by an eclectic and fragmentary process of acculturation. It lacks an organised structure and exists only in the marginal spheres.

Another type of primary Westernisation refers to the process of general diffusion of Western cultural traits, such as the use of new technology, dress, food and change in the habits and styles of life of people in general, resulting from the cultural contact with the West. It implies mere imitation of external forms of culture. Unlike the first process, it is diffused both among general public as well as the intelligentsia among the villagers as well as the urban dwellers.

In the earlier period these types of Westernisation produced the sub-culture of middle-class elites especially in Calcutta, Bombay and Madras, where the contact with the West started and was more intense. Gradually this sub-culture grew into a Great tradition of modernisation.

Some of the institutional developments which have directly been instrumental in the creation of the major trend of modernisation in India are: 1) the growth of a universalistic legal superstructure; 2) expansion of education; 3) urbanisation and industrialisation; 4) increased network of communications; and 5) the growth of nationalism and the politicisation of society. Each of these factors had a pan-Indian significance and was not a sub-cultural or localised process as primary Westernisation was.

Diffusion of legal norms marks a change from status to contract, from hierarchy to universal equity and equality. In the Great tradition of Hinduism (and Islam) the norms which constituted the foundations of the legal system were an extension of the principle of hierarchy. The *dharmashastras* clearly lay down differential standards of legal rights based on the recognition of the status of various castes and classes.

From a cultural point of view the new legal system caused a major breakthrough in the principles of hierarchy and holism, the two pivotal values systems of traditional culture. Hierarchy was abolished in the new system and justice founded upon new legal forms based on equitable standards, and on the recognition of the individual as the unit in all matters of negotiation.

These culture trends are pan-Indian in character, have their centres in the urban and cosmopolitan areas, are highly structured and sophisticated in form and integrated with the world-view of science and liberalism. Hence, they comprise the upper stream of cultural modernisation. Besides, another process of modernisation is also going on in India, at the grass-root level. This relates to the daily lives, customs and habits of people in general in India. It conforms to the characteristics of Little tradition.

It consists of changes in dress, food habits, rituals, vocabulary, material culture, mode of travel and types of conveyance and customs. Traditionally, home-made clothes were worn by villagers all over the country, a custom which now survives only among a few castes in some regions in India. The factory-produced clothes now have replaced the home-spun clothes and occasionally one might come across modern synthetic fabrics even in the remote parts of the country. Even in poorer homes now women do not tailor clothes for their family members; professional tailors do this job. Even the mode of dress has changed considerably in these villages.

A change in food habits has also taken place, which brings people nearer to modern food technologies. New items of food are gaining popularity even at the village level. Meat-eating and the use of eggs among the higher caste members is on the increase. Formerly upper caste men used to avoid eating at restaurants and public places, but now fewer people observe these restrictions.

Many terms from the English language have now become an organic part of colloquial expression of rural folk, also bringing with them meanings of cultural modernisation. Increasingly, themes from urban life, contemporary politics and social economic issues are being borrowed by the cultural media of the folk tradition. Folk songs now often use metaphors, idioms and tunes of popular cinema songs; many of them refer caustically to contemporary feuds and tensions among various castes and groups; election propaganda is often made through the media of folk dramas, songs and devotional meettings.

Cultural Contradictions of Modernisation in India

As the process of modernisation becomes all-encompassing, it also generates inter-structural tensions and conflicts between past traditions and contemporary factors. In many developing countries in Asia modernisation causes a structural and cultural breakdown in society. The cases of China, Indonesia, Burma, Pakistan, and Iran can be cited. The only successful case of modernisation in Asia is that of Japan, but there too its institutionalisation has not been without a breakdown following the Second World War.

In India modernisation in its initial stages did not lead to any serious breakdown because of the peculiar structural characteristics of Indian society. Here, primarily, the cultural system was fairly independent of the political system. And there was also independence between the political system and the system of caste stratification. This inter-structural autonomy facilitated the assimilation of modernisation innovations, without inducing major breakdown. However, this means that modernity developed mainly as a sub-culture and a sub-structure without pervasive expansion in all sectors of life. The more modernisation becomes encompassing, the more structural autonomy ceases to operate as a shock absorber. Changes in the political system begin increasingly to impinge upon the system of stratification (caste, class, ethnic community), and these together create serious stresses for the cultural system as a whole. The cultural prerequisites of a comprehensive modernisation necessitate adaptive changes in the system of values which come in direct confrontation with traditional cultural values and norms. For instance, secularism, untouchability, non-parochialism are some cultural demands of modernisation in contemporary India which its traditional values system continues to resist.

The important questions arise: Under what structural or cultural conditions does modernisation lead to the integrative transformation of society? What are the structural prerequisites for the institutionalisation of changes without breakdown?

The answers to these questions can be formulated only through objective analysis of important trends of social and cultural changes in India in the process of modernisation. In the cultural sphere major changes have been introduced by legislation and brought about by the state policy. These seek to abolish the social inequality and exploitation handed down by tradition and accord democratic rights and constitutional privileges to all members of society. This has led to a trend away from Sanskritisation (emulation of the Great tradition) and towards the formation of new identities and associations of castes, regional groups and tribes. These processes are accelerated by urbanisation, industrialisation, the spread of education, and politicisation.

An important component of the general trend of modernisation consists in the mobilisation of the traditional structures and loyalties for objectives which are essentially modern. This phenomenon of "Modernity of Tradition" has become so important that it provided the title of a widely known book by two scientists.[1]

However, tradition also gets reinforcement in the process; modern media of communication and transport are increasingly used for spreading ritual order and for the rational organisation of religious groups and their mode of activities and social participation. Thus, there is a tendency among religious groups to organise themselves on a rational bureaucratic model, and the previous fission of each new part from the parent body has now changed into strong orientation towards fusion.

Major potential sources of breakdown in the Indian process of modernisation may, in one form or another, be attributed to structural inconsistencies, such as: democratisation without spread of civic culture (education), bureaucratisation without commitment to universalistic norms, rise in media participation (communication) and aspiration or expectation without proportionate increase in resources, verbalisation of a welfare ideology without its implementation as a social policy, overurbanisation without industrialisation and finally modernisation without meaningful changes in the stratification system.

The crucial variable lies in the mobilisation of people's motivation for change and in the institutional changes necessary for co-ordinating modernisation trends.

If you wish to study the subject in depth:

1. Rudolph, L. I., Rudolph, S. H., *The Modernity of Tradition. Political Development in India*, University of Chicago Press, Chicago, 1967.

---

[1] L. I. Rudolph and S. H. Rudolph, *The Modernity of Tradition. Political Development in India*, University of Chicago Press, Chicago, 1967.

2. Moddie, A. D., *India in Search of Values*, Allied Publishers, New Delhi, 1987,

3. Singh, Y., *Modernization of Indian Tradition. A Systematic Study of Social Change*, Oriental Press, New Delhi, 1974.

18

The Interaction of Cultures

In this chapter, consideration should be given to the following:

1. What is the difference between international political contacts and cultural interaction?
2. At what levels do cultures interact?
3. What is the mechanism of cultural interaction?
4. What is "cultural imperialism"?
5. What are the aspects of the West's cultural expansion in other countries?
6. What are the basic trends of modern cultural interaction? What is international culture?
7. What role does the struggle of the newly-independent countries to protect their cultural identity play in their intellectual life?

Along with economic and political contacts, cultural ties are a constant and essential component of international relations. All these components not only complement each other, but enter into complex interaction, in which each of them reveals its independence and specific features. Culture means principally society's intellectual life—the sphere in which intellectual values—knowledge, standards and historical experience—are created, accumulated and consumed. Culture is, therefore, the scene of the most stable form of interaction between peoples, and their mutual enrichment and understanding.

It is evident that the level of the given nation's development and its position of domination or dependence have a serious effect on the character of its cultural contacts with other nations. A state of dependence brings about growing resistance to the cultural expansion of the oppressor state and the cultural integration of the various ethnic groups of the given society, whereby it mobilises its cultural potential in order to affirm its unity and opposition to oppression.

The Structure of Cultural Interaction

Each form of culture — morality, law, philosophy, science, art, and political culture — has its own specific features. This encourages nations to borrow foreign cultural forms and adapt them to their own needs. Such are, for example, the processes taking place in literature: world literature is a tremendous wealth, which enriches the literature of every nation.

But each component of intellectual life is above all connected with its own cultural environment. Otherwise, certain sections of the intelligentsia might develop a superficial and transient attraction to the most modern foreign trends which actually do not meet their society's intellectual needs. In the political sphere Westernisation could trigger military coups overthrowing democratic parliamentary systems which do not enjoy much trust amongst common people. In the sphere of law, Westernised standards and practices are not accepted by the masses, which give preference to customary — albeit outdated — standards of common law.

Interaction also takes place on the level of subcultures and trends which are present in every developed culture. It consists above all in the cultural opposition between the dominant and oppressed classes, the culture of each of them has not only its own ideological tinge but also its own set of values. An analysis of the social aspect of cultural interaction shows us the extent to which the dominant ruling classes of the developing countries, culturally isolated from their own societies, find themselves under the influence of the capitalist West. This largely determines the status of the intelligentsia in those countries. The influence of the latest Western cultural achievements often leads to its isolation from its own national culture.

What are the basic principles of international cultural interaction?

International political relations involve above all states (and sometimes nations with no statehood of their own but striving for it), and also various international movements and organisations (such as the Non-Aligned movement and the United Nations). Therefore, not all nations take part in international politics.

Unlike politics, international cultural ties show considerable independence from state regulation and, moreover, are capable of influencing politics. The cultural influence of a given nation is often very different from its political role. Associations of states are also to a great extent based on established cultural ties and are largely stimulated by them.

Levels of Cultural Interaction

In Chapter 8, we considered the basic types of cultural communities and saw that it was convenient to classify them as ethnic groups, nations or civilisations. And it is above all between these that interaction takes place.

However, before considering these levels of interaction, let us make two more points. The first is that, as a result of long-established contacts between nations, there develops a regional type of culture; such cultures exist, for example, in the Mediterranean region, the Maghreb, the Middle East, North America, the Pacific region, and so on. The second is that there is the modern urban culture of industrialised nations, which is essentially supra-national and leaves its imprint on all present-day cultural processes.

Now let us examine each level of cultural interaction.

1. *The ethnic level* involves interaction between ethnic and meta-ethnic communities of various types: local ethnoses, ethno-linguistic communities, cultural-economic ones (having common material culture), historico-ethnological ones (having commonness of intellectual culture), ethno-religious ones and others.

This type of cultural interaction is contradictory. There is mutual enrichment and increasing integration on the one hand, and a growth of ethnic awareness and the desire to preserve one's ethnic identity on the other. Ethnic communication (as expressed in growing contacts, bilingualism, an increase in the number of mixed marriages, etc.) does not in itself bring about the establishment of community. The culture of an ethnos ensures not only its integration and stability as a system. Elements of this culture have another existence, as well, since they also show some of the differences between ethnoses, becoming the basis for the distinction between "us" and "them". Every ethnos views any other ethnos as something external, differing from it in many ways, including culture. Of course the former's attitude towards the latter can vary depending on different internal or external factors. There might be interest, but still no interaction. There might be mutual or one-way penetration, entailing the use of certain elements of the other culture without actually erasing the borderline between the two cultures. Undoubtedly, it is at this level as well that elements of inter-ethnic culture are formed—a culture on whose basis primary communities interact. Such culture includes above all languages of inter-ethnic communication, which are not necessarily spoken by any of the given ethnic groups. In Tropical Africa, for example these are not only Swahili and Hausa, but smaller ethnic languages as well, and even mixed jargons (pidgin English), which are used in trade and economic contacts.

However, such culture lacks the degree of maturity necessary to ensure intensive interaction and concordance between various elements. Disagreements and conflicts in which differences often become a pretext and criterion for enmity and violence, necessitate the achievement of stable unity at a higher level.

2. *The national level.* National unity takes shape both on a monoethnic and polyethnic basis as a result of common economic activity and state-political regulation. This is accompanied by the creation of a corresponding common culture (language, ideology, conduct norms, customs, etc). In Asia and Africa, national unity took shape to a greater extent on the basis of common historical experience accumulated during the period of colonial oppression and the struggle for national independence and self-determination. In the newly-liberated countries, national unification was above all effected by the state. In the sphere of culture, the state is a most important instrument of unity, too.

Nevertheless, the processes of cultural consolidation of a nation often turn out to be dual in character and in turn cause inter-ethnic conflicts. In India, the trends towards ethnic and language consolidation which trigger clashes between members of different ethnic and language groups, deserve condemnation. Many Indian social scientists and political leaders see local nationalism as the source of friction and conflict leading to the disintegration of state unity.

More often than not, measures aimed at consolidating territorial and state nationalism result in encroachment on the rights or even the expulsion of ethnic minorities. In the 1970's, the authorities in Guinea, Uganda, Kenya and Zambia drove out all immigrants, some of whom had lived in those countries for several generations, not only from neighbouring countries, but from further afield (from the Mediterranean and Asia). Underlying such measures were mostly economic motives, considering that the local bourgeoisie wanted to have less competition in enterprise (although this often caused long-term economic damage). Nevertheless, certain socio-cultural reasons are also evident. In Uganda, for example, an important factor was that the Hindu population was distinguished by its customs and norms (language, endogamous marriage, restrictions on repeated marriages for widows) in contrast to intertribal exogamy and levirate* among the Africans.

3. *The civilisational level.* The most tangible results in the exchange of intellectual, cultural, and scientific achievements were in the past reached through contacts between different civilisations. In the Middle Ages, European civilisation borrowed much from the Muslim region and later from India and China. There was also intensive interaction between the Muslim, Hindu and Buddhist regions. Conflicts gradually gave way to peaceful coexistence and fruitful co-operation.

Recent research has revealed that there were diversified contacts between the African continent and other regions, which were weakened in the period of colonial domination. Despite the undoubted similarity of the primary cultural substrata of Tropical Africa and Latin America, these parts of the world were for a long time in ignorance of each other. Only in the 1930's and 1940's, the upsurge of Indianism and Africanism (initially, Neg-

* Levirate is a custom under which a widow must or has the right to marry the brother of her late husband.

roism), accompanied by the intelligentsia's interest in the cultural roots of their peoples, brought about a growth in cultural relations. In has been discovered that the non-European cultural substratum had similar characteristics on both continents, especially in religion, language, and folk culture.

The achievement of independence by many countries in Asia and Africa helped overcome the former colonial limitations and realise the potential that were previously dormant in various ethno-cultural and national-political communities. Naturally, the state principles of national self-determination also largely determine the character of cultural ties between different societies. These relations are greatly influenced by various international organisations, such as ASEAN, the Arab League, and the Organisation of African Unity.

Mechanism of Interaction

The literature on problems of acculturation has described in detail the mechanism and consequences of cultural interaction. At the ethnological level one can single out both positive and negative cases: addition (complication) and impoverishment (erosion).

A positive impact is seen in cases where the absorption of elements of another culture is (1) voluntary, (2) organically combined with native cultural heritage, and (3) spread out in time. Lexical borrowings (e.g., by Eastern languages from European ones) are striking examples of addition while the spread of bilingualism, is a typical illustration of complication.

Cultural impoverishment can result both from the supplanting of the organic elements of native culture and from the superficial absorption of elements borrowed from other cultures.

Matters are different at the national level. A nation's self-determination (or at least its efforts to achieve it) provides a measure of independence enabling it to withstand negative foreign influences and absorb only the positive elements of other cultures.

In today's world, the whole system of cultural interaction is affected by the complex and contradictory cultural system, in which one should distinguish Western bourgeois culture and world urban culture.

There are clear differences in the ways different Western countries influence the newly-independent nations. In most cases, the former metropolises, even having lost their political domination and agreed to restructure their economic relations, still retain (and usually even expand) their cultural influence. Rivalry between leading capitalist nations for influence on the developing countries is often expressed in their growing "traditional" influence or in their striving to oust their rivals from the given developing country's cultural sphere to facilitate their economic penetration, as well.

The West's impact cannot be reduced to a simple sum total of influences of each West European state and United States. It assumes a large scale and can be described as civilisational. In this impact, one must distinguish components of the capitalist system of intellectual production (associated with the entire capitalist mode of production), on the one hand, and the progressive critical content in which the positive achievements of Western civilisation are reflected, on the other.

Modern Cultural Imperialism

In the past three decades, in the overall strategy of the leading Western states vis-à-vis the developing countries, a special role has belonged to influence through culture. Although after the collapse of the colonial system, Western imperialism has been using new economic and political forms of pressure, it has also been intensively trying to develop more subtle and flexible methods.

The leading capitalist states still control powerful levers of influence on those countries, and an important role here belongs to culture. Therefore, the cultural influence of the West and of Japan on the newly-independent states has deep inherent contradictions. It helps to perpetuate the economic domination of Third World countries by world capitalism, often causing the destruction of original cultural forms, moral standards and values without providing adequate substitutes for them and undermining society's intellectual potential. Therefore, the influence of Western imperialism comes up against a sharply negative public attitude in the developing countries, and the policies of many of them are aimed at resisting or, at least limiting Western cultural expansion. Such expansion is increasingly defined in international documents as "cultural imperialism".

Recent studies emphasise that imperialism can take on various forms and act in different spheres. Researchers usually single out five forms of imperialism: economic, political, military, communicational, and cultural. The concept of cultural imperialism is usually defined as the use of political and economic power to impose the values and customs of a given culture on another nation, and restrict the latter's own culture.

The above types of imperialism are constantly present, but the role of each can change, which results in a restructuring of the methods of influence, depending both on the world situation and on the opportunities which imperialism can use in a given country.

In the cultural sphere, imperialism has the following characteristics:

1) Transfer of the way of life and consumer attitudes of Western capitalist society;

2) Imposition of Western bourgeois culture as universal, ruling out any contribution made by other cultures;

3) A desire to achieve political ends through cultural contacts;

4) A one-way flow of information from the "centre" to the "periphery" (from major Western corporations in the entertainment industry and mass media to multimillion audiences in other countries);

5) Formation of a socio-cultural elite which must encourage the establishment of pro-Western principles and thus serve as a bastion of Western bourgeois influence.

Capitalist influence in ideology and culture has always been exercised on both the official and unofficial levels, the two permanently complementing each other and being co-ordinated in common programmes. But in the past two decades, the importance the West has been attaching to its methodical ideological and cultural influence on other countries has considerably increased. Culture has become not only a component part of other forms of official policy, but an independent sphere of such policy.

Governments assumed the role of co-ordinating all these forms and methods of cultural influence, including the education system, the news media, mass culture, cultural and scientific exchange, tourism, etc.

Transnational Corporations and Cultural Imperialism

Cultural expansion is an important component and essential condition of the activity of transnational corporations dominating various spheres of life in the developing countries. Their activity is not limited to the economy. It is complemented by political pressure on those countries' governments or on opposition forces, and by intensive social and cultural influence. To function successfully, transnational corporations introduce social and cultural mechanisms that ensure their successful functioning. This results not only in the change of consumption models, but a restructuring of the entire set of values, in which consumption becomes the main criterion.

Transnational corporations set great store by sociocultural investment, for this serves the interests of their own production. They ensure the production of a mass culture which leads to idealisation of the mother country's lifestyle, ideology, values, world-view and art and their uncritical acceptance, engendering a sense of inferiority in relation to one's indigenous culture.

Especially disastrous are the consequences of the cult of consumerism, which is so necessary to Western corporations to dominate the minds and actions of a certain section of society—the middle class, which can become the main consumer of their goods.

The transnationals claim that their activity is free from all ideology which supposedly amounts to the mere production and sale of goods and the maintenance of high-standard business and optimum consumption, thus solely meeting the material interests of the people. In actual fact, capitalism replaces the old myths which served to disguise human relations in pre-industrial societies with commodity fetishism, which is the cornerstone of bourgeois ideology and culture. Commodities are offered not only through the retail network. They function largely as part of the Western way of life, preached by the entire system of news media, mass culture, and advertisement. Here, too, there is a high degree of monopolisation. The largest cultural corporations (producing films, television programmes, music records, newspapers, magazines, books, games, etc.) are based in the United States, although today they have powerful rivals in Japan, Britain and France.

Advertisement encourages the exaggerated growth of material demands unsuitable for the developing countries. It serves to satisfy commercial interests, rather than the people's actual need of keeping up good health, nutrition, and clothing. It seeks to persuade the Third World consumer that instead of traditional drinks he needs Coca Cola or Pepsi, instead of natural milk he needs powder milk in a flashy carton, and so on. The need for food is transformed into that for Lion's Maid ice-cream and Cadbury chocolate, the need for transport into that for fashionable cars, the need for a home into dreams about a detached house with the most modern gadgets for maximum comfort. The breakdown of traditional needs and forms of consumption, which were closely linked with old customs and ethnic culture has a destructive effect on the whole system of customary attitudes and goals. However, this trend in consumption sometimes includes local exotica, which also serve the ends of prestigious consumption or leisure. The "wonders" of the East and Africa are now a source of profit.

Whereas the interests of the transnationals themselves are quite satisfied by the tangible increase of the consumption of their products, this cannot be said of the interests of the majority of the local population or the interests of society as a whole. They have to pay through the nose for the Western life-style, in more than one sense: by subordinating their life and labour to the laws of capitalist production, which turn out to be much more ruthless than the former taboos, totems, and religious bans.

Spreading to various spheres of life, such Western-type consumption patterns often have disastrous effects, not only socially, but even economically. A notorious example of the destructive effect of such consumerism imposed by Western advertisement using socio-psychological factors is the activity of the Swiss firm

Nestlé, which advertises in many countries its baby food. Its substitution for natural nursing results in considerable growth in import expenditure which exceeds in a number of African and Asian countries the budget of public health agencies. Another result of such imposed consumption patterns in a context of a low level of general consumption is a rise in child morbidity. All these consequences cost the developing countries approximately one billion dollars annually. And that is only one example of how cultural-psychological methods are used for increasing economic dependence.

Advertisement of the most up-to-date products is aimed at different sections of society, using different techniques in different cases, often including all sorts of guises such as "cultural" exotica. It is directed above all at the wealthier sections of society.

Mass Culture as an Influence Factor

An important tool used by Western imperialism to influence the developing countries is its mass culture. It is, in effect, a pseudo-culture which is closely dependent on the capitalist market and is meant to tie the consumer to it. That pseudo-culture is designed to replace real life and distract the individual from the hardships of his traditional or modernised way of life. This noisy, gaudy, highly accessible, ready-to-use quasi-culture, which requires no special preparation before consumption, mass-produced by the entertainment industry, is to mould a new type of individual, *homo consumens*, a person devoid of any distinctive personality, class or political principles, an easy object of manipulation by the capitalist economic and political system.

Bourgeois mass culture is designed to show the man in the street that there is another, easier life that has become available to him, thereby subconsciously convincing him of the advantages of the bourgeois lifestyle, making him accept it uncritically and idealise it, and at the same time producing in him an inferiority complex with regard to his own native culture.

Western mass culture is closely associated with consumerist philosophy, in other words, chasing after the things, fashions, services, and education which determine one's belonging to the cream of society. Encouraging such views, mass culture emphasises the priority of individual needs and personal interests over social ones. Such privatisation of interests is, of course, closely linked with the class factors.

Expressed in the dissemination of thrillers, pulp magazines, cinema and television films, mass culture destroys the old norms of conduct and consumption, well-established concepts and principles, replacing them with new myths and fetishes dictated by the capitalist market.

The Role of the Mass Media

The leading Western nations make extensive use of the great potential of the modern mass media to increase their influence in the rest of the world. The term "informational imperialism" has been long established both in political and academic literature.

The Western news agencies, particularly the four leaders—Associated Press, UPI, Reuter, and France Presse—impose their views on the greater part of the world. The importance of the news reports and other information presented by these agencies reflects the needs of the industrialised Western nations, for whom the problems plaguing millions of people in the Third World are of little interest. Those problems are of less importance to them than all sorts of sensations that excite the minds of the Western public, whereas the achievements of the developing countries, whether in the economic, social or cultural fields, cannot break into the information market. The Western mass media network not so much encourages free information exchange as it distorts one's view of truly important events in the world. And it is not only a question of the amount of information the leading industrialised Western nations provide to the developing countries being a hundred times greater than that which they receive therefrom. It is above all a question of the character of this information, which reflects the needs of the leading Western powers.

Moreover, the transnational news corporations have become extensions of industrial corporations. The information and ideas disseminated through periodicals, the radio, television, cinema, advertisement, etc., penetrate into people's minds and psychology, preparing fertile ground for accepting the values and norms that meet the needs of big business. The form and content of the information spread through the media reflect the ideological values of the leading Western powers. Along with ordinary consumer goods, cultural-information products constitute a means of influence by which the world capitalist system shapes the values, principles and conduct norms that meet the needs of that system.

Education and Cultural Imperialism

A major target of the Western transnationals, various foundations and research centres is the developing countries' educational systems. Taking advantage of the Third World countries' acute need for modern systems of education and training of intellectual personnel, the leading Western powers, under the guise of aid, assume control of key educational establishments—universities and research centres in the developing countries, figuring that in the future the educated young people in those countries will form a pro-Western elite. Instead of shaping good specialists, worthy citizens and active champions of progress in their societies, such education tears them away from their national roots and lures them over to the West, depriving their own countries of talented specialists.

Because of the acute shortage of their own specialists, Asian and African countries keep inviting school teachers and university professors from abroad. Moreover, a large proportion of local university students, and teachers and other specialists from Asian and African countries get an education and take refresher courses in the industrialised West. There is no arguing that this is an important channel for training much-needed national intellectual personnel. However, in the present situation, this system of education is divorced from the developing countries' interests. This reflects adversely on the kind of training, principles and world-view of young people getting such an education. National universities in Third World countries are often controlled from abroad, with curricula and requirements (examination questions, etc.) meeting the interests of the former metropolitan state, which fact encourages the moulding of an elite orientated towards cultural dependence.

Other methods of influencing social consciousness in the newly-independent nations are cultural exchange, the sending of religious missionaries, and the brainwashing of national specialists invited for various reasons to the West.

Fighting for Cultural Independence

The developing countries are struggling to restructure international relations in the field of culture. Elimination of cultural imperialism is just as difficult and important a task as elimination of political and economic dependence. Cultural policy pursued by most developing countries increasingly includes demands for an end to Western domination in culture and the mass media, and for independent cultural development.

This rejection of Western domination is accompanied by the affirmation of positive values (solidarity, universality, harmony, continuity) presented in the form of specifically ethnic or national symbolism and intellectual constructions which have taken shape in each particular civilisation and transformed in line with modern requirements.

Recent decades have shown that the Western sociocultural system is resisted by other cultures, which undermine its stable position there. This is not to say that Western culture does not penetrate into and spread throughout the Third World. But there are definite objective limits to such diffusion, and more often than not the dynamics of cultural interaction is such that the alien culture enters a hostile environment and is limited, rejected, and forced out. In their culture policies, the governments of most developing countries increasingly take into account their nations' demands for an end to Western domination in culture, education and the news media.

Cultural Synthesis and Identity

Many Asian and African thinkers insist that the self-determination and stability of non-Western societies depends on their ability to resist the Western cultural impact and preserve their own cultural values and standards. Most UNESCO resolutions usually conclude with statements of the need to preserve and develop the cultural heritage of every nation and to recognise its right to its own cultural identity, and it is culture which is treated in such documents as the basis for equal interaction with other nations and as a crucial factor in international relations in general. In fact, the status accorded to "cultural identity" now bears comparison to the concepts of "independence" and "sovereignty" on the political plane.

No matter how significant and self-evident the cultural-historical differences between nations or ethnic communities, special theoretical and practical importance is today attached to differences in types of culture between the capitalist West and the non-Western world, each of which has its distinct forms of universalistic organisation of material and cultural aspects of public life.

The emergence of new ideologies such as "the Islamic society", "Buddhist socialism", "Dharma Raj", political and philosophical "Africanism" testify to the intense search for new forms of socio-cultural organisation that would correspond to the given nations' cultural roots.

Although each of these concepts is dressed up in the garb of its cultural environment a typological similarity is evident between them. Many Asian and African researchers themselves insist that there are fundamental differences between the East or Africa as a whole and Western civilisation.

The emphasis on the cultural identity of Asian and African countries and the demand for their cultural self-determination are persistently accompanied by the idea that in their present form, Eastern and African cultures cannot successfully solve today's problems of self-determination and development. Taking the form of protest against the destructive impact of alien modernisation, and presenting urgent demands to the modern world, the various movements championing cultural identity so far lack comprehensive programmes of social reform that would meet today's needs. This is fraught with the danger of social dynamics scaling down.

Aware of the equally ruinous effect that both extreme

traditionalism and total Westernisation would have on their cultures, the Third World nations are intensively looking for a happy synthesis (or symbiosis) of the two. Ethnic and Western, old and new elements in fact exist side by side, often intermingling, and yet remaining within certain bounds. Everyday practice keeps giving rise to numerous combinations of various social and cultural principles: Eastern morality and Western technology, politics and ethics, rationalism and humanitarianism, science and human values, the personal and the social, and so forth.

Despite numerous calls for a more intimate blend of all these different principles, it is hard to bring them all together. The various models that are being offered are still too eclectic, motivated by an abstract desire to combine the best of both worlds, mechanically bringing together autochthonous and borrowed, traditional and modern elements.

In recent years, social scientists on different continents have increasingly been coming up with theories of independent development of various non-Western civilisations which are to coexist with the Western ones. The impossibility of applying the Western model to the whole planet has necessitated a revision of the geopolitical and civilisational principles underlying relations between the West and the Third World.

These new models of inter-civilisational understanding and unification remain largely abstract, based on the philosophical-culturological idea of the similarity of the basic values of non-Western civilisations. Despite the efforts of many prominent public figures, the practical implementation of such mutual understanding comes up against many difficulties, which are often aggravated by political conflicts. It is often difficult to establish cultural contacts between the Hindu and Buddhist, Islamic and Hindu, Arab and African regions. And yet calls for inter-regional co-operation gradually bear fruit.

Modern Trends of Intercultural Contacts

The newly-independent countries' active role in international relations intensively helps to improve international relations in general, on the one hand, and promotes cultural pluralism in each particular country, on the other. These trends usually operate simultaneously since they can affect various elements and levels of culture.

Apart from the culture of obviously Western capitalist origin, there is a world industrial-urban culture. In the most general terms, it includes both the high-standard arts culture of various regions, mass culture, features of everyday life (clothing, food, houses, household utensils), forms of leisure (tourism), sports and psychophysical training (football, calisthenics, yoga, karate, etc.), social behaviour and organisation (forms of marriage and family), political culture, and so on.

This culture combines the achievements of different nations. However, it primarily takes shape in the West. Masterpieces of art usually gain recognition through UNESCO, at Western festivals and competitions, or through international awards, and only later in the rest of the world. Similar processes take place in the social sciences, because philosophical and ideological trends of Western origin rapidly penetrate into the minds of the intelligentsia of other countries, coming into complex interaction (synthesis and symbiosis) with autochthonous trends.

An important element of world political culture is international law, which regulates political relations between states and between inter-state organisations (above all the United Nations) and also within the national liberation movement. International law began to take shape back in the period of colonial expansion of Western powers and was at first largely superficial, being subordinated to the expansionist and hegemonistic aims of the capitalist West (and later Japan). The influence of the foreign policy of the Soviet Union, and later of the world socialist system, encouraged the formation of a new type of international relations and the establishment of effective international law. A most important principle of such law is peaceful coexistence, in the context of which the structure and mechanism of international relations embracing various spheres was elaborated. In the field of co-operation on social, cultural and humanitarian issues, the following basic principles are implemented: assistance to social progress of all nations, observance of human rights and fundamental freedoms, respect for the rights of ethnic minorities, a ban on racial discrimination, liquidation of the social consequences of colonialism and neocolonialism, and exchange of cultural and intellectual values.

An important consequence of international legal culture which incorporates the principle of national sovereignty is the establishment of the principles of cultural pluralism. The emergence of dozens of "new" states has created a complex field of interaction of newly recognised cultures.

Characteristically, in the 1960's, Western bourgeois ideologues started speaking about a crisis of international law. For them this crisis consisted in the "exorbitant" claims of many newly-independent countries of Asia, Africa and Latin America which entered the international scene but refused to accept standards of international law based on Western criteria of civilisation. They demanded a revision of earlier principles of international law discriminating against the developing countries. The persistent efforts of the young states supported by the socialist countries brought about a radical change in the character of international law, including the recognition of the principles of cultural identity and independence of all sovereign states.

An important element of world culture today is science, both as a sum total of knowledge and as a world-view. Undoubtedly, in its intellectual and technological achievements, science transcends, not only national boundaries, but the bounds of local civilisations, and for that reason is proclaimed the common heritage of all nations and the basis of communication, interaction and mutual enrichment. In the newly-independent states, science has become an inalienable component of educational programmes, while its popular elements have become part of people's everyday life. And yet, to even a greater extent than in the history of international law, there are mixed feelings towards science in these countries. On the one hand, acceptance of science is seen, not only as assimilation of achievements of world significance, but also as a source of building up the given nation's strength, which often turns it into an object of national rivalry. But on the other hand, science is viewed in many ways as a means of subordination of various aspects of life to the pressure of imperialism. Science is often believed to have a dual intellectual nature, because it is not an organic part of the structure of intellectual production and the values which have taken shape in non-Western societies.

A detailed legal presentation and the practical implementation of the principles of international cultural co-operation are seen in the documents and activity of the United Nations and UNESCO. A general declaration of these principles was adopted at a UNESCO conference in 1966, on the 20th anniversary of its establishment. The declaration above all stated the need to respect and preserve the identity of every culture, because each culture has its own value, being part of the common heritage of mankind. The aims of cultural co-operation are the mutual enrichment of and the strengthening of friendship among nations and the mutual understanding of each other's way of life. It was specially emphasised that cultural co-operation must highlight ideas and values which help create an atmosphere of peace.

The important role of culture in promoting understanding and friendship among peoples is a constant theme of official declarations and other materials of UNESCO and other international organisations. The World Conference on Cultural Policies, held at Mexico City in 1982, called for "cultural and scientific co-operation on the basis of equality and mutual interest as an important factor in the strengthening of peace, friendship and reciprocal understanding among people".* Culture reveals and embodies the interdependence of different nations. Therefore, efforts should be directed towards establishing a new world cultural order, based on the recognition of the cultural identity of each people, the principles of equality, justice, freedom and solidarity—in other words, a cultural order based on the recognition and affirmation of the unity and variety of all peoples and cultures.

The principle of cultural pluralism on the international plane implies a certain degree of self-determi-

* *World Conference on Cultural Policies. Mexico City, 26 July-6 August 1982. Final Report,* UNESCO, p. 187.

nation of various independent cultural communities (local ethnoses, nations, regions, civilisations), which preserve a certain measure of cultural identity. The right to cultural self-determination and to the independent development of ethnic or national culture is expressed in one form or another in all constitutions and official governmental programmes of the newly-independent Asian and African countries.

The growing diversity of cultures and a trend towards self-determination on the basis of not only political factors but cultural community is an objective reality of our time, determined by the involvement of broad sections of society in public life. Intellectual culture is a natural sphere of their self-expression. Nonetheless, the artificial extension of pluralism could exacerbate the difficulties facing the newly-free countries. Recognition of the naturalness and inevitability of cultural self-determination is bound to lead to a weakening or a split, and undermine the trend towards unification on the basis of which these countries seek to resolve their problems.

For many polyethnic societies in Africa, the abovementioned artificial extension of pluralism would mean perpetuating ethnic disunity, which has such a baneful effect on the whole life of society. In the tiny country of Malawi, for example, which only has a population of four million there are thirteen ethnic groups, and communication among them within the framework of production is insufficient to establish stable relations in other social spheres.

The defence of cultural pluralism is opposed by many national leaders. Such pluralism, when extended to the level of ethnos and tribe, obviously goes against both the trend towards national consolidation and the general desire of most Asian and African countries to jointly resist Western expansion. This kind of pluralism inevitably leads to the disintegration of large political and cultural entities and bitter conflicts—from inter-tribal to inter-regional ones. Moreover, such pluralism is mostly expressed in fields which hardly put any restrictions on the all-pervasive world capitalist market.

In the newly-independent countries themselves, such

trends are often condemned by advocates of national and pan-national unity, who reject everything that might conceivably undermine or weaken it. Thus the young nations face a dilemma: how to prevent the disintegration of the primary cells of society and establish stable cultural communities without generating conflicts between tribes, ethnic groups and nations and weakening the primary cells?

While approving of cultural pluralism and accepting it as a reality, the advocates of capitalist modernisation view the economy as the basis of intra- and international interdependence, which they claim will remove the negative effects of cultural pluralism. The latter is assigned the function of maintaining the vitality of various ethno-cultural groups, nations, and even civilisational complexes, on condition that they don't hold back economic integration.

Both in India (within one country and in the ASEAN countries (within an inter-state alliance) there are numerous deep divisions between ethnic, language, religious and economic communities, which greatly encumbers the establishment of cultural unity. Therefore, for the most part the problem of cultural pluralism is solved through the principle of "unity in diversity", which means the preservation and autonomy of various cultural communities, with the creation of a stable network of cultural exchange supplemented by general political and administrative structures. An auxiliary role is given to such elements of cultural community as religion, language, law, education, and mass media.

Thus the principle of cultural self-determination cannot serve as a universal criterion in dealing with cultural issues, since it is relative and dependent on other social factors. The independence of cultures is complemented by their interaction either on the basis of common intellectual life or through a well-established system of mutual understanding.

The Influence of the Socialist Countries

There is a fundamental difference in the way the socialist and capitalist countries influence the developing countries. Socialism influences these countries by its intellectual values, the ideals of humanitarianism, progress and peace, on the one hand, and by its achievements in building a new type of society which abolishes exploitation of man by man and eliminates acute social antagonisms. Socialist culture attracts the social consciousness of the developing countries by the fact that it has given expression to the principles of human solidarity and eliminated the mutual alienation of people arising from the domination of private ownership, and the pursuit of profit and material values. Socialist culture removes the antagonism between culture for the elite and culture for the masses, broadens the internationalisation of intellectual life, and ensures the continuity of progressive traditions and experience accumulated by society. This humanitarian content makes socialist culture appeal to the developing countries.

Of great importance to the nations struggling for the acceleration of progressive development is the experience of cultural development accumulated in the Central Asian and Transcaucasian republics of the USSR during their transition from backwardness, illiteracy and poverty to high achievements of modern culture. The intensive development of all spheres of cultural life, the development of mass education, the creation of a large new intelligentsia—all these are good examples for the newly-independent countries which must also tackle the effects of age-old backwardness and conservative traditions that fetter the creative forces of society. The utilisation of this experience has become an important part of the newly-freed countries' social reform programmes.

Inter-cultural Understanding

Societies and world systems differ primarily in their socio-economic foundations. The capitalist principle of private ownership generates deep social conflicts. By contrast, socialist society, which affirms public ownership of the means of production, eliminates social antagonisms and builds firm foundations for the organic unity of society. The Third World combines traditional solidarity with private ownership which are not yet connected with modern production. Economic and social pluralism of Third World societies results in political and cultural factors being largely given the function of integrating society.

For all the differences between the civilisations of today, the world is united by a tremendous need for communication. Of course, the essence of capitalist society is not limited to capitalist principles alone, it also incorporates the achievements of mankind as a whole. Trade and other economic contacts as such are constantly complemented with human contacts, in the course of which people enrich each other with their cultural achievements and expand each other's intellectual horizons. In the world of today, against the background of a tremendous growth of the material productive forces, the intellectual and cultural achievements of all societies, great and small, retain their significance, constituting the common wealth of mankind.

The degree of the cultural identity of each community—great or small—is relative. There is interaction between different communities, which includes contacts within a culture that is common to them. However, this relativity does not cancel out mutual understanding, without which interaction is often reduced to "extra-cultural" methods, such as war. The increasing importance of these problems in today's world is demonstrated by the rapid growth of research and the development of special scientific programmes in the field of international communication.

Mutual inter-cultural contacts began in time immemorial and are a constant feature of communication among human communities. Modern culture as a whole is the result of the endeavour of the whole of mankind and the interaction between different cultures. But it is not a question of assimilation and levelling out of cultures. It is important that both modern and ancient civilisations preserve their cultural wealth and identity.

The assertion and protection of cultural identity is, as we have seen, an important feature of present-day world processes. But at the same time there is a broadening and intensification of cultural intercourse, as a result of which national cultures enrich one another, assimilating each other's achievements. And finally, an important component of the cultural processes today is the expansion of a supra-national, universal human culture, which is closely associated with modern forms of production and the mass media.

In the world of today, the population of each country is becoming increasingly influenced by other cultures—through personal contacts and through assimilation of some elements of other cultures. But this is not necessarily accompanied by the erosion of former cultural communities. On the contrary, there is often a tendency to preserve or revive the given people's old cultural identity. Nevertheless, very promising is the dissemination of knowledge about different peoples, which is accompanied by the assimilation of skills of communication in a foreign cultural environment. This enhances mutual understanding and therefore strengthens peace and encourages respect for human rights and the elimination of all forms of discrimination.

Cultural co-operation helps establish an international climate conducive to disarmament and the solution of economic and ecological problems. This ultimately stimulates the establishment of worldwide prosperity and the successful development of mankind.

However, left to themselves, these processes are slow and they keep coming up against serious obstacles. Constant, rationally organised efforts are needed—and they depend on extensive knowledge of the principles of inter-cultural communication.

If you wish to study the subject in depth:

1. *Afrika: vstrecha tsivilizatsii* (Africa: A Focus of Civilisations), Nauka, Moscow, 1970.
2. Burlatsky, F. M., Galkin, A. A., *Sovremenny Leviafan. Ocherki politicheskoi sotsiologii kapitalizma* (A Modern Leviathan. Studies in the Political Sociology of Capitalism), Mysl, Moscow, 1985.
3. Arutyunov, S. A., *Narody i kultury. Razvitiye i vzaimodeistviye* (Peoples and Cultures. Development and Interaction), Nauka, Moscow, 1989.
4. *Strany i narody* (Countries and Peoples), Vol. I: *Zemlya i chelovechestvo* (The Earth and Mankind), Mysl, Moscow, 1978.

5. *Bonds Without Bondage. Explorations in Transcultural Interactions,* Ed. by K. Kumar, University of Hawaii, Honolulu, 1979.

6. Condon, J. C., Yousef, F. S., *Introduction to Intercultural Communication,* Bobbs-Merril, New York, 1975.

7. *Cultural Dialogue Between the Peoples of the World,* UNESCO, Paris, 1980.

8. *Cultures in Contact. Studies in Cross-Cultural Interaction,* Pergamon, Oxford, etc., 1982.

9. Mazrui, A. A., *World Federation of Cultures. An African Perspective,* Free Press, New York, 1976.

10. Samovar, L. A., and Porter, R. E., *Intercultural Communication: A Reader,* 4th ed., Wadswart, Belmont (Calif.), 1985.

19
Culture and Personality

In this chapter, consideration should be given to the following:

1. What role does personality play in the system of cultural regulation of society?
2. What is the difference in attitudes to personality in the cultural systems of East and West?
3. What are the basic stages and types of socialisation of personality?
4. What changes in the socialisation of personality are brought about by modernisation?
5. What characterises the marginal individual?

The elements of culture that we have examined in previous chapters — norms, values, knowledge, and principles — constitute a certain system and as such interact with other factors of social regulation, such as the economy, social structure, and politics. However not only the above-mentioned social institutions are the bearers of culture which reproduce and disseminate its elements. Another important factor determining its functioning is personality. The latter reflects (or does not reflect, as the case may be) the customs, norms and values forming parts of culture, sometimes subjecting them to various degrees of transformation.

---

* In writing this chapter, the author made use of the works of V. S. Starostin, a Soviet sociologist specialising in the developing countries.

The Social Essence of the Personality

The problems of personality are the concern of several sciences. Of special importance here is social psychology, for which personality is a focus integrating various mental processes.

According to some of the latest psychological theories associated with the school of the Soviet psychologist Lev Vygotsky, the inner processes of the human psyche are based on inter-personal relationships in the course of a person's socialisation. The sociological plane involves relationships and structures which determine the behaviour of an individual as part of various social groups and communities: classes, nations, elites, and professional, age, sex, and other groups.

The sociology of culture examines, not only the objective, impersonal aspects of the elements and structures of culture, but also the subjective aspect, as reflected in a person's inner world. An individual's qualities are not explained by his social or cultural status alone. There is also his inner world, which reflects objective factors (albeit in its own peculiar way). On the one hand, culture shapes a particular type of personality; on the other, personality brings its own demands and interests into the norms, requirements and behavioural patterns of a given culture. Without considering personality factors, we cannot explain the actual functioning of cultural norms and values (in contrast to their ideal existence) or the deviations from the norm, which inevitably occur in society. It is only by considering the problems of personality that we can reveal the contradictions and conflicts caused in a person's mind by the discrepancy between the general norm and a given situation, which often results in serious psychological stress or social upheaval.

A special place belongs to the problem of the self. On the subjective plane the self is related to an individual's self-awareness, his awareness of his potentials and his difference from others. But it is not so easy to discern the objective characteristics of the self, so there are very few people who can answer the question: "Who am I?"

Each culture and each social order mould their own kind of personality, with the degree of uniformity or variety depending on what is acceptable within the framework of a particular culture. The extent of individualisation varies greatly from culture to culture, since not all societies have a developed concept of personality.

The socio-cultural factors of an individual's behaviour can be considerably revealed if one examines the roles accepted in each particular subculture in a given community. The role of any social group is a set of certain statuses: the class status (employer, worker), the occupational status (industrial worker, peasant, serviceman, scientist), the family status (husband, wife, child), and so forth. At the same time, every person can combine several roles, which vary depending on the form of activity, situation, or personal inclination (hardworking or lazy pupil).

In the cultural aspect, the assumption of roles reveals a great deal in society's life, shaping the character and identities of individuals, social groups, and nations. It is essential in communication between individuals belonging to different groups, and also in the social mobility of individuals and groups.

The Cultural Variety of Personalities

By far not every society can shape stable individuality, and consequently needs it as an essential component of the overall system of culture. In a traditional ethnic culture, the degree of individualisation is still very low, being limited to a few secondary spheres of behaviour. In such primitive cultures, a person sees himself only as a member of his family and tribe, his life and death being an integral part of the life and death of that family and tribe. The constraints of individual and society are mutual. Instead of thinking how to act in each particular case, a person simply follows the patterns established by his ancestors. The ancestor, a generalised image of past generations, is the ideal and the limit of his potential.

In more developed cultures, it is the emergence of individuality that is conducive to cultural variety and enrichment. However, attitudes to individuality can considerably vary depending on the cultural-historical type of society.

In the history of European culture, starting with the Renaissance, the prevailing tendency was to view the self as an important moral, intellectual and social asset. An individual is seen as an integral and active being, possessing the right (moreover, the obligation) to exercise his potentials in this world.

The European cultural tradition maintains that man is an autonomous subject of activity emphasising his identity in all his manifestations. The recognition of several role-functions generally does not contradict this principle, whereas the fragmentation of the self is seen as something abnormal. In Eastern cultures, by contrast, role-functions largely eclipse the individual's self-awareness. A person sees himself and is seen by others to a great extent depending on the environment or sphere in which he lives and acts during a particular period. He is viewed above all as a focus of specific duties and responsibilities arising from his belonging to his family, commune, clan, religious community, and state.

In classical Chinese tradition, the supreme virtue was one's subordination to recognised standards of conduct and the suppression of one's self. Confucianism taught the need to control one's emotions and express them in a strictly conventional way. In a context of all-prevailing official bureaucracy, the only way of circumventing this requirement was to withdraw from public activity into the seclusion of a monastery. A sophisticated system of physical and mental training gave one a sense of being dissolved in the Universe.

Somewhat different was the individual/society relationship in classical Hindu tradition. The human self enjoyed a very high status in Hindu philosophical systems; however, it was determined, not by any specific factors, but by a supreme spirit, in relation to which the bodily and empirical self was seen as transient. Moreover, faith in karma, a chain of reincarnations, made the life of each individual rather relative, devoid of independent value. The individual achieved self-realisation by negating his own empirical nature, and by breaking off all concrete earthly links with other people, with society, with the world, and with his own actions.

A person's real life is affected by the correlation of his social environment, his subjective desires, and his potentials. All these elements however are mobile and changeable. It would be sociologically rather useful to compare Molière's Jourdain and Bernard Shaw's Eliza Doolittle. Both seek to enter high society, but from different sides. Jourdain has the wealth but lacks the finesse of expression, whereas Eliza could well be taken for a duchess, after being trained by Professor Higgins, but lacks the requisite income. In both cases the plot is built on the characters' active desire to ascend to what they view as a more glamorous, prestigious social stratum. But what if high society lost its prestige and glamour in the eyes of the "lower" classes? In this case, too, various personal positions are possible. A revolutionary stand means struggle to change the social order which cannot be tolerated any longer. But one could also eliminate the emotional stress and avoid a nervous breakdown by various forms of inner relaxation.

Types of the Individual's Socialisation

Every society has its own system of socialisation—a system that helps a person develop as an active, full-fledged member of society. In the course of socialisation, the individual assimilates his community's social memory and traditions. Through various social institutions and mechanisms, he acquires essential work skills, and knowledge about his natural and social environment, and cultural standards and values accepted in his society. There are many definitions of the process of socialisation but, apart from certain differences in points of emphasis, its essence is interpreted as the assimilation by the individual of socio-cultural experience vital in his particular society.

The essential features of socialisation depend on the historically concrete socio-economic structure and the prevailing type of culture. One speaks, therefore, of the specific features of socialisation and essential differences in the individual's status under different socio-economic systems: primitive society, ancient society, feudalism (European), serfdom (Eastern), capitalism, or socialism. Within the same society, one's socialisation largely depends on what class one belongs to.

Among the factors determining socialisation are the individual's social, cultural, religious and ethnic environment, the character of the work the community as a whole and each particular family is engaged in (this is the main and primary mechanism of socialisation), the economic and social status of one's parents and other close relatives, etc.

Despite the great variety of pre-capitalist societies, the process of socialisation in all of them has much in common. Traditional (primitive) societies had no specialised institutions, and socialisation was characterised by the scarcity of the skills and values that had to be assimilated by each individual. The primitive economic level and socio-cultural rigidness of such societies, coupled with a short average life-span determined the stereotyped and accelerated character of socialisation. Its climax was the initiation rite in which adolescents were transferred into adulthood, symbolising recognition of their social maturity and granting them a set of rights and obligations sanctified by tradition.

The weak differentiation and limitations in space and time of the transfer of socio-cultural experience restrict the possibilities of primary social groups. Because of the absence of cultural institutions, a special educational system and means of communication, collective experience was passed on primarily by word of mouth (including folklore), worldly wisdom and experience, which an individual accumulated with time and which were in direct proportion to his age. The individual's life-span was an important condition of accumulation and preservation of socially significant information, which made old age a factor of prestige. The veneration of the tribe elders was in effect the equivalent of an institutionalised mechanism for transferring cultural experience.

But today too, in the developing countries a child's socialisation during his first years of life is as a rule effected by traditional methods and traditional institutions. In the countryside the entire commune is traditionally responsible for child upbringing. The child usually spends his early years (up to age 3 or 4) in close contact with his mother. In time, his grandparents, elder siblings, aunts and uncles and other relations also begin taking part in his upbringing. As in any society, adults use minor errands and games to involve their children in work, teaching them to be obedient, respect their elders and betters, learn the morals and culture of their people, and observe the norms and rules of conduct.

Respect for one's elders and age hierarchy is an important feature of the way of life and the process of socialisation. Its significance has been preserved in the age-groups that remain to this day and underlie the traditional educational system, and in the special speech formulas used in addressing members of different social and age groups and in the special prefixes attached to an individual's name depending on his age and social status.

The traditional system of upbringing is based on observation, imitation, and participation. Socialisation includes diverse physical exercises (which reflect elements of traditional work processes and cultural rituals), instruction in handicrafts, religion, and customs. The assimilation of all this is stimulated by both encouragement and severe punishment. Another important means of transferring tradition from generation to generation is dance, music, and folklore.

By the late 1980's, the number of children of preschool age vastly exceeded the I billion mark. The overwhelming majority of the world's children were born in the developing countries. How this young generation will be socialised, what information it will assimilate in the process, and what ideals and values it will have—all this will largely determine the existence of the greater part of mankind at the start of the third millennium.

But the family is not the only socialising factor in the developing countries responsible for passing on cultural traditions and values from generation to generation. Another important socialising mechanism is religious schools, which have always had a tangible impact on upbringing.

There are many other traditional socio-cultural institutions which continue to perform socialising functions in the developing countries. Traditional folk performances—including the puppet theatre and religious rituals—far from being ossified remnants of the past, are active and significant cultural institutions. They have a great vital and creative potential and play an important role in society. These traditional means of communication are not only a source of information and entertainment: through them young people assimilate generally established norms and values, in other words, they perform a general socialising function.

Modernisation and Personality

Today, the character of socialisation is undergoing radical change because the information an individual must assimilate in his formative years has grown dramatically in size, become more diverse and sophisticated. All these changes are to a greater or lesser extent characteristic of any society, but those taking place in today's Asia and Africa are more diverse than those any society has had previously.

The break with traditionalism and the advent of cultural modernisation gradually destroy the former uniformity and stability. The pluralism of values reflects the technological progress in production and the growing complexity of the social structure, i.e. the formation of various social and occupational groups, classes, and strata. The variety of values in its turn becomes a condition of social mobility and progress, and is conducive to individualisation of the personality.

All this changes the mechanisms and increases the rate of the individual's socialisation, and tears down the partitions which used to surround the socio-cultural field within which socialisation used to take place.

The criteria of the personality's modernisation include:

1) Openness to new practice — both in one's relationships with other people and in one's assimilation of new production skills;

2) Increased independence from traditional factors such as family and religion; greater trust in modern political, public, trade union, co-operative, etc., leaders;

3) Faith in the efficacy of science and medicine as a whole, and abandonment of the former passivity and fatalism in the face of adversity;

4) Desire to raise one's own and one's children's occupational and educational standards;

5) Planning one's actions and punctuality;

6) Growing interest and involvement in public and political affairs;

7) Desire to keep abreast of the news; more interest in national and world news, compared to local news.

Despite socio-economic, political and ethno-cultural differences, school and other types of education everywhere play a dominant role in shaping new, more modern and dynamic personal qualities in the adolescent. Apart from elementary literacy—reading, writing, and arithmetic—pupils assimilate new values, principles and behaviour patterns, which are highly significant for their personality development and the future development of their countries. Those adolescents who have gone to school for a longer period are not only better informed and are not only better speakers; they develop a different perception of time and a stronger sense of personal and public responsibility. They are more actively involved in public affairs and are more receptive to new ideas and people, and interact differently with others. They have more respect for science, are quicker to respond to any change, and will in the future be more responsive to birth control measures.

The wealth of the personality consists in the breadth of its horizons and the content of its relations with society. Achievement of the full measure of this wealth is the humanitarian ideal. The opportunities for attaining it depend on the development of the productive forces.

The comprehensive development of the personality does not at all coincide with the ideal of the all-round consumer. Reducing human needs to those for manufactured goods and entertainments is the result of a person's alienation from the actual process of production and from other people, which they are to "compensate for". Truly human consumption consists not in appropriating things, but in assimilating a mode of activity and contacts with others, which bring people closer together and implies the individual's active self-realisation in creative work and communication.

The Marginal Individual

Many studies in the sociology of culture in recent decades have focused on the marginal individual. This research has helped reveal important patterns in the character of cultural change taking place in the newly-liberated countries in the course of modernisation.

The marginal individual is a person who lives and consciously participates in the cultural life and traditions of two different nations. He can never completely break with his past and its traditions (even when given a chance to) and will never be completely accepted in the new society where he now seeks to get assimilated. He exists on the border-line of two cultures and two societies which will never completely coincide.

The marginal individual is the product of migration and the various accompanying processes as a result of which a person of a certain culture is forced to assimilate other, alien cultural values, social roles, and another way of life.

The state of marginality, if it assumes a stable character, makes the individual a conglomerate of heterogeneous social roles and cultural principles. Such ambivalence often leads to depersonalisation, causing psychological tension, mental disorders and nervous breakdowns. At the same time, such combination of elements from different cultures can enrich the personality and provide prerequisites for its creative potentials to develop.

Socialisation is conducive to instability and eclecticism in the structure of the personality (especially in a marginal individual) in a transitional (post-colonial) society and to the predominance of ambivalent personalities. Such personalities have strange combinations of tradition and modernity, mysticism and rationalism, knowledge and prejudice, religious contemplation and political dynamism.

The personality reflects modernisation in a highly subjective way. Each specific individual forms part not of culture in general but of a concrete social and cultural field, which is but a fragment of a given society, with its own mechanisms of socialisation and set of cultural values.

One of the most important factors influencing man in a transitional society is the "revolution of expectations", which promises to improve his economic status, give him land, cheap food, a job—in other words, to satisfy his basic needs. Such expectations largely restructure man's inner world, both in town and country. But this is sometimes accompanied by bitter disillusionment when expectations clash with reality. In the city, the individual (often a peasant in the recent past) finds he has no job, no home, no proper food or medical assistance. These hardships and privations dissolve the sweet mirage, deepening the new city dweller's disappointment. At the same time his outlook broadens as he learns about another way of life, other religions and political views, and becomes more tolerant towards other behavioural standards and habits which often contradict his own. But tolerance has its limits and can turn into envy, resentment and indignation at outrageous injustice, economic and political inequality and the growing abyss between ostentatious luxury and utter poverty.

All these factors create the social soil that breeds the "transitional individual"—an isolated, lonely, defenceless person, plucked out of his native environment and searching in vain for a niche in a hostile world. Only a few are lucky—those who manage to acquire a trade or profession, assimilate urban ways and join the ranks of skilled blue-collar workers, officers, intellectuals, and entrepreneurs.

The majority, however, remains in the transitional state. Having lost the relative calm of his traditional little world, the marginal individual seeks a new stability and new idols to replace the toppled ones so as to get clear-cut instructions from them on how to live and what to do next.

Thus, the personality is the bearer of culture. It translates values, norms, knowledge and faith into the given individual's behaviour in his particular social environment and into his attitudes to other people and to the world at large. Without the individual, without his systematic and intelligent activity, culture cannot take on material form and exists merely as a set of abstract principles. And yet the personality cannot be wholly identified with the entire culture of a given community. It embraces only part of this culture—the elements that correspond to the given individual's social status and the character of his socialisation. At the same time, in a context of intense interaction of different cultures, personality may come in closer or looser contact with other values, norms and behavioural patterns. Such situations require knowledge of another culture and the ability to adjust to another cultural environment. The sociology of culture is meant to help develop this ability.

If you wish to study the subject in depth:

1. Starostin, B. S., *Osvobodivshiyesya strany: obschchestvo i lichnost* (The Newly-Independent Countries: Society and Personality), Mysl, Moscow, 1984.
2. Kon, I. S., *Sotsiologiya lichnosti* (The Sociology of the Personality), Politizdat, Moscow, 1967.
3. Kon. I. S., *Otkrytiye "Ya"* (Discovery of the Self), Politizdat, Moscow, 1978.
4. *Culture and Personality. Contemporary Readings,* Ed. by R. A. LeVine, Abdine, Chicago, 1974.
5. *Culture and Self. Asian and Western Perspectives,* Ed. by A. J. Marsella *et al.* Tavistock, New York-London, 1985.
6. Stonequest, A., *The Marginal Man. A Study on Personality and Culture Conflict,* Russel and Russel, New York, 1961.

Conclusion

Having mastered the fundamentals of the sociology of culture, you will have acquired an ability to find your way about not only in your own culture, that is, form a better idea of its general character and logic and understand the sets of values, norms and views, which to a large extent determine people's behaviour. In the world of today, every individual constantly comes in contact with the norms and values of other cultures. He finds himself involved in a world of inter-cultural communication. It is extremely important, therefore, not to reduce this communication either to a purely exotic interest or to pragmatic gain. A new system of inter-cultural relations must be established.

Both within separate states and in international relations, cultural development and the co-ordination of cultural activity are becoming more and more systematic. Special attention is devoted to culture as a factor of international understanding. Culture can help resolve the complex problems standing in the way of normal relations between many countries. Cultural understanding and dialogue is an important means of settling many economic and political conflicts and an essential condition of building a harmonious world.

Such activity demands professionalism—in other words, training experts capable of addressing complex problems on the basis of scientific knowledge of how culture functions in society. The authors hope this manual will be a first step in mastering this vital science. However, they have only meant to give a few recommendations not claiming to take the only correct view of cultural processes of past and present.

Name Index

N

O

P

Q

R

S

T

U

V

Subject Index

N

O

P